MW00795125

St. Maximus the Confessor's Questions and Doubts

ST. MAXIMUS
THE CONFESSOR'S
QUESTIONS AND DOUBTS

TRANSLATED BY
DESPINA D. PRASSAS

Northern Illinois University Press

DeKalb

© 2010 by Northern Illinois University Press

Published by the Northern Illinois University Press, DeKalb, Illinois   60115

Manufactured in the United States using postconsumer-

recycled, acid-free paper.

All Rights Reserved

Design by Shaun Allshouse

Library of Congress Cataloging-in-Publication Data

Maximus, Confessor, Saint, ca. 580–662.

[Maximi Confessoris Quaestiones et dubia. English]

St. Maximus the Confessor's Questions and doubts /

[translation and introduction by] Despina D. Prassas.

p.   cm.

Includes bibliographical references and index.

ISBN 978-0-87580-413-2 (clothbound: alk. paper)

1. Bible—Examinations, questions, etc. 2. Theology—

Miscellanea. I. Prassas, Despina D. II. Title.

BR65.M39673Q3413 2010

230'.14092–dc22

2009028407

To my parents,

Πάτερ Γεώργιος Ε. Πρασσᾶς

and Αἰκατερίνα Μαχείρα Πρασσᾶ

and to my γιαγιὰ, Δέσποινα Τάκης Μαχείρα

who believed and instilled in all her children,

"the education, this is the most important thing"

CONTENTS

ACKNOWLEDGMENTS

Where to begin? I was unbelievably fortunate to receive a telephone call from Amy Farranto, acquisitions editor at Northern Illinois University Press, as I was emerging out of my post-doctoral coma—that period after the dissertation is over, when one is settling into the new academic position and trying to figure out how to teach 18–21-year-olds, a population not the least bit interested in what you have spent many years of your life learning. With my strength improving every day, I was able to take up, again, the dissertation.

Therefore, I must begin with Amy. She has been incredibly generous, patient, kind, accommodating, are there really enough descriptors? Perhaps not. But had it not been for her professionalism and willingness to walk a newbie through the process of converting a dissertation into a book, this work would have taken much longer to see the light of day. It is with tremendous gratitude and an immeasurable feeling of indebtedness that I say, "thank you, for everything."

Many thanks, also, to the friends who have always provided the essential support and been anchors as I continue to maneuver my way through the field of academia: Lili Murad, Samantha Elizabeth Papaioannou, Kyriaki FitzGerald, Donna Anton, Pamela Hamilton, Niki Lambros, Fr. Tom FitzGerald, as well as Jane Lunin Perel, Paola Cesarini, and Richard Strasser. Special thanks to Susan Ashbrook Harvey, Michael Penn, Robin Darling Young, Susan Holman, and Paul Blowers. Also, I am grateful to the Dominican

Friars at Providence College, especially those in the Theology Department, who have continually encouraged me without ever asking for anything in return. Thank you.

The two anonymous reviewers of the manuscript provided excellent feedback, much of which I have included in the revised text. The staff at Northern Illinois University Press has been most accommodating and enthusiastic throughout this entire process—Susan Bean, Julia Fauci, Linda Manning, Barbara Berg, and Alex Schwartz—many thanks for all your help. A special thanks, again, to Pam Hamilton, who worked as copy editor of the text, and Peter Gilbert who provided support with the translation. At the same time, all errors are my own. Hopefully, there are not many.

Lastly, how to thank my parents, who have endured the many years of the dissertation, the tortuous and tension-filled first years of teaching, and the seemingly unending process of putting together the first book. A dedication may not be enough. It is my hope you will be as proud of this work as I am and maybe even more so. But the person to whom I am the most indebted is my maternal grandmother who came to this country decades ago with her fourth-grade education and instilled in her children and grandchildren not only a love for education and learning but the confidence to realize our dreams. May her memory be eternal. And I thank our gracious and loving God whose generosity is never ending.

St. Maximus the Confessor's Questions and Doubts

INTRODUCTION

The late nineteenth and twentieth centuries were a time of renewed interest in the writings of Maximus the Confessor (580–662), the seventh-century monk whose theological teachings contributed significantly to early Byzantine monasticism and the decisions of the Sixth Ecumenical Council (680–81).[1] This interest in the writings of the Confessor has continued into the twenty-first century, inspiring a new generation of scholars.

The new millennium finds the ongoing production of scholarship addressing the works of the Confessor. There are critical editions of the *Liber Asceticus* (*LA*);[2] recensions of the Greek Life of Maximus,[3] the *Ambigua ad Thomam* (*Amb.Th.*),[4] and the florilegia;[5] and translations of various *Ambigua* and the questions and responses of the *Quaestiones Ad Thalassium* (*QT*),[6] of records of the trial and letters produced as a result of Maximus's arrest and exile,[7] and of the Mystagogy (*Myst.*)[8] and the *Centuries on Charity* (*CC*).[9] There are numerous monographs in various languages dealing with the topics of Christology,[10] the body and deification,[11] and with Maximus's philosophical contributions,[12] hermeneutics,[13] cosmology,[14] monothelitism,[15] and, of course, anthropology.[16] More and more often we find comparative works presented to better understand the Confessor's antecedents and influence,[17] and lastly, there has been a proliferation of master's theses and doctoral dissertations that will continue to expand the field.[18] Maximus has emerged as an essential church father in that he is regularly mentioned in general texts on Christian theology and the development of Christian thought.[19]

This book provides the first English language translation of Maximus the Confessor's *Quaestiones et dubia* (*QD*), a series of 239 questions and responses found in José Declerck's *Quaestiones et dubia* in volume 10 of Corpus Christianorum Series graeca.[20] The primary witness of the critical edition is a manuscript found in the Vatican Libraries approximately fifty years ago, *Vaticanus graecus 1703* (*Vat.gr. 1703*). There exists a French language translation of Maximus's text by Emmanuel Ponsoye;[21] however, in several places my translation departs from Ponsoye's. The current volume is not meant to include an exhaustive treatment of the *QD*; that would be a major undertaking and goes far beyond the scope of this work. The purpose of this part of the book is to introduce the *QD* and to provide a brief historical and literary contextual background to help ground and familiarize the reader for a reading of the translation.

HISTORICAL AND CULTURAL CONTEXT
The Life of Maximus the Confessor

There exist two renditions of the life of Maximus the Confessor. One is the tenth-century Greek *Vita* composed by Michael Exaboulites,[22] a Studite monk, which also contains paraphrased interpolations from the *Vita* of Theodore the Studite.[23] The other version is the Syriac *Vita*[24] written by George of Resh'aina shortly after the death of Maximus.[25] Neither has been proven to be definitive.[26] The Syriac *Vita*, whose author claims to have been a disciple of Sophronius of Jerusalem, states that Maximus was born in the village of Hefsin, east of Lake Tiberias. According to the text, Maximus was the product of an adulterous relationship between a Samaritan merchant from Sychar and a Persian slave girl who was owned by Jews from Tiberias.[27] Maximus, named Moschion at birth, was baptized a Christian under the protection of a priest named Martyrius. After the death of both parents, he moved to the monastery of Palaia Lavra and was taken in by the abbot, Pantaleon.[28] It was Pantaleon, described in the Syriac *Vita* as "the wicked Origenist," who changed the name of the child from Moschion to Maximus.

Maximus confirms the year of his own birth, 580 CE, when he states in 655, at the trial that resulted from his involvement in a council that condemned monothelitism, that he is seventy-five years old.[29] Born during the reign of Tiberius II Constantine (578–82), he was of noble descent and received a good education.[30] It is unknown whether he received the broad humanist education for which the university at Constantinople was renowned.[31] This education would have included grammar, rhetoric, philosophy, arithmetic, music, geometry, and astronomy, the ἐγκύκλιος παίδευσις (egkyklios paideusis), an education common to all boys anticipating a life of imperial service. Maximus tells us he received a private education and was not formally trained in rhetoric.[32]

While in his early 30s, Maximus became the ἀσηκρῆτις (asekretis), the first secretary, at the court of Heraclius, and he oversaw the imperial chancellery from 610 to about 614.[34] Though this information comes from the Greek Vita,[35] Maximus himself states that he had served in the imperial secretariat.[36]

After Maximus left the imperial service, he continued to maintain good relations with his friends at court. The person with whom Maximus corresponded most often, according to the surviving corpus of letters, is John the Cubicularius, who oversaw the imperial household.[37] The correspondence was regular[38] and took place throughout the saint's life, though only three letters written before 626 are extant; this date is significant because it is believed by Polycarp Sherwood to be the year that the QD was written.[39]

Maximus may have left imperial service sometime between 613 and 614.[40] He withdrew to the monastery of Philippikos, near Chrysopolis (modern-day Scutari), on the Asiatic shore of the Bosphorus, opposite Constantinople.[41] He left imperial service in order to engage, according to the Greek Vita, in ὁ καθ'ἡσυχί αν βίος (ho kath hesychian bios), the quiet life.[42] Maximus wrote about the importance of calming the soul through hesychia, inner quietude,[43] but the Vita states he left because of the growing theological controversies of monenergism and monothelitism.[44] Most scholars question the accuracy of this statement since these controversies had not grown to such a degree at that time as to warrant his leaving court.[45]

One wonders whether Maximus knew General Philippikos, the founder of the monastery there, and whether a relationship with the general from Maximus's time in imperial service would have influenced his choice to begin monastic life at Chrysopolis. It is possible. And while there is no indication of why Maximus left the first monastery, the choice of St. George's at Cyzikos as his next monastery may have been a result of his relationship with the archbishop of Cyzikos, John. Maximus wrote to the archbishop while at Chrysopolis.[46]

The Greek *Vita* states that the monks at Chrysopolis persuaded Maximus to become the *hegoumenos*, abbot, at the monastery. This has been disputed,[47] although the argument that his literary production could not have allowed him to attend to the responsibilities of a *hegoumenos* does not seem all that convincing.[48] Georges Florovsky concludes that although Maximus may have been elected *hegoumenos* by his fellow monks, he may not have accepted the position.[49] The tenth-century *Vita* refers to the saint as *abbas* (whether this term was one of respect for his literary achievements or his actual title within the monastery setting is unclear); however, the signature on record of the Acts of the Lateran Council of 649 reads *monachus* following Maximus's name.[50]

Maximus probably left Chrysopolis sometime between the years 624 and 625.[51] No source provides a reason for the move from his first monastery. One cannot help but wonder, however, whether the area surrounding Constantinople was in danger of attack from either the Persians or the Avars; the Emperor Heraclius had narrowly escaped an ambush during a meeting with the Khan of the Avars in Heraklea in June 617.[52] It is also possible Maximus simply needed another, perhaps more knowledgeable, guide for his monastic development. If Sherwood's dating of Letter 6 is correct, Maximus already would have been in contact with Archbishop John of Cyzikos while at Chrysopolis. Sherwood suggests that this letter, addressed to Archbishop John, was written prior to his departure from Chrysopolis.[53]

Maximus, along with a disciple named Anastasius, transferred to the monastery of St. George at Cyzikos, a town located at the base of a peninsula extending from the southern coast of the Sea of Marmara.[54] Maximus left Cyzikos before the arrival of the Persian army in the spring of 626.[55] The attack of Constantinople by Persians, Avars, and Slavs could have dealt a death blow to the city. Fearing the worst, Maximus, along with several fellow monks, travelled south to North Africa,[56] possibly stopping in

Cyprus and Crete and arriving at Carthage in 628.[57] He joined the Euchratas monastery where Sophronius (who was to become the Confessor's teacher and spiritual father) was abbot.

During his African stay, in 645, Maximus engaged in a theological debate at Carthage with the deposed patriarch, Pyrrhus.[58] Ten years earlier, Pyrrhus, then abbot of the monastery at Chrysopolis, had written to Maximus asking his opinion of Patriarch Sergius's *Psephos,* a document forbidding any mention of the operations in Christ.[59] Maximus supported the *Psephos* at the time, and after their debate in 645 Pyrrhus accepted the dyothelite position. Maximus accompanied the patriarch to Rome, where Pyrrhus made his confession to Pope Theodore regarding his former monothelite position.[60] By 647, the confession was retracted, and Pyrrhus was excommunicated by the pope.[61]

The Emperor Constans II, under the guidance of Patriarch Paul II of Constantinople, published a *Typos* the same year (647), which stated there should be no discussion or disputation regarding the theology of one will/energy or two wills/energies of Jesus Christ. Two years later, Martin I, newly consecrated Pope of Rome, convened the Lateran Synod, which condemned the *Typos.* Maximus had been living at a monastery in Rome for two years prior to the council and took an active part in the synod by preparing some documentation.[62]

Emperor Constans, upon hearing of the decision of the Lateran Synod, sent an exarch to Rome to force the acceptance of the *Typos.* In June of 653, Pope Martin and Maximus were arrested for noncompliance. Maximus was tried in 655 for crimes against the empire,[63] exiled to Bizya in Thrace,[64] and after being visited by two imperial emissaries in 656, was deported to Salembrie and then to Perberis. He was recalled to Constantinople to come before the patriarch in 658. Along with Martin and Sophronius, he was anathematized and sentenced to have his right hand amputated and his tongue cut out. He was exiled with his disciples, Anastasius and Anastasius the Apokrisarios, to Lazika, located on the southeast coast of the Black Sea.

After being separated from his disciples, Maximus arrived at the fortress of Schemaris in the Caucasus mountains on June 8, 662. He died two months later on August 13, 662. Less than two decades later, at the Sixth Ecumenical Council held in 680, he was vindicated. His doctrine of the two wills and two energies was recognized as canonical.[65]

The issue of the two *vitae* remains central in the minds of some Maximus scholars. While one would be challenged to make a final decision regarding which *vita* contains the more accurate material, at the very least the existence of two *vitae* demonstrates the varied responses to the major theological issue of the seventh century, monothelitism. Even though the dating of the Syriac *Vita* is inconclusive, it does predate the Greek *Vita*, suggesting that the Syriac *Vita* may be more reliable.[66] To some extent, however, the Syriac version may be considered somewhat biased since the author tends to malign Maximus; it is frustration with the decision of the Sixth Ecumenical Council (681) against monothelitism that prompts this approach by the monophysite author.

But the main issue lurking in the background of the *QD* is not monothelitism, which does not come to the fore until the late 630s. The issue that emerged in the monasteries in the late sixth and early seventh centuries was that of Origenism. Therefore, a question that the Syriac *Vita* seems to imply is, was Maximus an Origenist? This question will be addressed below.

Monasticism in Constantinople and Its Surroundings

Monks were present in Constantinople from the second half of the fourth century. By 518, the capital and its immediate surroundings counted at least sixty-seven monasteries for men and many for women.[67]

From the start, the monks engaged in the religious controversies, challenging archepiscopal authority and involving themselves in the deliberations of the councils.[68] In the Acts of the Council of 536, we find the signatures of representatives from sixty-eight monasteries in Constantinople and forty monasteries in Chalcedon.[69] There were also many hermits, including one Daniel the Stylite, who ascended his own pillar in the late fifth century in the town of Anaplous.[70]

The reputations of the monks seemed to vary. The early monasteries were established outside the walls of the city, and the presence of monks in the city was prohibited by the law of Theodosius I (379–95).[71] The law was repealed shortly after it had been enacted,[72] but concern about the presence of the monks in the capital was expressed long before the establishment within the capital of the first monastery. Several of the patriarchs, notably John Chrysostom and Gregory Nazianzus, believed that asceticism, and therefore monasticism, could best be practiced in the desert.[73] More often than not, a bishop needed to recall a monk who had been sent to the capital on business and had been "tempted to mingle with the world and busy themselves with secular matters."[74]

From the fourth to the seventh centuries, many civil disciplinary canons were promulgated that addressed the activities of the monks and monasteries.[75] Justinian ruled that no monastery could be established without the consent of the local bishop, who would also appoint the abbot. All novices were to undergo a three-year probationary period, and monks were to be discouraged from changing monasteries.[76]

Ecclesiastical disciplinary canons that emerged from the church councils of the fourth century spoke to concerns regarding monastic discipline and administration. The Council of Gangra (340) addressed certain monastic practices and, specifically, the behavior of those considering the vocation. Such behavior included women dressing like men in order to join monasteries;[77] women leaving their husbands for the monastic life;[78] parents neglecting their children for asceticism[79] and children neglecting their parents;[80] women cutting off their hair for the sake of asceticism;[81] and ascetics behaving poorly and neglecting the fasts of the church.[82]

The Council in Trullo (691–92) produced 102 canons, several of which addressed the activities of monks and nuns. Canon 34 outlawed any conspiracy by the monks against the local bishop;[83] Canon 41 required a three-year probationary period for all novices entering the monastery; Canon 42 required that hermits no longer be permitted to roam the cities but attach themselves to monasteries or risk being expelled from the cities; Canon 43 allowed anyone to become a monk, including convicted criminals and slaves;[84] Canon 44 outlined a discipline for the monk who had taken a wife or committed fornication;[85] Canon 45 prohibited nuns from wearing jewels and silks when tonsured;[86] and Canon 80 dictated that the priest and abbot of a monastery must be selected from among the monks of the same monastery, thereby protecting the monks from a bishop trying to introduce his own personal candidate to oversee the monastery.[87]

By the end of the seventh century, imperial and ecclesiastical authorities had addressed serious problems resulting from the activities of the monks. This included the activities of wandering monks and preachers who were not subject to any ecclesiastical discipline. The hermits were popular among the refugees who had been moving throughout the empire as a result of the wars. These itinerant holy men engaged in the lucrative work of predicting the future and offering prophesy.[88] Canon 61 of the Council in Trullo raised concerns regarding the use and sale of amulets and the prevalence of fortune-telling.[89] The canon also focused on whether prophesying or fortune-telling by means of random searches of Old and New Testament texts was to be permitted.[90] Not surprisingly, Canon 19 of the Council in Trullo required that clergy and bishops interpret Scripture in accordance with the teachings of the Fathers of the church and without improvisation.[91]

Educated monks, many of whom espoused the Origenism that was circulating in the monasteries of Egypt and Palestine in the fifth and sixth centuries, were causing disturbances in the monastic communities.[92] Maximus speaks of adversaries from among his fellow monks and is referring to the Origenists.[93] His concerns were genuine. A century earlier, problems with Origenist monks were so great that the mother of Cyril of Scythopolis feared that her son (who was entering the monastic life) might be led astray by the Origenists who were gaining power in Jerusalem.[94]

There were also internal quarrels among the Origenists that resulted in monks travelling to Constantinople in order to defend their positions. In 553, Justinian finally convened a council at Constantinople that anathematized Origen and Theodore of Mopsuestia, and the teachings of Evagrius and Didymus the Blind (313–98 CE) on the preexistence of souls and *apokatastasis*.[95] By the end of the sixth century, many Origenist monks and their disciples found their way to the capital. Whether their motivation for leaving Palestine was the anti-Origenist environment or the raiding tribes who captured monks in order to ransom them—Persians, tribes of Saracens, and "Hebrews" looking for money attacked monks and others—there was a movement of the monks northward.[96]

Monastic Education and Literature

Many of the monks, especially those who had been farmers or soldiers, were not well educated prior to entering the monastery. Some education, namely, the ability to read, was necessary for the monks if they were to be able to perform the liturgical services correctly. Cyril of Scythopolis tells of a Palestinian monk named Euthymius who was carefully educated in "secular culture" as well as in Scripture.[97]

The Byzantine monk, with few exceptions, remained formally uneducated throughout his life.[98] He read Scripture, chanted the Psalter, and learned the tradition of the church. It was expected that a monk would educate himself by reading—this had been part of the monastic tradition since the beginning of organized Christian monasticism.[99] After learning the basic rules of the monastery, Pachomius insisted that his monks learn to read. They began by reading the Psalter and proceeded to the Epistles of Paul.[100] By the ninth century, Theodore Studite set aside certain days when the monks, in lieu of physical labor, would gather in the library and read until evening services.[101] The discussions on the benefits of a Christian education over and against a secular education were not important in the Byzantine monasteries, though they were to some in Byzantine society.[102]

The monks also read *apophthegmata*, miracle stories, and biographies.[103] This was the world the monks knew, and this type of literature was more easily accessible than Scripture, since there were no concerns regarding personal interpretation.

The monastic literature of the fifth and sixth centuries included a variety of genres:[104] *apophthegmata*,[105] centuries,[106] miracle stories,[107] lives of the monks,[108] homilies,[109] and, equally as popular—and which brings us to the translation—*quaestiones*.[110]

MAXIMUS AND THE *Quaestiones et dubia*

Background of the Text

It is believed that Maximus's literary activity began while he was at St. George Monastery in Cyzikos.[111] Sherwood has dated the following texts to the period before 626: *LA, CC, Expositio in Psalmum LIX* (*EP*),[112] and three surviving letters.[113] It was also at

Cyzikos that Maximus states he worked out some of the more difficult passages of the *Orations* of Gregory Nazianzus,[114] which would be clarified in the *Ambigua ad Iohannem* (*Amb.Io.*)

Though Jean-Claude Larchet also believes that the majority of Maximus's early literary works were written while he was at Cyzikos,[115] it would have been difficult for Maximus to have produced so many treatises in less than two years' time. One questions whether an arrival date at Cyzikos of 624/25 is possible. However, it was during his time in Africa that Maximus would complete the majority of his writings.[116]

Other works that have been dated to the early period include the seventeenth theological and polemical opuscule[117] and the *Life of the Virgin*. Larchet believes the latter was "sans doute" written during the early phase in Maximus's literary career,[118] though the text is "sous réserve de l'authenticité, encore mal établie, de cette oeuvre."[119]

The *QD* is also considered to be an early work of Maximus since there are no references to any christological disputes.[120] The work has been dated to 626 by Sherwood,[121] as early as 624/25 by Epifanovich,[122] and has been called a "young work" by M.-Th. Disdier.[123] Hans Urs von Balthasar has proposed criteria to categorize the Confessor's writings into two groups: the writings that contain allusions to monenergism or monothelitism (which he concludes would have been written later than 633/34) and the writings that carry no trace of these two themes (dated to before that time).[124]

The literary genre of *QD*, that of *quaestio-responsio*, served a function that was primarily pedagogical,[125] and the majority of Maximus's works are in this form. This genre is a merging of two *quaestio* traditions: the patristic exegetical ἀπορίαι tradition and the spiritual-pedagogical tradition of monastic questions and responses.[126]

Maximus's primary source of information was Scripture, though he was very familiar with the works of many Christian writers and tried to cite his sources whenever possible.[127] In the *QD*, Maximus makes direct references to two writers very popular within the monastic community, Diadochus of Photike[128] and Dionysius the Areopagite.[129] However, there are two writers whom the Confessor does not mention by name but whose work was clearly influential: Origen[130] and Evagrius Ponticus.

It has been shown that Maximus was influenced both by the writings of Origen and by those who read Origen.[131] Though the Syriac *Vita* accuses Maximus of having been trained by an Origenist, few literate monks would have bypassed the writings of Origen;[132] many would have been familiar with his exegetical method.

Evidence of Maximus's familiarity with the writings of Origen is present in his early works.[133] In the *QD*, in particular, we find Maximus drawing from Origen's exegetical style and content. In *QD* 17, Maximus interprets the passage, "the pupil of the eye," in the exact way Origen has in the past.[134] But the question that seems more present, and one that the author of the Syriac *Vita* seems to raise, is whether Maximus subscribed to the teachings of Origen that later would be condemned at Constantinople in 680. Therefore, we must turn to *QD* 19, where Maximus takes up Gregory of Nyssa's teaching on the *apokatastasis*.

In *QD* 19, while answering an interrogation regarding a reference to the *apokatastasis*, Maximus provides an explanation and in doing so might lead a reader to suspect Origenist sympathies. Maximus defends Gregory's writings (and refers to his thinking as "lofty") and outlines three different types of restoration: the restoration of virtue in a person, the restoration of human nature in the resurrection, and the restoration of that which has fallen into sin. It is the third restoration that Maximus applies to Gregory; it is necessary for the powers of the soul, which have become sinful, to return to that state for which they were created. The memories of evil that are lodged within the soul must be separated from the soul, so that the latter will be able to return to God. It is specifically the third restoration, whereby all who have fallen into sin will return to God, that harkens back to Origen's teaching on the subject. Origen's teaching on the *apokatastasis* is found in the *De Principiis*.[135] Given that this is the only direct reference to any teaching of Origen in the *QD* and that it is not entirely clear whether Maximus's explanation is precisely the same as Origen's, the conclusion drawn by the author of the Syriac *Vita* cannot be accepted.

Maximus also knew the writings of Evagrius, upon whom he depended for his *CC*.[136] One similarity between the writings of Maximus and Evagrius occurs in *QD* I, 68, which addresses the clothing of a monk. The discussion on the clothing of the monk also takes place in Evagrius's *Introductory Letter to Anatolios*,[137] though the interpretations of the articles of clothing—the hood, the belt, and the scapular—differ. Dionysius the Areopagite,[138] Dorotheus of Gaza,[139] and John Cassian[140] also offer interpretations of the monastic schema.

While it is beyond the scope of this work to delve into a full explanation of Maximus's exegetical style or to attach him to one exegetical "school," in the *QD* he clearly applies, to quote Manlio Simonetti, "scripture to the various circumstances of the community's life . . . so as to adapt it to the needs and purposes with which it may not have had an immediate or obvious link."[141] In his exegesis he attempted to respond to questions arising from the practical application of a text (either biblical or patristic) to everyday life and to educate the reader/listener. From his explanation of anthropomorphisms to his progression from the literal to the allegorical interpretation of a text, Maximus appears to be working within the so-called Alexandrian school of exegesis and draws upon the style of Philo and Origen. Philo's name came up several times during searches on specific interpretations using the online search engine *Thesaurus Lingua Graeca* (*TLG*). I realize the limitations of the *TLG* as a research tool; any errors in the transmission of texts to electronic form and the general concern over the reliability of Migne's Patrologia graeca (PG) will affect results. Yet, the information obtained is worth considering. In *QD* 25, a search on the interpretation of "Joseph" as "set apart" yields one other reference, in Philo's *De somniis*.[142] Didymus expands on Philo's interpretation of "one set apart by the Lord,"[143] though Maximus maintains the interpretation of Philo. In *QD* 27, the phrase "*logos* of discretion" appears,[144] and in *QD* 53, in a commentary on Isa 40:12, the word "hand" is interpreted as "action."[145] There are two questions where Philo as well as one other author—Cyril of Alexandria in *QD* 30, Procopius of Gaza in *QD* 47—appear as potential sources for the interpretation. Yet none of these biblical exegetes is mentioned by Maximus.[146]

However, numerous searches on specific phrases and sentences of the *QD* through the *TLG* result in the names Origen, Evagrius, and Didymus the Blind emerging again and again. This reflects a certain continuity of thought that should be attributed, at least in the case of Maximus, to a familiarity with the writings of these authors. By incorporating phrases and images from the writings of others, Maximus is situating himself within the patristic exegetical tradition and is using the basic grammar by which many of the earlier writers constructed their own readings of the texts. Similar interpretations will be noted in the footnotes of the translation.

Similarities between certain passages in the QD and the writings of Origen and Evagrius have been noted above. Is there any connection between the writings of Didymus the Blind and Maximus? Didymus, the fourth century teacher at the Catechetical School of Alexandria, was a biblical exegete who functioned within the allegorical tradition of Alexandrian biblical exegesis. But his task was not simply one of interpretation of Scripture; Didymus lived during the time of the great Trinitarian controversies and the rise of monasticism in Egypt. While Didymus would become known as a great allegorical interpreter of Scripture, his biographers, Rufinus, Jerome, and Palladius, preferred to describe him as an ascetic rather than as a theologian.[147]

With the decisions of the Fifth Ecumenical Council at Constantinople (553) that condemn the writings of Origen, Evagrius, and Didymus, a void will be created within the monastic communities. Maximus, in his biblical exegesis, will draw on the exegetical style of Didymus that includes both the literal and allegorical interpretation of Scripture with the goal of clarifying difficulties within various texts (biblical and patristic) and disclosing their inner meanings.[148] He will affirm what Didymus knew, namely, that the literal sense of Scripture can uncover the mysteries of Scripture but that it is the anagogical sense of Scripture arrived at through allegory that brings one to a deeper understanding of the word of God.[149] And, like Didymus, Maximus will use all the tools of Alexandrian exegesis: etymologies of names, symbolic value of numbers, and interpretations of animals, of plants, and of parts of the body, etc. All Scripture has a spiritual meaning.

Why would Maximus incorporate the style and interpretations of three writers who had been condemned? After the decisions of the Fifth Ecumenical Council, the monasteries in Egypt and Palestine were thrown into confusion. What would the monks read, now that the writings of the most popular Christian exegetes and expositors on prayer were to be destroyed? Or, for our purposes, without legitimate allegorical interpretations of Scripture, how would the monks understand Scripture? I believe the *QD* is an attempt to answer that question.

The *Quaestiones et dubia* has not enjoyed as much scholarly attention as have the larger works of Maximus that provide insight into his discussion and refutation of monothelitism.[150] The *QD* does not appear as often in the later manuscript traditions[151] as do the smaller works that provide spiritual guidance.[152] The publication of José H. Declerck's critical edition in 1988, was a significant step in *QD* scholarship, and the first four chapters of Declerck's work have added to the understanding of the manuscript tradition of Maximus's corpus. Until now, an English translation of the *QD* has been unavailable.

There is some secondary literature on the *QD*.[153] The situation expressed by Sherwood almost fifty years ago in his study on the *Amb.Io.* regarding contemporary and past Maximian scholarship— "One of the outstanding deficiencies has been a knowledge of the Confessor's writings in their own context"[154]—holds true for the *QD*. Though the text treats patristic, theological, philosophical, dogmatic, and liturgical concerns, it has been seen primarily as a series of interrogations and responses providing spiritual and moral interpretations of difficult or confusing biblical and patristic passages. For the purposes of this study, the term "question" refers to each individual text, which consists of the interrogation and the response.

The interrogations of the *QD* have been categorized as artificial by Paul Blowers[155] and are believed by Blowers to have been posed by the author himself.[156] The position of Blowers has been called into question by Larchet.[157] I would suggest that, like the other works of Maximus that fall within this genre of the *quaestio-responsio*, there exists the possibility that the interrogations of the *QD* may have been asked by someone other than the author.

The other works of Maximus that employ the *quaestio-responsio* format (*Amb.Io.*, *Amb.Th.*, *QT*, and *Quaestiones ad Theopemptum*) have been given their titles from the name of the recipient of the responses and, in some cases, the texts provide information regarding the request for the response.[158] The extant manuscripts of the *QD* have no title or first page attached.[159] Therefore the recipient, who may have been the person who requested the responses, is unknown. Yet, as Larchet states, Maximus was consulted by numerous people regarding spiritual and theological issues,[160] and it is clear Maximus wrote to clergy and laity alike, as his letters show. Therefore, there are many to whom the *QD* could have been directed and by whom the interrogations could have been provided.[161]

Though it is unlikely that Maximus received a list of over two hundred interrogations from one individual, the entire lot could have been a compilation of the most frequently asked questions or, more likely, a combination of questions from different individuals or members of a monastic community. Perhaps Maximus had answered these interrogations orally at one time or another.[162] It is also clear that not all the questions are the product Maximus's thought. There are three instances of interpolations in the *QD*.[163] The recipient may have been an individual, though it is more likely to have been a community of monks or nuns.[164]

Among the many topics Maximus addresses in the text are interrogations regarding etymology and the interpretation of names,[165] arithmology,[166] the soul,[167] and the *logoi*,[168] an important aspect of Maximus's cosmic theology. Though one finds no direct reference to certain typical Maximian themes in the *QD* (for example, the distinction between γένεσις and γέννησις [*genesis* and *gennesis*],[169] the triad "existence-movement-rest,"[170] refutations of monophysitism[171] or monothelitism[172]), one does, however, find many of the characteristic themes in the thought of Maximus.

Perhaps what is most interesting about the *QD* is that even though the interpretive style has been characterized as anagogical,[173] the language employed throughout the text would seem to belie such a purely anagogical or spiritual emphasis.[174] The word τρόπος (*tropos*) appears more than twice as often as the word ἀναγωγὴ (*anagoge*).[175] This text may be characterized as focusing on θεωρία (*theoria*) rather than πρᾶξις (*praxis*), but the words πρᾶξις and ἀρετὴ (*arête*) appear almost twice as often as θεωρία.[176] Based upon the terminology used by the Confessor, this text appears to be focused on the "active" life of the monk and how to live that active life. This idea will be addressed below.

While there is no indication in the critical edition of the *QD* as to why Maximus committed his thoughts to written form, perhaps the best expression of his motivation can be found in *Amb.Io.* 45:

the texts are written, he says, "for your nourishment,"[177] that is, for the spiritual edification of the reader, whoever that reader may be.

José H. Declerck's Critical Edition

José H. Declerck compiled the critical edition of the QD, which, after the elimination of secondary recensions, consists of four principal recensions.[178] The main recension is *Vat.gr.1703*; the three other recensions are designated as Selection I, Selection II, and Selection III by Declerck.[179] Each recension contains at least one question that is not found in the other three.[180] There is one question that all four recensions share: QD 86 in the first recension, QD I, 22 in the second recension, QD II, 4 in the third recension, and QD III, 17 in the fourth recension. *Vat.gr.1703* constitutes the most important and most ancient[181] source, since it contains the largest number of questions and responses, and, for reasons to be explained below, it is the closest to the original work. Yet the second recension, Selection I, has known the greatest propagation.[182] Selections I, II, and III contain a considerably smaller number of questions than *Vat.gr.1703*, and Declerck has suggested a reason for this.

The author of Selection I has collected what would be considered the more literal interpretations of the biblical and patristic passages. The responses to these questions do not contain anagogical interpretations. Declerck suggests that this was done for a reason.[183] The compiler of Selection I also seems to avoid questions addressing the Evagrian doctrine of the three states of spiritual perfection (πρακτικὴ φιλοσοφία, φυσικὴ θεωρία, and θεολογικὴ φιλοσοφία, *praktike philosophia, physike theoria, theologike philosophia*),[184] and the collection is limited to texts that emphasize the acquisition of certain virtues.[185] This compiler was also interested in the *nomina sacra*[186] and in physiological concerns.[187]

Selection II focuses on interpretations of passages from the Psalter[188] and ends with an exhortation to asceticism.[189] The compiler of Selection III has also omitted questions containing allegorical explanations.[190] The reason for the brevity of Selections I, II, and III resides in the omission of most anagogical interpretations of biblical and patristic passages.

There are also questions found outside the branches of the direct tradition. Certain questions were preserved in other texts in a more isolated way, either singly or in groups of two to five questions.[191] Why the existence of these shorter collections? One reason might be the popular and didactic character of these questions. For example, *QD* I, 1, a listing of the vices and virtues, would have attracted attention since it would be beneficial (especially to a monastic audience) and easy to memorize. *Quaestiones et dubia* I, 68, on the meaning of the monastic schema, as well as *QD* I, 26, on how one obtains the remission of sins, would also be of interest to a monastic community. The "errant" questions and those from the small collections constitute an important contribution to the construction of the critical edition.[192]

It is unknown whether the sum of the questions of the four recensions equals the entire original work, and Declerck suggests that a large part of the original text still may be unknown.[193] However, he hypothesizes that Questions III, 1 and III, 2 should be situated at the beginning of the original redaction.[194] These two questions are not found in *Vat.gr. 1703*, yet the main manuscript for Selection III maintains the same order of the questions as *Vat.gr. 1703*. Declerck suggests that the Selection III manuscript is a copy of *Vat.gr. 1703*, before *Vat.gr. 1703* was mutilated and lost its first few folia.[195]

Lastly, of the four recensions, three (*Vat.gr. 1703*, Selection I, and III) have a southern Italian provenance, while Selection II has an "eastern" provenance. Among the many similarities between Selection II and the *catenae* on the Psalter (the most ancient of which come from Palestine) are the characteristics of the material of the folia (parchment, paper, or silk), the style of the script, and the color of ink.[196] Declerck concludes that the compilers of Selection II came from the East.[197]

It is impossible to reconstruct the original order of the questions. The compilers of the various manuscripts that make up the four recensions would have had their own reasons for copying the text and therefore would have had specific goals in mind that may have affected the order of the questions. Some manuscripts are ordered by length, others by thematic content, and others in groupings relating to biblical or patristic passages.

Declerck's numeration does not offer any indication of the way in which the questions were numbered in the original work.

Therefore, it is impossible to draw any conclusions regarding the position of each question within the context of the entire work.

Vat.gr. 1703 consists of 195 different questions, and it is the largest manuscript. The majority of the questions in the *QD* are found in *Vat.gr. 1703,* with the exception of thirty-six found in Selection I, seven found in Selection II, and one found in Selection III.

The oldest witness of Selection I dates to 994 and consists of eighty-three questions though there are some anomalies;[198] these anomalies include repetitions and questions not considered to be true ἐρωταποκρίσεις (*erotapokriseis*). Since a large number of questions are attested to in many recensions, the questions of this translation are numbered according to *Vat.gr. 1703* and Declerck's Selections I, II, III.[199]

With regard to the study of the indirect tradition, several questions come from exegetical chains,[200] spiritual *florilegia*, and specific citations from patristic writers. The *catenae* and *florilegia* that comment on the Old and New Testaments have recovered the biblical exegetical texts.[201] The questions found in these texts are used by Declerck to recover fragments not preserved in the direct tradition. Maximus is rarely cited in the *catenae*, given that many *catenae* were already constructed by the seventh century.[202] However, another possible reason for the lack of references to Maximus among the *catenae* is the anagogical character of his interpretations. These did not contribute to the information a catenist might hope to convey, namely information related to Christian practice.[203] However, one finds that Maximus is often cited in the *catenae* on the Psalter, and the citations are numerous.[204]

Maximus is cited most often in the spiritual *florilegia* that provide the reader with contemplative material. His writings are also found among the *florilegia* offering practical prescriptions for the Christian life and are directed to laypeople and new monks.[205] Often the interrogations and responses in the *florilegia* address the different forms of *apatheia*, the principal virtues, the divine and human operation of Christ,[206] and the virtues of the body and soul.[207] However, some of the material found in the *florilegia* suffers from false attributions.[208]

Declerck admits that his examination is not exhaustive. He did not comb the entire, as he calls it, "forest" of *scholias* on the discourses of Gregory of Nazianzus[209] but hopes to have located the most important pieces. The study of the indirect tradition has not affected the construction of the critical edition of *Vat.gr. 1703*, though.[210] The information regarding the indirect tradition has contributed to the knowledge of the history of its transmission and reception.[211]

Several questions emerge regarding *Vat.gr. 1703*. Is it possible for the text genuinely to be attributed to Maximus, or is the manuscript an amalgamation of texts borrowed from various sources and labeled under the name of Maximus in order to assure its success? Could the work be that of an imitator who has composed the collection of ἐρωταπόκρισεις (*erotapokriseis*) by copying the style and methods of Maximus, after having been inspired by the *Amb.Io.* or the *QT*?[212] Given the incidence of interpolation in the Combefis edition, are any other questions interpolated?[213] While Declerk admits he is unable to guarantee the authenticity of each question, he believes that any argument for inauthenticity is weak.[214]

Of the 239 questions of the critical edition, the length of each question ranges from one line[215] to several pages.[216] Of the four recensions, the majority of the questions address biblical topics, mainly from the Old Testament,[217] with the largest number of citations from Genesis.[218] Of the questions on passages from the New Testament,[219] the majority come from the Gospel of Matthew.[220]

Among the patristic writers Maximus mentions by name, Gregory Nazianzus is cited the greatest number of times.[221] Other patristic writers include Gregory of Nyssa,[222] Dionysius the Areopagite,[223] Basil of Caesarea,[224] Diadochus of Photike,[225] Irenaeus of Lyons,[226] Cyril of Alexandria,[227] John Chrysostom,[228] Nemesius of Emesa;[229] there is one reference to Aristotle.[230] While the name of Jesus Christ is mentioned most often,[231] Maximus draws on the experiences and activities of other biblical personalities, such as Paul (usually referred to as Ὁ Ἀπόστολος), Moses,[233] and Peter.[234] One question treats the Nicene-Constantinopolitan creed.[235]

Methodology—Teaching the Ascetical Life through *Theoria* and *Praxis*

There are two dangers when attempting to provide some introduction to a text of interrogations and responses produced by Maximus the Confessor. The first danger lies in the temptation to search out and identify Maximian *topoi*, an activity many readers immediately embark upon when reading the Confessor's works. The second danger, or perhaps difficulty, lies in determining something universal to say regarding a series of seemingly disjoint interrogations and responses. The approach of this writer lies somewhere in between the two, hence the subtitle of this introduction to the translation. Maximus's *QD* is primarily pedagogical. He is attempting to teach the reader about the ascetical life, which can only be learned by engaging in both *theoria* and *praxis*.

Maximus applies specific **principles** to his writings, emphasizes certain monastic **topoi**, and uses a variety of **tools** to convey his thought. A distinction must be made between principles, *topoi*, and tools.

A **principle** reflects a framework in which the writing has been developed by the author and interpreted by the audience. As one reads the questions, there are several principles[236] that emerge from almost every question: interpretation (primarily biblical),[237] theological anthropology, anagogy, and typology and also, perhaps less noticeably, the importance of the ascetical life. Maximus's audience, presumably a group of monks, would most likely have read the text searching specifically for teachings on the ascetical life.

Some of the more common monastic **topoi** include the passions, the virtues, and evil. Paul Blowers notes that specific monastic *topoi* are found in the questions posed to Maximus by Thalassius in the *QT*.[238] Two of the most predominant monastic *topoi* (and Maximian *topoi*) found in the *QD* are *theoria* (contemplation) and *praxis* (action), both of which lead, in the writings of Maximus, to *theologia*.[239] In the *QD*, Maximus's discussion of *theoria* and *praxis* is not simply that of defining the terms and their relationship to one another. He also provides an example of *theoria* and *praxis* within the specific responses to each question. This will be discussed in more detail below.

Maximus incorporates several **tools** for conveying his thought: allegory, typology, etymology, number symbolism or arithmology, military terminology, multiple interpretations, and techniques of anthropomorphosis, to name a few. These tools are literary devices to help the reader better understand the message Maximus is trying to convey, and they, therefore, serve a pedagogical function. For example, by providing multiple interpretations of specific biblical passages, Maximus enables his reader to choose the interpretation that best suits the reader's need or would most easily be remembered. The use of military language would have provided his fellow monks, some of whom were likely retired military personnel, with an easier and more familiar way of understanding Scripture.[240]

Maximus would have been exposed to these literary devices or tools through his education and reading of patristic texts.[241] These tools are mentioned because they provide the reader with familiar terminology or methods of analysis to help the reader better understand the interpretations of biblical and patristic texts.

TEACHING TECHNIQUES

Several pedagogical, or teaching, techniques are employed by Maximus in the *QD*:[242]

Etymology. The use of etymology is found throughout the *QD* and primarily in reference to geographical locations. Shinar, where the tower was built (Gen 11:1–9), is translated as "keenness of the teeth" (*QD* 2); Mount Garizin is interpreted as "circumcision" (*QD* 15), Cana as "possession," and Galilee as "revelation" (*QD* 35). Proper names are also subjects for etymological investigation. David is "one who is despised" (*QD* 49); Daniel is the "judgment of God" (*QD* 20); Joseph is "in addition" (*QD* 25); and Jacob/James is "the vanquisher" (*QD* 30 and 191). Samson, is called the true Nazarite or "one fenced about" (*QD* 47) and is "portraying a likeness" (*QD* 47). Herod is "skin-like" (*QD* 71), and Satan is translated as "adversary" (*QD* I, 12). Peter is "obedience," and John is interpreted as a "dove"(*QD* 191).

In *QD* 126, the questioner specifically asks, "What is the etymology of gluttony (γαστριμαργία, *gastrimargia*)?" to which Maximus provides a partial answer of lustfulness (μαργοῦ, *margou*) and cites Aristotle. There is one question where Maximus interprets the spelling of Abraham's name (the inclusion of three a's) in terms of Abraham's ability to see three angels, as compared to Lot who saw only two angels (*QD* 39).

Maximus provides one word that has a double meaning, ἀνατολὴ (*anatole*), both "rising" and "east" (*QD* 44).

Arithmology. The QD, perhaps more than any other text of the
Confessor's, is replete with examples of number symbolism.[243]
Maximus provides different interpretations for specific numbers:[244]
the number two represents body and spirit (*QD* 17), matter and
form (*QD* 39 and 164), soul and body (*QD* 44), perceptible and
intelligible (*QD* 44), law of the spirit and law of the flesh (*QD* 38),
anger and desire (*QD* 73), desire and pleasure (*QD* 39), and the
written (Jewish) and Gospel laws (*QD* 39).

The number three, which was often interpreted as the powers
of the soul (reason, desire, irascibility, which should be balanced,
QD 48), is also interpreted as knowledge (ethical, natural, and
theological, *QD* 29), the laws (natural, written, and grace, *QD* 58),
and a way of life (practical, natural, and theological, *QD* 58). The
number three indicated completeness, since the created order is
composed of three parts (heaven, earth, and the underworld),
and the Godhead is composed of three beings (Father, Son, and
Holy Spirit).[245]

The number four represents the four basic elements (earth,
water, fire, air, found in *QD* 80, 124, 22, 17, 116), the virtues
(prudence, courage, discretion, justice, found in *QD* 48, 116, 41,
46, I, 30), the perceptible things (*QD* 155), the four foundations of
the Gospel (*QD* 116), and the combination of the active, natural,
and theological states with prayer (*QD* 46).[246] The number five
represents the five senses (*QD* 17, 183, 80) and nature (*QD* 41,
124), and Maximus refers to five powers of the soul (*QD* 92).

All the multiples of two, three, four, and five are also significant.
For example, the number twelve is the product of the addition of
three (powers of the soul), four (virtues), and five (senses), or the sum
of five (nature) and seven (time) (*QD* 41). The number ten is a sum of
the addition of five (intellectual senses) and five (bodily senses) (*QD*
43). Ten also represents the Ten Commandments (*QD* 49).

The number twenty is interpreted as earthly attachment,
since the four basic elements are multiplied by the five senses
(*QD* 80). The number forty signifies the perceptible things (*QD*
164) since it is divisible by four, which represents the basic
elements (*QD* I, 30); forty is considered to be a number that
brings about distress because it reminds the reader of the forty
years the Hebrews wandered in the wilderness and experienced
great suffering (*QD* 193).[247]

The number six signifies the creation (QD 35), the creative state, and the perceptible world (QD 176), since the world was created in six days (Gen 2:2). Perhaps one of the most important numbers is the number seven. Seven is referred to many times: the seven activities of the spirit (QD 67), the seven spirits of wickedness, the seven passions of evil, and the seven-fold vengeance (QD 77). Seven also represents the way in which to refine the commandments (QD 148) and the seven-fold punishment of seventy times seven (QD 78).

For Maximus, the number seven also signified time (QD 41).[248] In Gen 41:1–36, Pharaoh's dream speaks of seven years of prosperity and seven years of famine. The number seven represents completeness and perfection, where seven days completed the week and the seventh day is the Sabbath (Gen 1:1–2:4). The land was also to have a Sabbath whereby no crops were to be planted on a specific field on the seventh year (Lev 25:2–7). After Jacob worked seven years with the hope of being given Rachel as his wife, he received Leah and worked seven more years for Rachel (Gen 29:15–30).[249]

Multiples of seven are expressed by the Jubilee, which is celebrated after forty-nine years. At that time, all servants are released and land sold is given back to its original owner (Lev 25:8–55). The number forty-nine is also the time between Easter and Pentecost. Maximus refers to the number fifty as the superlative of weekly time (QD 56) but may specifically mean forty-nine (seven multiplied by seven).[250]

There are two other notable examples of Maximus's use of number symbolism. In QD 56, Maximus mentions the 153 fish discussed in John 21:11, a number that is the sum of the numbers one through seventeen. In QD I, 31 and I, 33, Maximus makes reference to a series of numbers, one through four. This series describes both generations and transgressions. The first through fourth generations represent the stages of the development of a sin. The first generation is the attack of the devil or the seed of evil being planted within the human being. The second generation is the desire for some object. The third generation is the person's consent or willingness to pursue that desire. The fourth generation is engaging in the actual deed.[251] This connection between numbers and stages of sin would have been a useful tool in enabling the reader to commit to memory the anatomy and progression of a sin.

Anthropomorphosis. Throughout the text, Maximus interprets geographical locations, inanimate objects, and animate objects as having specific human attributes, passions, or activities.[252] A city has been interpreted as redirected *askesis* (*QD* 90), human souls (*QD* 90 and 145), and virtue (*QD* 169). A tower has been interpreted as the carnal passions (*QD* 2). Wool has been called ethical activity (*QD* 17), and two pillars have been interpreted as anger and desire (*QD* 67). Animals and plants are found throughout the *QD*. The lion (*QD* 3), the dog (*QD* 156), and grapes (*QD* 47) are interpreted as anger. Both the bear (*QD* 3 and 147) and the ass (*QD* 80) represent desire.

The representation of animals as the passions is found in the writings of Philo.[253] The lion and the bear appear often in ascetical literature: Sabas tames the lion by singing psalms;[254] Poemen refers to anger as a lion and fornication as a bear.[255] Therefore, the use of these animals to convey certain passions would have been familiar to a monk.

Multiple interpretations. Maximus often provides two or three alternate interpretations of a scriptural passage when responding to an interrogation. The best example is found in *QD* I, 29, where when asked for an interpretation of a passage from Psalm 103, "What is, 'here they build their nests'?" Maximus provides three interpretations, addressing sparrows, souls, and the different virtues.

In *QD* 185, Maximus offers two interpretations of Elias's time spent in the brook and having been fed by the raven. In one interpretation, Elias represents the knowledgeable *nous* sitting in the brook of temptations and the labors of *askesis*. The raven represents nature blackened as a result of disobedience. In the second interpretation, Elias is a type of the Lord coming into the world and accepting the temptations and sufferings that await him. In *QD* 187, the first sea is interpreted as both baptism and the active life. The second sea is the resurrection and knowledge.

In other questions, rather than provide alternate interpretations, Maximus adds to theexisting interpretation. In *QD* 39, the author explains why Lot only sees two angels while Abraham sees three. The two angels are first interpreted as matter and form, since Lot is unable to worship the divine except through visible things. Maximus goes on to say that Lot is unable to hold firmly to knowledge regarding the monad and the Trinity—and therefore he sees two angels.

Military terminology. In several questions, Maximus addresses scriptural passages regarding military actions taken during the combat of the Israelites with their enemies. In *QD* 80, Gideon rejects the soldiers who are afraid to engage in battle, and Maximus interprets these ten thousand as those who run from the hard work of virtue (Judg 6–7). Gideon goes on to reject another twenty thousand (the biblical passage says twenty-two thousand), whom Maximus interprets as those who betray the perceptible things with the senses (or, those who rely on the senses). The author concludes by saying that the *Logos* rejects those not fit for the spiritual troops, and only three hundred remain.

Quaestiones et dubia 82 discusses the divine troops who are led by the trumpet of the Gospel. In *QD* 165, Maximus interprets a parable from the Gospel of Luke (14:31–2) where Jesus emphasizes the importance of one relinquishing all for the sake of the Gospel. Maximus discusses the king who prepares the ten thousand troops (interpreted as the kingly *nous*) for battle against the king of the twenty thousand troops (interpreted as the "lord of the world who stands in formation with the perceptible things and the senses"). It is through the senses that the enemy prepares for battle within each person. The one who pleads for terms of peace during war is interpreted as one who is satisfied with what has been imposed upon the human being by nature after having experienced the original transgression of Adam and Eve. This person is unable to live by "the precepts of the Gospel."

If the *QD* was written while Maximus was at the monastery in Chrysopolis, which may have housed several retired military personnel, it is possible the author may have included military terminology to help his fellow monks better understand his biblical interpretations.

Nature imagery. Of the 239 questions of the *QD*, twenty-seven refer to animals, plants, and/or natural events. The anatomy, physiology, and behaviors of animals and plants are interpreted. These questions refer primarily to Old Testament texts.

Quaestiones et dubia 37, which addresses Levitical laws of cleanliness, discusses the position of the fins on a fish. The fish with fins on its belly represents the one whose reason is being threatened by pleasure. Therefore, the fins on the belly prohibit pleasure from entering the belly, and the obvious reference here is to the passion of gluttony. The fish with fins on its back swims powerfully through life and patiently endures all difficulties. The fish with fins on its tail skillfully avoids the grip of the demons. The fish with fins on both sides of its head has a mind that strengthens its own ability to take part in contemplation.

In *QD* 17, the goat that leaps from mountain to mountain is interpreted as the soul that leaps across "the cliffs of temptations" and "ascends the prophetic mountains" to "seek the summit of knowledge and to delight in this." The heron, before engaging in sexual intercourse, mourns first for forty days, and then, after the action, mourns for another forty days.[256]

The plump stalks of wheat seen in Pharaoh's dream (Gen 41:1–7) are interpreted as knowledge, while the thin stalks are ignorance.[257] Stones are interpreted as both the apostles (*QD* 15) and the divine *logoi* (*QD* 76 and 82). The rainbow placed in the sky by God after the deluge (Gen 9:12–17) is a covenant between God and Noah. This is interpreted as the flesh of the Lord,[258] signifying the incarnation as the covenant between God and humanity.

Sacramental symbolism. Throughout the *QD* one finds references to liturgical and sacrificial activity. *Quaestiones et dubia* 13 questions the practice of the distribution of the bread and wine during the celebration of the Eucharist. Maximus responds by explaining the mystical nature of the symbols of bread and wine, calling them representations of the divine essence. In *QD* 115, Maximus addresses 1 Cor 15:29 and discusses baptism as a *typos* of the burial and resurrection of the Lord, assuring the reader that by taking part in baptism one should expect the resurrection, and *QD* 80 interprets the fleece of Gideon as Judaic worship.

Most of the questions discussing sacramental issues refer to the sacrificial laws found in the Old Testament. *Quaestiones et dubia* 17 explains the five sacrifices mentioned in Leviticus: the sheep, the ox, the goat, the pigeon, and the dove, and *QD* 153 questions the use of flour in the lawful sacrifices: what is the meaning when it is mixed with oil, or mixed in an earthen vessel, or mixed in a frying pan? Fine flour is interpreted as nourishment for rational beings but when mixed with oil it is reason illuminated by knowledge. When flour is mixed in a frying pan, it is understood as reason that has been tested by internal temptations. When mixed in an earthen vessel, flour represents reason remaining steadfast throughout the testing by external temptations.

In *QD* 154, Maximus explains the celebration of the festival of the Lord (Num 29:12), where, beginning with fourteen bulls, seven are sacrificed on seven consecutive days. Maximus compares the young bulls to boys reaching puberty (age fourteen), who begin to experience "passionate movement." The Confessor concludes by suggesting that the law shows the necessity of offering sacrifice to God in order to decrease the effect of the passions until perfect detachment is attained.

Use of legal texts. The majority of the questions that discuss legal issues refer to passages from the Old Testament (approximately twelve, excluding questions regarding passages from Proverbs that could be considered legal pronouncements). Some questions address sacrificial laws (*QD* 154, previous paragraph), purification laws (*QD* 37), and other laws regarding the murder of human beings and livestock (*QD* 24, *QD* 76, *QD* 151).

Of the eight questions that address legal precepts from the New Testament, *QD* 18 provides a good example. Maximus explains why the Lord is required to pay taxes (Matt 17:24–7). The tax collectors are interpreted as the natural passions that make demands of all people. The Lord, as a result of his freedom, agrees to pay the taxes, and, according to Maximus, that agreement signifies his acceptance of the innocent passions. These natural passions are accepted by the Lord, who will perfect them. The coin pulled from the mouth of the fish (which is to be paid to the tax collectors and is interpreted as the suffering of sin that swims in the sea of life) is the *logos* of the flesh. By taking human form, the Lord releases the *logos* of the flesh from suffering. The *logos* of the flesh is the human condition of need. By taking human form, according to Maximus, the Lord restores human nature from the passion of self-abuse.

Use of lists. There are six questions that provide lists for the reader to consider. In *QD* 17, the sheep is described as offering three things to its owner: wool, milk, and a lamb. Wool is interpreted as ethical activity, milk as natural contemplation, and the lamb is one who has benefited from teaching. *Quaestiones et dubia* 59 describes the seven ways in which human nature has fallen: through Adam, through Cain, through Noah's generation, through the construction of the tower in Shinar, through Abraham's generation, through Moses's generation, and through the generation whose actions led to the coming of the prophets.

In QD 92, Maximus lists the seven laws of nature. In QD 137, there is a list of eight offerings for atonement and their interpretations. *Quaestiones et dubia* I, 45 mentions six "stillnesses" that are necessary for one to know God fully. One maintains stillness with regard to sinful activity, the exciting way of life, the intermingling with those who live recklessly, living an unsuitable life, a slanderous existence and disruption of the *nous*, and with regard to willfulness. These lists would have provided the reader with a way to categorize the teachings and may have helped the monk in committing to memory the ways in which to live the monastic life in a practical way.

Alteration of scriptural passages. There are two questions where Maximus provides what appears to be an alternate reading of the scriptural passage. While it is not clear whether the Confessor may have had a copy of Scripture that has since been lost to us or whether the mistaken recollection of Scripture is accidental, it is possible he altered the biblical story to suit his pedagogical needs.

In QD 80, Maximus first confuses the two groups of soldiers. According to the biblical passage (Judg 7:3), the first group to leave the army consists of twenty thousand soldiers (actually, twenty-two thousand[259]) and the second group consists of ten thousand soldiers.[260] The group of twenty thousand are afraid and leave, while the ten thousand are those who lap the water with their tongues rather than scoop up the water with their hands.[261] Maximus reports that the first group consists of the ten thousand and the second group, the twenty thousand. This confusion may have facilitated Maximus's interpretation of the twenty thousand as those who are betrayed by the senses since the number four (the elements) multiplied by five (the senses) equals twenty.

In the same question, Maximus states that there are twenty thousand soldiers instead of twenty-two thousand, which is the number found in the biblical passage. This change in number would satisfy his purpose of producing a more cohesive arithmology, since the multiplication of the four elements by the five senses equals twenty (or a form of twenty), not twenty-two.

In another example, King Adonibezek of Jerusalem is hanged along with four other kings after having been slain.[262] The King of Ai is hanged on a double tree, ἐπὶ ξύλου διδύμου (*epi xylou didymou*), also translated as a gallows.[263] Maximus seems to confuse the two stories in *QD* 174, stating that King Adonibezek is hanged on the double tree. If the mistake was purposeful, the goal would have been to further his ascetical teaching on the body and soul.

Typology. In *QD* 122, Maximus specifically asks about the types found in Exodus, including Moses and Pharaoh. Maximus does not hesitate to use the word τύπος (*typos*) in the interrogations as well as in his responses. In *QD* 115, he calls baptism a type for burial and resurrection, and in *QD* 68, Samson bears the type of Christ. There are other instances where Maximus creates his own typology. For example, in *QD* 32, he calls Ahab a type of ruler of Israel, and in *QD* 193, Elias bears the type of prophetic grace.

Allegory. The word ἀλληγορία (*allegoria*) is found only three times in the *QD*.[264] In *QD* 90, Maximus provides an allegorical interpretation of a city as redirected *askesis* (Matt 10:23) and in *QD* I, 8, provides a definition of allegory and compares this to tropology.[265]

Anagogy. While the word ἀναγωγή (*anagoge*) appears only eleven times in the *QD*, most questions are interpreted anagogically. In *QD* 8, after providing a literal explanation of the meaning of dressing a fig tree, Maximus interprets a herder "according to the method of anagogy."[266] In *QD* 30, anagogy and contemplation are considered ways in which the soul separates itself from evil. The interrogation of *QD* 44 specifically requests an interpretation of the garden planted in the East "by anagogy."[267] Though the word itself is not often mentioned, many interpretations of biblical and patristic texts in the *QD* are, as Maximus himself has attested, anagogical.

THE ASCETICAL LIFE

Maximus understood *askesis* as a life-long endeavor that consists of the struggle and discipline to maintain control over the passions. The ascetical life includes the pursuit of virtue, and his personal dedication to this life prompted him to write about it.[268]

Maximus's understanding of the ascetical life can be best expressed by *QD* 10, where he responds to questions regarding Jewish feasts. The reader is encouraged to (1) cease from engaging in evil deeds; (2) cease from consenting to evil thoughts; (3) not allow the provocation of desire; (4) put to rest the memories of evil and imaginings; and (5) build up perfect detachment.

He also provides details about *askesis*. *Askesis* affects both the mind (*QD* 84) and the body (*QD* 80), and if directed in the wrong manner, it can lead one to pridefulness (*QD* 90). It is considered to be a protection (*QD* 90) against the temptations (*QD* 94) but consists of hard labor (*QD* 127). *Askesis*[269] only takes place through self-control (*QD* 68, 151 and II, 18), is important for the *nous* (*QD* 52), and is dependent upon the ethical way of life (*QD* 97), which includes engaging in hard work (*QD* 185, and I, 27) and undergoing sleeplessness (*QD* 150).

Maximus mentions the vices of gluttony and sexual impurity (*QD* 2), but the responses more often provide instruction regarding how to avert such difficulties, namely, through self-control.[270] More importantly, though, Maximus provides two examples of the person who is living the ascetical life. The first example is Samson, called a Nazarite or ascetic.[271] Samson is also a type for Christ.[272] The relationship between Samson and Christ is found in the similarities between them: both were bound and handed over by their own people to foreigners.

Samson kills the passions by engaging in good deeds, and he thirsts for divine knowledge. When he finds himself trapped beneath the walls of the temple (the perceptible things), it is by action that he is able to elevate the senses and move them toward higher knowledge.[273] These actions of Samson (the destruction of the passions by engaging in the active life, seeking divine knowledge, and moving beyond the senses to higher knowledge) are characteristics of the ascetical life that Maximus would have wanted to convey to his reader.

The Nazarite or ascetic in *QD* 47 is one who wishes to purify himself by not partaking of grapes or any grape products, namely, any type of wine or liquor.[274] He is to grow his hair long and is not to come into contact with any dead flesh. In the Old Testament, these were called the Nazarite vows.[275] Purity in the Old Testament conveyed the meaning of being free from any physical, moral, or ritual contamination. Contamination resulted from one's contact with a corpse, from the involuntary emission of fluid from sexual organs, from eating prohibited foods, and from having contracted diseases of the skin, such as leprosy.[276]

The Nazarite has been told to abstain from wine, which Maximus interprets as causing the manic drunkenness of evil. The vine from which the wine comes (the "vine of Sodom") is interpreted as irrationality or derangement. One is to abstain from the wine of irrationality but also from the source of the wine (grapes) and the source of irrationality (anger). The biblical passage cautions the Nazarite against eating raisins, which Maximus interprets as the aging of anger (the aging of the grape), or resentment. Wine that has soured is interpreted as the sadness that results from the inability to achieve certain goals by pleasure. The fortified drink is the pleasure in taking vengeance against one's neighbor; and the pressed remains of the grapes (the stems, seeds, skins) are called the intentional and guaranteed forms of evil.

Maximus carefully deconstructs the passion of anger and lists the accompanying emotions and behaviors. Anger causes one to develop resentment, sadness, and pleasure in taking vengeance.[277] Maximus's inclusion of this lesson on the dangers of anger within the context of a discussion on the ascetic Samson clarifies that one is not able to lead the ascetical life without working to overcome the passions.

THEORIA AND PRAXIS

Theoria (translated as contemplation)[278] is mentioned fifty-one times in the *QD*. *Praxis* (translated as action) is mentioned sixty-one times. There are few nouns mentioned more often than these two words in the text.[279] Yet, as frequently as the individual words appear, they do not often appear together in the same question.[280] In *QD* 190, Maximus provides a good example of the relationship between *theoria* and *praxis*. He states that the person engaging in action or deeds (ὁ πρακτικός, *ho praktikos*) will depart from the battle with the passions and come to natural contemplation (φυσικὴν θεωρίαν, *physike theoria*). This person becomes occupied with the contemplation of existing things and, by engaging in action, brings the battle to an end. One then moves beyond natural contemplation, leaving behind all things, and moves toward the Cause, namely, God, through apophatic theology. One no longer makes positive statements about God that result from the affirmation of existing things but develops understanding by means of "the theology according to negation."[281] There seems to be a progression from action to contemplation.

However, in QD 87, after comparing the basic elements that make up the body with the basic elements of the soul, Maximus states that the source and elemental matter of the soul come from the four universal virtues and the right ordering of one's ethical behavior. At that time, contemplation is given bodily existence, and Maximus concludes the question by stating that action is the manifestation of contemplation in a person. Therefore, it is by contemplation that action occurs, and it seems as if one moves from contemplation to action.

Finally, in QD 130, he presents the question of "whether contemplation precedes action." His answer provides information about the modes of *theoria* and *praxis* but not *theoria* and *praxis* themselves. He responds that the mode of contemplation is two-fold: that which precedes actions and that which arises out of actions. Therefore, the issue here is not that of the importance of *theoria* over *praxis*, or a sense of progression from one to the other, but the intermingling that takes place between the two. In QD 182—the interpretation of Acts 20:9—where Eutychus falls from the third-story building after having fallen asleep while listening to Paul preach, Maximus assigns the active life to the first story of the building, contemplation to the second story, and theology to the third story. *Praxis* produces *theoria*, and *theoria* produces *praxis*.

Maximus is not always clear when distinguishing between content of a thing and mode of operation of that same thing. It is not always clear whether he is discussing the *logos* of some "thing," the meaning or content, or the *tropos* of that same "thing," the way in which that "thing" is manifested. The confusion arises, in particular, when the word for the content and the mode are the same.

Such is the case with the word *praxis*. *Praxis* is both the way in which something occurs as well as the object (manifestation) itself. For example, in QD 186, action is the object, or the *logos* (represented by meat), but in QD 145, it is by action and contemplation that souls are built, and action becomes the mode or *tropos*. However, there are instances when *praxis* as objective *logos* is described more specifically.[282] In *QD* 80, *praxis* is specified by the ethical way of life (ἡ ἠθικὴ φιλοσοφία, *he ethike philosophia*).

Theoria is described differently. *Theoria* as *tropos* is found in *QD* 145. Contemplation is the means by which souls grow. But Maximus is not very precise in describing the objective form, or *logos*, of *theoria*. Most often he mentions knowledge (γνῶσις, *gnosis*),[283] virtue,[284] and teaching. Knowledge and action work together to advance the soul. It is by the labors of action that one draws upon the waters of knowledge. Also in *QD* 80, Maximus states that appropriate knowledge is necessary for the accomplishment of moral virtue. In *QD* 86, one is able to attain the divinely inspired teaching and take part in virtuous action only through the mortification of the body. The relationship between *theoria*, virtue, knowedge, and teaching is a fluid one.

Maximus also conveys the meaning of *theoria* and *praxis* in yet another way. He constructs his sentences[285] and paragraphs in such a way that the resulting teaching can be seen structurally as another form of *theoria* and *praxis*.

In the response to almost every question, the structure is as follows: a biblical or patristic quotation to which he must respond, a preliminary explanation of that quotation, and then an expression of Maximus's experience, though he never calls it such.

In *QD* 21, Maximus begins his explanation of the passage from 1 Cor 15:23–24 ("Christ is the beginning; then they who are of Christ in his coming, [and] then the end") by interpreting the word "beginning" as the resurrection, "they who are in Christ" as the faithful, and "the end" as the salvation for all. This is the preliminary explanation or general interpretation of the passage. He then provides another interpretation that could be called personal: "beginning" is faith in Christ, "they who are in Christ" are works of faith, and "the end" is interpreted as being bound to God. While this may seem to be two parallel interpretations, there is something else going on.

Maximus continues his interpretation by offering the next scriptural passage, "death is the last enemy to be destroyed,"[286] and interprets the passage as the experience one has when one submits one's entire "self-determining will" (τὸ αὐτεξούσιον θέλημα, *to autexousion thelema*) to God. This second interpretation is most likely an expression of personal experience. The structure of the responses of most questions includes a formal interpretation, *theoria*, and a more personal interpretation, *praxis*.

Another example is found in *QD* 27. In the interpretation of a passage from Exodus ("to become rancid for those who considered it to be insufficient"[287]), Maximus first calls "manna" the word of God, which, through activity and knowledge, nourishes the soul. This is the formal interpretation, or *theoria*. The personal interpretation, or *praxis*, follows.

One gathers manna sufficiently when one follows the "middle way of the virtues" (τὴν μεσότητα τῶν ἀρετῶν, *ten mesoteta ton areton*) and avoids both the excesses and the deficiencies of all things. The example Maximus provides is the way in which a person who demonstrates discretion looks upon marriage. If by avoiding licentiousness one sees marriage as abominable, that person is making an excessive judgment. When one is unable to measure one's judgment as excessive, one will be led to other, more destructive, passions. The *logos* of discretion then becomes rancid and the other passions are similar to worms that result when food, in this case manna, becomes rotten.

This second interpretation is an expression of Maximus's experience. It is highly probable that a monk in the monastery might consider marriage to be an abomination, and Maximus may have felt the need to address this situation. Even though Christ was considered the model of virginity and those who remained celibate were living in imitation of him,[288] Maximus would have understood the importance of providing a more balanced approach to the passions and by doing so would offer an example of what it means to practice virtue by "the middle position and the royal way."[289]

In both of these examples, Maximus provides a biblical passage and a more formal interpretation that can be called *theoria*. He then provides his own personal experience as an expression of *praxis*. While the more formal interpretations of Scripture were necessary in order for Maximus's works to be taken seriously as functioning within the biblical exegetical tradition of Christianity, the inclusion of his personal experience, and the emphasis on *praxis* as well as *theoria*, was equally important. In the *QD*, Maximus the Confessor highlights the need to balance one's spiritual life by engaging in both *theoria* and *praxis*, and he concretely demonstrates how easily it can be done—well, maybe not that easily.

TRANSLATOR'S NOTE

This translation of Maximus the Confessor's *Quaestiones et dubia* follows the format of Declerck's critical edition. The footnotes contain both biblical (including variants in the Septuagint) and patristic references. The remaining footnotes provide brief explanations of specific transliterated Greek or technical terms. The Greek transliterated terms fall into two categories: (1) Hebrew words that have been transliterated into Greek and then transliterated again into English (for example, *raka*[290]); and (2) Greek words that have been transliterated rather than translated into English.

Of the Greek words transliterated into English, several may be familiar, *logos*, and *Theotokos*[291] for example. Rather than providing multiword translations for a single Greek term, more often than not I have retained certain words, such as *askesis, nous,* and *gnosis*,[292] in their Greek transliterated form. Maximus's understanding of the terms *logos, askesis, and nous* are clarified as follows.

The word *logos* takes on a particular significance in the writings of Maximus the Confessor.[293] Declerck's critical edition does not differentiate, perhaps for good reason, between *Logos* as the Word of God (the second person of the Trinity), and *logos* (which is translated in various ways, including word, reason, passage, and, most importantly, in terms of the concept of the *logoi*). Though the word has a long history in philosophical and Christian thought, for Maximus *logos* is used to express three realities: reason, Word, and principles. This presents a classic translation problem in Maximus's writings, where *logos*, having so many different meanings, can be translated as word of Scripture, reason, Word, argument, or principle(s).

The *logos* of a being is one's principal or essential reason, that which fundamentally defines and characterizes the being. The *logos* of a being is, in a double sense, its principle and its end. Every being has a *logos* that predefines its mode of existence. There is one *logos* for each thing that does exist or will exist. The *logos* is not only the divine will in the sense that it corresponds to the creative intention of God *for* that being but also in the sense that it corresponds to the divine intention of God. It is through their true *logos* that beings have something in common with one another.[294] Establishing harmony with one's *logos* is equivalent to moving in accordance with the purpose of God.[295]

Maximus also uses the term *logos* to refer to the second person of the Trinity, the creator of the universe and the lawgiver.[296] It is the incarnate *Logos* who holds together all the other *logoi*, "for the wisdom and sagacity of God the Father is the Lord Jesus Christ, who holds together the *logoi* of beings by the power of wisdom."[297]

The *logoi* are the divine intentions for creation,[298] and the *logoi* of all beings have been determined together with God before time, held together in their differentiation within and by the *Logos*. The concrete world in which human beings live is brought into existence in accordance with the preexistent *logoi*, which are identical with God's purposes for the world. They are not manifestations of the essence of God but of the creative will of God. The highest *logoi* of God that are accessible to the human being are his goodness and love.[299] The preexistence of all *logoi* in God safeguards their unity in him, but their differentiation safeguards their independence and individual existence.

The ancient idea of the *logoi* of creation, though found in Stoicism and Neoplatonism, was well developed by Maximus, who drew from Dionysius the Areopagite, though Thunberg mentions other possible predecessors.[300]

Askesis has been translated in various ways depending on the context of the sentence. *Askesis* was considered by Maximus to be essential for one to overcome fallen humanity. The primary model of *askesis* is the struggle of Christ with the Devil, who tempted Christ not only in the desert but also through the Pharisees.[301]

Askesis, according to Maximus, is integral to the Christian life and is considered a personal response to the self-emptying (*kenosis*) activity modeled by the life of Christ in the incarnation. The motivating force for any type of *askesis* is the desire for God, and the concept of *askesis* is more response than willed action. It is an urge to single-mindedness that is God-given. And it is the love for Christ that compels one to engage in the ascetical life not the will to fulfill a specific ascetical goal.

The *nous*, according to Maximus, is the spiritual center and the image of God in the human being. The term is found in Scripture and is translated as "mind." Maximus also calls the *nous* "the inner man," who gives consent to sin. The highest function of the *nous* is to contemplate the divine realities, in particular, the Holy Trinity. The term appears most often in Maximus's ascetical writings, where the work of the passions is addressed, and the passions are said to distract the *nous* from contemplation. It is the *nous* that is responsible for the relationship between the human being and God, where the *nous* represents the human being as a whole.[302]

Through contemplation (*theoria*), the *nous* perceives the divine energies present in creation (the *logoi*, passing through them to God by the Spirit). The *nous* that has a longing for God through the desire for love spends time with God, becoming wise, good, powerful, a friend of humanity, compassionate, and long-suffering. In short, the *nous* takes on the properties of God.[303] But it also receives the knowledge of God by being passive and becoming receptive (in a pure way) to the revelation that takes place within it.[304]

Maximus's understanding of the *nous*, though very similar to that of Evagrius (similar use of the trichotomy, *nous*, soul, and body, though for Maximus this trichotomy is not ontological), is central to Maximus's ascetical and mystical understanding of the human being. The *nous*, engaging in prayer, withdraws from all thoughts. Without love, self-control (*egkrateia*), and prayer, the *nous* is unable to devote itself to God.[305]

Apatheia has traditionally been translated as "dispassion," or "impassibility."[306] Throughout the translation I have chosen to translate the word *apatheia* as "dispassion" or "detachment," depending on the context. The word "dispassion" connotes an emotionalism while "detachment" connotes a choice of removing oneself from something else, a volitional act.

The monastic life was one in which the emphasis on volition outweighed that on emotion. Monastic texts were replete with references to the will, free choice, and self-determination. The words *pathos* and *pathe* were most often used to describe suffering. Therefore, *apatheia*, appearing twelve times in the QD, should be translated with that volitional sense intact.

Traditionally, *theosis* has been translated as "divinization" or
"deification."[307] The difficulty with these translations is that both
give the sense of the individual person being acted upon rather
than the person actively engaging in his or her own *theosis*. For
this reason, more often I have chosen to translate *theosis* as "union
with God."

Known biblical and patristic quotations that Declerck has
identified are enclosed by double quotation marks. Brackets are
used in the translation to provide additional explanation that
might clarify the meaning of the sentence. Parentheses are used
when supplying the original Greek term transliterated into English
and when it seems that Maximus was making parenthetical
statements. Declerck does not include parentheses in his critical
edition, but there are times when Maximus suggests examples or
adds commentary for clarification of his thought.

The lacunae found in the text are denoted by three asterisks
(***). Numbers are translated in two ways. Since some numbers in
the critical edition of the *QD* are written out (i.e., fourteen, five
hundred) while others are expressed in numerical form (i.e., 1, 3,
100), I have followed the same pattern in the English translation.

Twice I have chosen an alternate reading than that found in
Declerck's critical edition (but found in the apparatus). In *QD*
44.25, κακοῦ has been selected instead of κακοῦσθαι, and in *QD*
I, 68.4, τόπον has been chosen instead of τρόπον. Because of
the possibility of an orthographic variation that is phonetically
significant, I have replaced ἐτυμολογοῦντας by ἐτοιμολογοῦντας
in *QD* 76.20.[308] It is my opinion that the latter word is more
appropriate for the context.

The particles μέν and δέ are found in combination throughout
the *QD*. These two limbs of the grammatically coordinated
antithesis have been translated as "on the one hand" and "on
the other hand." In the following translation of the *QD*, since the
force of the two particles is not as strong as the above-mentioned
translations, the words are not always translated.[309] Throughout
the text Maximus provides multiple answers to questions. He
rarely provides a single answer to one question, and when offering
his responses, he uses the μέν/δέ construction to help clarify that
there is not one definitive answer to these questions; there can be
several. Because he provides several answers to any one question,

he does not consider his own responses to be definitive. The μέν/ δέ construction helps to clarify this.

The word ξύλον appears twenty-three times in the QD. I have chosen to translate the word as "tree" or "wood," instead of as "cross." The theological references to the cross of Christ are made specific by Maximus with the use of the word σταυρός. Though there may be other references to "tree," for example, δένδρον,[310] ξύλον will be translated as "tree" also, when the context dictates.

I have chosen to retain the Greek spelling of the word "Cyzikos." Lastly, the scriptural passages of the Old Testament are from the Septuagint, hence references to 4 Kings and the differing numeration for the psalms.

ST. MAXIMUS the CONFESSOR'S
Quaestiones et dubia TRANSLATION

Question 1

*** and it is restored again to its original form, that is, to the desire according to nature *** . And the 'placing of the hand "into the bosom"'[1] means our Lord Jesus Christ, the Word of the Father, who was made flesh in our laboratory of nature; for this is what "the bosom"[2] and "the white hand" signifies. And again, by the hand's restoration to its original form is shown how, after the resurrection, when the Lord was taken up, he was restored to the Father's bosom. For Moses, since he became a mediator between God and the people, at times gives a face to "the God and Father,"[3] and at times to our nature.

Question 2

What does the tower built in the land of Sennar mean?[4]

✛ We, too, build a tower whenever we move "from the East,"[5] that is, whenever we move away from knowledge. And we come into the land of Sennar, that is, into the passion of gluttony.[6] For Sennar is translated as 'the keenness of the teeth.' Then, we also build a tower, that is, we value the carnal passions and we build by linking together passion to passion. And "up to heaven";[7] for, having focused their care upon vanities, they never wish to stop, but [also] have an insatiable appetite for these things. But God stops the construction of the tower and "confuses their languages"[8] whenever he, instructing [us] for our benefit, thwarts our evil. For whenever he instructs one who has given way to the depravity of sexual impurity by sickness, or tempers one who has become enslaved to gluttony by poverty, it is as if he creates a hindrance to [the construction of] the tower of passions, at the same time "confusing the languages." For, by sickness, he restrains the fornicator who is always concerned with sexual impurity, causing him to be completely preoccupied with the health of the body, as if confusing the language of the continuous pursuit of passion.

Question 3

What does it mean that David sang and stopped the evil spirit in Saul?[9]

✥   Everyone who, like the blessed David, shepherds the sheep, that is to say the reasoning part of the soul, and is victorious over anger and lust just as he was over the lion and she-bear,[10] this same person, by making use of the word of teaching, along with [that of] a certain lofty contemplation, delights the hearer and puts to sleep the passions of wickedness that are in him.

Question 4

Since it has been written in the Gospel, "Unless one is born of water and the Spirit"[11] and again, in another place, "He will baptize you with the Holy Spirit and fire,"[12] I beg to learn, what is the difference?

✥   In each person in whom the Holy Spirit comes to be, it cleanses, like water, the defilement of the flesh, it washes away, like the wind, the stains of the soul, as Holy Spirit, it establishes the ways of the virtues, like fire, it makes [one] a god by grace, causing to show in him the fiery, divine marks of virtue.[13]

Question 5

Since, according to the theologian Gregory who said in the discourse on Pentecost[14] that the apostles have attained perfection through three charisms: first, in healing sicknesses and driving out demons; second, his [Jesus] breathing [upon them] after the resurrection;[15] third, the Spirit itself essentially in the form of tongues of fire, please provide an example by which it can be explained how, if someone should become equal to the apostles with respect to virtue, he or she is able to receive the above-mentioned graces and how should one understand the word 'essentially'?

✠   It is possible also for us, if indeed we strive to become imitators of the apostles: first by action to take command over the passions [in the right way] and to cure thoroughly the sicknesses of the soul; second, through natural contemplation[16] to restore nature to itself; third, through the teaching of the word[17]—for this is the "tongues"—to become a fire to those who hear, both consuming their passions as fire [does] and at the same time enlightening them. And, as to how, at first, the Holy Spirit was at work in the apostles, and how, in the end, he descended upon them essentially, one must explain this by way of an example. Just as, when wood is placed in a frying pan, when the wood is lit from below, the wood receives the heat of the fire through the pan, so at first the Spirit operated obscurely in the saints. But if keeping to the same image, someone removes the pan from in-between, and the fire takes hold of the wood directly, straightaway the wood is assimilated to its proper nature. Thus, it is possible to describe [the meaning of] 'essentially' through perceptible examples.

Question 6
Since the Scripture does not clearly state that Abraham gave the tithes to Melchisedek,[18] but speaks differently—and if he gave back everything, as he himself says that he took nothing even to the "strap of a sandal"[19] how is it that he gave the tithes? For he himself, when he departed for battle in a panic, did not bring anything of his own with him.

✠   Since the Divine Scripture says that Melchisedek is "a priest of God,"[20] Abraham, as occupying the place of a layperson, is fittingly believed to have given tithes to the priest. But that he had also [some means] from which to provide them is clear from the following: for the kings who had encamped against Sodom had taken, not only the things belonging to the Sodomites, but also had with them spoils from other places that they had captured beforehand. So, when Abraham had defeated them and had taken all of their possessions, those which belonged to the Sodomites he returned to them, while the other things he kept for himself, and, from these, he offered the tithes to Melchisedek.

Question 7

Why were the priests according to the Law not forbidden to have wives, but priests according to Christ are forbidden, as far as custom goes?

✚   The most ready answer is that it is because the Gospel is higher and because virginity has become accessible to many ever since the Master of all was pleased to be born through virginity, a thing which was rare among the ancients. And since the priesthood of the Gospel is believed to exist according to the order of Melchisedek[21] and not according to the order of Aaron, and Melchisedek is not recorded as having had a wife,[22] therefore it is also unfitting that bishops, who serve as priests according to his order, should have wives.

Question 8

Since it has been written that the prophet Amos was a "goatherd," "a dresser of fig trees,"[23] what is a "goatherd" and what is "to dress"?

✚   A "goatherd" is a herder of goats, and "to dress" is to cut. Therefore, since the sap of the fig tree is coarse and thick and toxic, they who dress it cut the fig tree with knives, causing the sap to flow down [the tree]. And insects crawl inside it, and, when the sun's ray penetrates, they sweeten and soften it [the sap]. This is, on the one hand, the literal sense; but according to the anagogical method [i.e., the way of interpreting that leads the spirit upward], a herder of goats is someone who, through reason, shepherds the desiring part of the soul. And the person who, through self-control, mortifies the body and drains off the moisture of the passions, is the one who dresses fig trees. For he receives divine thoughts, which are likened to insects, and by the "sun of righteousness"[24] he is sweetened and softened in soul and is appointed a prophet from God and a teacher to others.

Question 9

What does the bronze[25] snake signify, which was raised up by Moses on high in the wilderness according to God's command?[26] The spiritual snake, who from the beginning deceived the human being, through disobedience infused the law of sin in our flesh, slithering like a snake in us through pleasure; for this reason, if the one who walks the way of virtue (a desert for the passions) should turn again to Egypt, that is, to the benightedness of sin,[27] he is struck by the noetic snakes. But if he shall gaze upon the crucified Lord, whose flesh, hung on high, has made dead and inoperative the law in our flesh of the snake of sin, he is saved. And the snake is bronze, since the nature of bronze neither disintegrates nor permits rust, just as the rust of sin[28] had nothing to do with the Lord "nor did his flesh see corruption."[29]

✤   Since Gregory the Theologian is recalled as having said, "the bronze snake is hung up against biting snakes, not as a type of him who suffered for us, but as an antitype,"[30] and that "the one who believes 'puts to death the powers beneath him,'"[31] it is necessary also to clarify these things. The one who, through virtue and knowledge, completely purifies the soul's power of vision knows clearly that evil is without substance and exists, not in any of things that are beings, but only in being done. Since therefore the snake, the author of evil, mingled the crookedness of sin[32] in the human being through disobedience, Moses was commanded to lift up the bronze snake, hinting at what was going to come to pass at the time of the Lord. For he and he alone, through the suffering of the Cross, exposed sin and showed it [to be] inoperative and dead. And so whoever looks intently upon him and believes the enemy has been put to death and become inoperative, this person also "puts to death the powers beneath him." For neither by the senses nor by the perceptible things through which it held power is it able to do damage. Therefore, it is said by the [Church] father, "not as a type but as an antitype," as it hints at the devil's own being put to death.

Question 10

Since "the law is spiritual,"[33] how should we [Christians] celebrate the Sabbath of days[34] and the Sabbath of weeks,[35] which is Pentecost, and the Sabbath of years,[36] the seventh year, and the Sabbath of the seventh year,[37] which is the Jubilee?

✤   We celebrate the week of days whenever we stop the activity of evil deeds, and we also celebrate the Sabbath of weeks whenever we stop consenting to evil thoughts. And we also celebrate the

Sabbath of years when we do not allow the provocation of desire, since the year experiences the burgeoning of fruit and the desire that arises in these. And we also celebrate the Jubilee when we fully put to rest the memories of evils and imaginings that happen accidentally because of the preconceptions [that exists with]in us. For the Jubilee is translated as 'a loosening of the bonds of the living person' or 'a respite from the grief of [being] a living person.' For when someone develops perfect detachment,[38] then he is released from the bonds of sin and, being set free from grief, establishes joy in the soul.[39]

Question 11

What does Elisha raising the son of the Shumannite[40] woman mean?[41]

✛   The prophet Elisha indicates the Lord, and the child of the Shumannite woman indicates human nature. For since human nature became sick through the transgression and was killed by the diabolical fever, the Lord sent Moses working miracles through his staff,[42] (as Elisha, likewise, sent Giezi[43]) and he did not raise up the man, nor did the prophets have the power to do so. And he, the Lord himself, because of his love for humankind, took on our flesh and, through the suffering of his flesh, gave life to our mortified nature.

Question 12

Why does one of the evangelists render the genealogy from earlier to later[44] and the other the opposite way?[45]

✛   I think that this was not done not unintentionally but rather in an exceedingly mystical way. For some of the faithful are led down from the promises to the practice of the commandments, and others beginning with the practice of the promises are brought up to the statements. For this reason one leads the genealogy down and the other leads the genealogy up.

Question 13

For what reason, in the preparation[46] of the precious body and blood of the Lord, is there in the church the custom of setting out the loaves of bread and the cups of wine unequally?

✛   All things that are accomplished in the church have a reason that transcends nature. Since these symbols, especially, are mysteries and representations of the divine essence, and it [the essence] is incomposite—every creature is composite but only, as it is said, is the Holy Trinity simple and incomposite—for this reason, therefore, the church sets out the loaves of bread and the cups unequally, characterizing the divine in these things.

Question 14

Since some people are at a loss, because [they say], "Why is the Lord's incarnation said to remain unseen by all the heavenly powers, when we find that the prophecies concerning the Lord have occurred through angels, and Gabriel announced the conception of the Virgin,[47] and angels instructed the shepherds in the mysteries[48]?" What therefore is it that the angels fail to see?

✛   That the angels knew the Lord's incarnation, which, for the salvation of humanity, was going to come to be, must not be doubted. But what escaped their notice was this: the Lord's incomprehensible conception and the manner in which, while being entirely in the Father and entirely in all things and fulfilling all things,[49] he was entirely in the womb of the Virgin.

Question 15

Why on earth is Joshua the son of Nave ordered to build an altar and write the law on Mount Gebal,[50] the mountain on which the curses were given?

✛   Garizin means 'circumcision,'[51] and Gebal 'dough.' And so, in the dough of the Gentile part, which has been cursed, our Lord Jesus Christ sets up an altar, that is, the Church, inscribing the law, "not on a tablet of stone but on a tablet of the fleshly heart."[52] And it says the altar was built from the perfect stones, "which the axe has not touched,"[53] indicating the intelligent stones, the apostles, who were unhewn because of the plainness and simplicity of their manners, from whom the church of the Gentiles was formed.

Question 16

What does it mean when the prophet warns those who are making "cakes for the army of heaven"[54] that they are to be delivered over to Nabuchodonosor so that he should set his throne in the gate of Jerusalem?[55]

✛ "Cakes" are little bread [loaves] of various kinds which the Jews and their wives used to make and would place on the windowsills of their house so that they would receive the glow of the moon and the morning star. Since then "cakes" are interpreted to mean "windowsills," this suggests one understood that whoever, through pleasure, delectably offers his senses to sensible things, this person makes "cakes." For this reason he also welcomes the spiritual Nabuchodonosor into the Jerusalem gate, that is, into the soul, to rule within it, oppressing it as a slave. For Nabuchodonosor is interpreted as 'prophesying a judgment of affliction.'

Question 17

What is indicated by the five sacrifices offered according to the Law: the sheep, the ox, the goat, the pigeon, and the dove?[56]

✛ According to one reading, the ram, as the ruling beast, is understood as the rational part, the bull as the irascible part, the goat as the desirous part, the pigeon as discretion, and the dove as sanctification. But if one must also seek the natural qualities of each animal, and embrace the contemplation offered by each of them, they who are knowledgeable in such things say that the sheep offers three things to his owner: the wool, the milk, the lamb. And 'the pupil of his eye revolves with the sun,' and it excretes 365 pieces of dung each day. So the rational sheep, the human being, if indeed he has striven to offer himself as a sacrifice to the God who owns [him], has, as his proper debt, to offer, as *wool*, his ethical activity, and, as *milk*, his natural contemplation—for this is what nourishes the mind—and, as a *sheep*, one who has been instructed to produce further offspring through the same teaching, who is in all ways similar to himself and perfect to set before God. But such a person also has 'the pupil of the eye accompanying the sun in its revolution,' that is to say he accompanies, i.e., follows with his mind the "Sun of Righteousness,"[57] which bears the things that pertain to us through his providential administration of whatever exists; for, giving thanks both in afflictions as well as in prosperity, he follows upon that providence that rightly guides all things. And such a person excretes, each day, 365 pieces of dung, that is, those things which are subject to time and becoming he casts away every time as perishable and superfluous.

Concerning the ox: they say that it has a triangular-shaped heart[58] and a kidney with five projections. And it also has three stomachs[59] and light-like eyes by day and fire-like eyes by night. And, while looking eastward a third of the day and a third of the night, it breathes snorting. Its right nostril emits a sweet calf scent, and its blood is poisonous for all tamed animals except the dog.

And so, it is necessary also for us, who, like an ox, bear the yoke of Christ and employ the plough of reason, to cut open the stony hearts and to root out the thorns of the passions, and to spread out the earth of the heart[60] for the reception of the divine word (*logos*).

And we must have a triangular-shaped heart, that is, we must have in our heart the wholesome doctrine concerning the Trinity, so that just as the heart physically distributes life in the body, so also the reverence for God unites the limbs of the soul.

And we must have a kidney with five projections, that is, must have the desiring [part] not turned toward the passions, but through the five senses we must look upon creation solely [to develop] a desire and love for the Creator.

And we must also possess three stomachs. The stomach first receives food and through its digestive ability transmits to each of the limbs pure nourishment, giving the remainder to the bowel. And so, in like manner, it is fitting that we should be guided through active, natural, and theological contemplation, and impart the things appropriate to all the limbs of the soul, and provide for the weaker part, that is, for the body. For this is the bowel.

And we should breathe, looking towards the east 'for a third of the day and a third of the night,' that is, looking towards the three-fold providence of God, which preserves and corrects and instructs [us], so as to give thanks both in the night of temptations as well as in the day of prosperity. Moreover, we should have fire-like eyes by night and light-like eyes by day, that is, having our contemplative power in the day of virtues receive the rays of knowledge from the "sun" of "righteousness"; and in the night of temptations, which, for the sake of virtue, are introduced one after the other, having it understood the reasons for these abandonments.

Also we should have a sweet-smelling right nostril. The right side of the human being is the soul, since we are two-fold, of body and soul. And so, the one who, through the virtues of the soul, has drawn down the grace of the Holy Spirit becomes sweet-smelling to others. And the blood of such a person is poisonous for tamed animals, that is, the anger that leads astray is poisonous for the human beings who imitate it, but nourishment for the demons who howl like dogs against us.

Now the goat has this kind of nature: easily ascending the mountains, and it climbs on precipices and rejoices in musical songs; and if its right horn is burned so as to produce smoke in any place,[61] it creates an illusion of an earthquake. And it excretes 200 pieces of dung each day. It is necessary, therefore, for our soul to leap courageously across the cliffs of temptations and, that, ascending the prophetic mountains, we should hunt for the summit of knowledge and experience delight in this, and not only be delighted but also, by teaching with the shepherd's pipe, that is, with the active word, we should impart delight to the listeners. And the right horn signifies that the one who brings the contemplative [part] of the soul close to God through prayer, by becoming sweet-smelling to the listeners, and violently shakes the habit in them of the fleshly passions. Such a person, on each occasion, rejects the deceit of the senses regarding the perceptible things. For the senses are entangled together with the things of perception. As such, the number four multiplied by ten makes forty, and this being multiplied by five completes the 200.

Question 18

What is the two-drachma tax which the Lord was to pay, and what is the fish Peter was ordered to catch, so as to take the coin that was in it and give it to those who demanded it?[62]

✢   They who demand the two-drachma tax bear an image of the natural passions within us. These [tax collectors] came to Peter, that is, to the one who is the Lord's active and humble [disciple] and who, in the manner of a disciple, is obedient to the Father, and they make demands since it is customary for a man to exact from people whatever they have in tribute. And the Lord demonstrated, as God and Master, his own freedom through the parable. But since, having taken on our flesh, he had also accepted its innocent passions, to perfect these things in [human] nature he also bore with them, "without sin."[63] For, given that he had, in the beginning, molded the human being and had placed in him two overall principles,[64] the leading one being that of the soul, and the other, by his providence, that of the flesh, but [the human being] remained steadfast in neither of these but had wounded the one by the transgression of the commandment, the other by the abuse of nature's limitations, whichever *logos* he had hid in passion he allowed to swim in the sea of the troubled life; for this reason, when it is demanded of the Lord to pay the tax of nature, as master and corrector of nature, through the *logos* of action, he grasps the slimy passion of sin that is swimming in the sea of life and draws out [from the fish] the *logos* ingested within it, that is, the boundary of our neediness that has been given from the beginning as a way towards forgiveness, [and] separating it, he returns it to nature free of abusive passion.

Question 19

Since Gregory of Nyssa, in his own writings, seems to those who do not understand the depth of his lofty thinking to hint in many places at a restoration (*apokatastasin*), I entreat you to say everything that you know about this.[65]

✠   The church knows three restorations: the first, that of each [person] according to the *logos* of virtue, in which one is restored fulfilling the *logos* of virtue in him; second, that of the entire nature in the resurrection, the restoration to incorruption and immortality; and third, which Gregory of Nyssa, above all, made use of in his own writings, is this, the restoration of the powers of the soul that fell into sin, returning to that for which they were created. Just as it is necessary for the entire nature in the resurrection to recover again the incorruption of the flesh at the hoped-for time, so also must the distorted powers of the soul in the duration of the ages again throw off the memories of evil lodged within it and passing through all ages and, not finding a resting place, return to God, who is without limit; and, thus, by full understanding (*epignosin*),[66] not by sharing in the good things, it must recover again its powers and be restored to its original

[form], such that the Creator may also be revealed as not being responsible for sin.

Question 20

What does the story about Bel mean, and who is Daniel, and King Darius, who knew that the footprints of those who had entered [the temple] had belonged to men and women and children?[67]

✠   Every human being who comes into the confusion of life— for this is how Babylon is interpreted—makes his own soul a temple to Bel,[68] that is, to the devil, to which if Daniel should come, that is, the law of God—for Daniel is interpreted as 'a judgment of God'[69]—he teaches Darius, that is, the kingly *nous*, that the footprints in the temple, that is, of the soul, are of men and women and children who are walking, that is, of anger and desire and ignorance; whereby the kingly *nous*, knowing this, hands it over for judgment to the law of God for the complete destruction of all of them. And the sprinkled ashes[70] reveal *askesis* and humility. For through these, the footprints of the passions that run back and forth in the soul become visible to the *nous*.

Question 21

How should one think about the saying by the Apostle, "Christ is the firstfruits; then they who are of Christ at his coming; then [comes] the end."[71]

✠   "Christ" became the "firstfruits" through his resurrection; "then they who are of Christ," are they who believe in him; "then the end" which is the salvation of all the nations through faith. And if you desire to understand the statements relating to each one, "Christ is the firstfruits" the beginning" is the faith in him, "then they who are of Christ" are the works of faith, "then the end" means being separated from all things, both perceptible and intelligible, and being joined to God by knowledge. And "death is the last enemy to be destroyed"[72] means whenever we, ourselves, submit the entire self-determining will (*autexousion thelema*) to God, then the last enemy is also abolished. And it is called "death" since God is life, and that which is opposed to life is fittingly called death.

Question 22

What does the rainbow mean, which God placed in the cloud as a covenant with the human race?[73]

✠   Since the rainbow is four-colored, it shows the flesh of the Lord having come to be like us from four elements[74] though without having a cause for its composition, just as the rainbow also does not have a cause. He placed this in the cloud, that is, in the world. And the world is a cloud because of the wrath of God, that is, the penalty of death. Now sometimes the cloud is taken as indicating good, as it gently waters and provides shade from the burning heat, and at other times it is taken for wrath, as it brings about ruin through rain and violent hail. And so, according to this, it says that the rainbow is placed in the cloud, that is, the incarnation of the Lord in the world of wrath, so that the human race is no longer to be washed away by the waters of evil. And it is a rainbow because of this, so we know that the reconciliation of God with us is a war with our enemies and adversaries, or, even more, the war of the Lord with the enemy has become a reconciliation for us.

Question 23

For what reason does the law forbid one from consuming any blood of the beasts or of other things?[75]

✠   "Beasts" not only means the wild animals but also the tamed animals that are unclean under the law, such as the ass, the pig, and others. And these are the more violent and untamed passions of evil. And so, we must not use them as the sustenance of our vices. But because blood is understood as the sustenance of [our] life, and many times is also understood as anger because of murder, it suggests the consideration that we should place all of our life before God and live not for ourselves but for God,[76] just as the law says, "you shall pour out the blood before the altar,"[77] or, again, that we must not allow the irascible [part of the soul] to serve in its own defense or for its own passion, but only that it should strongly and vigorously cling to God and cling to God and divine things.

Question 24

What is, according to the law, the goring bull, and why is it murdered although it is an irrational beast?[78]

✦   A "goring bull" is one who has acquired an irrational zeal as if this were in accord with God and who uses it for the defense of others. And so, one must kill such passion so that it may not murder the many whom it will strike, and cause endangerment to its own master, that is, the soul.

Question 25

What is the multicolored garment of Joseph and what is the meaning of the fulfillment of the dream that his father and brothers bow down to him?[79]

✦   Every Israel, that is, a *nous* that sees God, creates for his own son Joseph, that is, for the one born according to God, a multicolored garment, that is, he binds the ethical manner with the manifold variety of the virtues.[80] To such a one therefore—and Joseph is interpreted as an addition[81]—his father and his mother and his brothers bowed down [to him]. For to each person who adds and increases the measures of virtue and knowledge, the natural law and the fostering sense [faculty] bow down, bending with their natural and perceptive *logoi*. But since Joseph is also understood as the Lord, the God and Father[82] is said to make for his own natural son a robe of many colors, i.e., the body which, for us, he assumed from us, multicolored with the divine virtues, as it is said in the psalms, "And a body you have prepared for me,"[83] [a body] which his Jewish brothers, according to the flesh, stripped off and stained with the blood of suffering.[84] And his father and the mother and the twelve brothers bowed down to him, that is, the law and worship and the believers from the twelve tribes.

Question 26

What is the meaning of the pillar of the cloud leading the way by day and the pillar of fire illuminating the night?[85]

✦   By both of these [symbols] the word of God is meant. On the one hand, refreshing those who travel [by means of] action away from the burning heat of the temptations, it becomes "the pillar of cloud"; on the other hand, illuminating those who travel [by means of] knowledge and purifying the haze of ignorance it becomes "the pillar of fire."

Question 27
What does the manna mean, and what is meant by its becoming rancid for those who collected more than was needed?[86]

✛   Manna means the word of God, which is appropriately united with all through action and knowledge and which nourishes the soul. Therefore, whenever someone has used it properly and reasonably, that is, when one follows the middle way[87] of the virtues, equally avoiding an excessive or minimal use of them, he gathers the manna sufficiently. But whenever one does not use reason properly but excessively—for it would be well to show the meaning of the passage by a single virtue—such as, whenever someone who pursues continence avoids licentiousness but judges marriage to be abominable, already the *logos* of continence[88] "has become rancid" for him by the immoderacy of his excess, and it not only becomes rancid, but also brings forth worms, that is, it gives birth to other passions.

Question 28 (III, 7)
What is the meaning of the passage about the woman who is struck and "has an abortion," and "if the child comes out perfectly formed"[89] the law declares that the one who struck [her] must give "life for life."[90] But if the child falls out unformed, [why] is it only an accident?

✛   Literally, we understand the passage in this way: since the murder is of the body—for a soul, being immortal, is never murdered—for this reason "being not perfectly formed"[91] into the human form does not entail to danger but only mild damage. But if the human image is fully developed, it is reasonable to see such a person as committing the murder of a perfect human being. And in terms of spiritual contemplation we consider the following: the one who scandalizes a soul that has become pregnant with the divine word and has formed, through habit, the seed of virtue causing that soul to miscarry and lose such a form of the teaching, is liable to the penalty of death. But the one who violates a soul that received the seed of the word but did not give form to it through conduct and activity, is worthy of punishment.

Question 29

What do the "six cities of refuge"[92] mean and why were the three given inside the promised land and the other three outside it?[93]

✛   Since the tribe of Gad, because it had acquired many flocks, received the cities outside the promised land, the law set aside three from among these for refuge for anyone who had committed murder involuntarily[94] and the other three for the promised land. Therefore, according to the anagogic reading (*anagoge*), this means the following: since there are three ways according to which we sin unwillingly—from action by tyrannical constraint, from deception, and from ignorance—the one entangled in these must flee before the accompanying passion which follows in close pursuit kills him, making him sin of his own inner volition. The one sinning from tyrannical constraint must flee to the city of abstinence; the one sinning from deception must flee to the city of experience and good wiliness; and the one who sins from ignorance must flee to the city of learning. And these places are assigned to those [engaged] in the active life, because of its productivity and its suitability for pasturing flocks. For the active life is both productive in virtues and pastoral for those who are rather herd-like.

And the inner cities are assigned to those who practice *gnosis*. For, since the gnostic is preoccupied with three things, ethical, natural, and theological knowledge, it is necessary that whoever commits murder involuntarily, that is, gains an apprehension without experience, if, on the one hand, with regard to ethical teaching, he stirs up anger and desire contrary to reason, he must flee for refuge to the city of meekness—for meekness is the goal of ethical philosophy—but, again, if he has erred in natural contemplation and gives attention to things without scientific knowledge, he must flee for refuge to the city of science (*epistemes*); and, finally, if he has erred with respect to theology he must flee to the city of faith, lest in some way the accompanying passion of ignorance proves strong enough to overtake [him], and should destroy him who partakes of it.

And what is [the phrase] "until the death of the high priest"?[95] Such a person must remain and then return to his rightful land, as can be understood by what follows. "The high priest" is our

Lord Jesus Christ. And so, whenever we might come into perfect detachment[96] and no longer offer to him any of the things of this world, whether words or ideas, and simply, whenever we are beyond sense and the act of thinking, and no longer "do we know Christ according to the flesh,"[97] then the high priest has died for us, no longer receiving from us worship by means of any of the things that have come to be. And finally, we are resettled upon our rightful land, that land which is, that which is in God himself, in whom are the *logoi* of the virtues.

Question 30
What are the rods that Jacob, stripping off, has put into the water troughs,[98] and who is Rachel, the one who stole the idols,[99] and what is the terebinth in which Jacob hid these things?[100]

✛   Every Jacob, that is, the vanquisher,[101] strips off the rods,[102] that is, the *logoi* of beings, making them clean of the material forms which overlay them, [and] places them in the water troughs, that is, in the habit of knowledge, so that those who, in the manner of sheep, are being taught with instruction, by longing after it, may become stamped, as with a seal, so as to imitate it. And so, every soul that is taught in this manner steals the idols of her own father, who had earlier begotten her in an evil way, into evil. And the idols are not naturally inherent in visible things, but "from the" evil "father, the devil," [visible things] are given idolized forms, for the purpose of deception. And, according to the Apostle, the one who rightly steals these [idols] "leads all things captive into the obedience of Christ."[103] And she hides them in the camels' saddles; 'camel' here you should understand as the body because of its crookedness and because by the tracks of its feet making altogether an impression in the earth, [and] the camel depicts our body that, because of transgression, has become crooked and subject to passions. And saddles are the different methods of *askesis*, upon which the soul is seated that escapes from her father, who searches for evil and seeks after the idols he had invented for the purpose of deception. These idols the soul, after she had rightly tearing snatched them away from him through lofty spiritual reflection [*anagoge*] and contemplation concerning them, hid in the saddles of self-control that press [against] our body. But when she comes into the promised land, that is, into perfect knowledge, then she is ordered also to strip these things off, that is, the things rightly stolen for our spiritual uplifting, whether, like a cloak, they have more the character of ethical customs or, like earrings, they are given ear to, as the natural *logoi* that are [inferred] from them.[104] For the transparent *nous*, having taken these things, concealed them in the terebinth, that is, in the mystery of the Cross. For in it is all action and knowledge hidden.[105] And the Cross is compared to a terebinth since in the winter this tree is completely unpleasing and in the spring it is completely at its most fragrant and most pleasant. So, likewise, the Cross of the Lord also in the present life seems to have an appearance of something despised, but in the future life it sends forth a majesty of much fragrance and glory.

Question 31
What is the meaning of the story concerning Judah and Thamar?[106]

✥   Our Lord, Jesus Christ, who was born "according to the flesh"[107] from the tribe of Judah and on the road of life came to "the lost sheep of the house of Israel,"[108] found the church of the Gentiles on the road of error, a prostitute, lusting "after other gods";[109] and, having united himself with her, he offered to her a staff and a signet-cord and a ring,[110] that is, the mortification through the Cross and pious opinion concerning beings and the grace of the Spirit, or, to speak plainly, practical, natural, and theological knowledge.

Question 32
From St. Cyril of Alexandria concerning Nabouthai and Ahab.[111]

✥   The things said about Nabouthai refer to Christ; now Israel, according to Isaiah, is a vineyard, while Ahab is taken as a type of the rulers of Israel, who desired to have [the vineyard] "for a garden of vegetables, watering" it "with the thick dregs of subversion."[112] And Christ represents Nabouthai, who did not want to relinquish it [the vineyard] as it was his paternal inheritance. Hence, the spiritual Jezebel, that is, the synagogue, when he was denounced, sought to destroy him.

Question 33

Whom are Jephtha and his daughter taken to represent?[113]

✠   Jephtha represents the Lord and his daughter [represents] the Lord's completely undefiled flesh. For just as Jephtha was one born of a prostitute[114] and was banished from his own family[115] and, after he left, fought and defeated the adversaries,[116] having made a promise to God to offer in sacrifice whomever should come out to meet him from his own household,[117] so also, "with regard to the flesh"[118] the Lord came forth without sin from our prostituted nature and from his own household and became the sower of his own flesh [and] was banished by those Jews who appeared to be his own,[119] and having won the war for our sake, offered his very own flesh "to God, the Father."[120] For Jephtha is interpreted as an opening of God.

Question 34

What does the passage from Proverbs mean, "a roof will be brought low by slothful neglect, and a house will fall to pieces by the idleness of hands"?[121]

✠   The roof is understood as the natural powers of the soul. For just as the beams fall down when neglected and warped because of the weight that has been placed [upon them] fall down, so likewise, the natural powers of the soul, when care is not taken for them by the study of the Holy Scriptures, become warped by the weight of the voluntary and involuntary temptations,[122] and fall down towards the perceptible things. And "a house will fall to pieces by the idleness of hands" whenever the soul, by inactivity in good deeds chases away the indwelling grace, taking in through the [ways of the] senses the phantasms (*phantasias*) of the material things, after the likeness of dripping rain.

Question 35

What does the wedding at Cana show and what are the mysteries that were performed in it?[123]

✠   Cana is interpreted as possession and Galilee as "revelation." And so, every *nous* that has a revelatory skill with regard to the divine things, when it is joined with virtue or even with sense perception, is in need of the mediation of the *Logos* so that, on the one hand, when virtue is joined to the mind's knowledge,[124] it may be harmonious with it and, on the other hand, so that sense perception may bow down to the authority of the mind, which naturally gives order to it. And since the gnostic condition has become watered down by the diffusion according to pleasure that occurred as a result of disobedience, the *Logos* came, restoring to the land its original firmness. And the mother who makes the request[125] is faith, or again, humility, or again, scientific, experiential wisdom. For each of these has engendered in human beings the condition for giving birth to the highest divine form.[126]

And "my time has not yet come"[127] shows the following: since the teaching takes precedence over signs—for it is on account of those who do not believe in the teaching that the demonstration by signs [miracles] comes about,[128] and he had not yet taught them and received experience of their disbelief—for that reason he said, "my hour has not yet come."

And the servers[129] indicate the prophets, who through their own teaching *** that nature made empty by the transgression *** . But the Lord came and transformed [it] into spiritual knowledge and, through faith, elevated their nature into what is beyond nature. And this shows forth the person of the *Theotokos*.[130] For just as the *Theotokos*, who exists by the workmanship of her Lord and son, herself brought him forth according to the same flesh, so also faith, which exists from the word,[131] by the activity of doing brings the word into actuality.

And the water jugs,[132] since there are six, indicate the habit of bringing good things into being, because the Lord, too, created the visible world in six days. And the host of the banquet is the discerning law. For this reason he says, "every person sets out the good wine first, and then the poor wine,"[133] for the unmixed and discerning law says, in its discernment, "the mind should first return in recognition to the cause and then, accordingly, [move on to] the things that come after it, which Adam did not do," or rather [it says] that "the teaching of the Lord should be drunk first, before the law and the prophets."

Question 36

How shall we consider the passage from the Gospel, "among those born, no one has arisen who is greater than John,[134] but he who is smaller than him in the Kingdom of Heaven is greater than him"?[135]

✠   Whoever will humble himself more than John—for this is "who is smaller"—is greater than John. Or, in another way: since John is believed to have attained the present knowledge, [which is] accessible through contemplation, the small and ultimate knowledge, according to the future, yet-to-be-revealed condition, is greater than what is known presently. Or, also, because the consummate theologian among human beings is inferior to the least among the angels. Or, also, the one who holds the lowest rank within the community according to Gospel is greater than the most consummate [person] according to the righteousness of the law.

Question 37

What do those birds, as well as the land animals and sea animals, that were held by the law to be unclean, indicate with regard to general reasoning?[136]

✠   We have interpreted the birds as representing, in general, the passion of vainglory and arrogance, a passion separated into different categories (*troupous*) according to the differences of the birds. And the land animals, universally, represent the passion of avarice, which is divided into different [categories] according to the difference of each disposition of the animals. And the water animals, universally, represent the passion of gluttony because of its [the passion's] sliminess and difficulty in moving and because they roll around in the earth, and the unclean fish which are unclean according to the law are an inflammation.[137] And the law defines those that have fins and scales to be clean, indicating by the one that has fins on the belly that the person who has developed against pleasure a high reason does not allow it to enter the belly; and the one that has fins on the top of its back swims in a manly way through the sea of life, bearing patiently the things that befall [it]. And the one that has fins on its tail is the person who skillfully runs away from the grips of the hunting demons, and the one that has fins on both sides [of the head] has a mind that secures the contemplative [part] on all sides.

Question 38
For what reason does the Scripture say that Esau, before he was born, had been hated by God but that Jacob had been loved?[138]

✛   In the literal sense, it is clear that God, "the one who knows all things before they have come to be,"[139] knew what sort [of person] each was going to be by free choice[140] and knowing, he already hated the one and loved the other. But if according to [an interpretation by] the anagogic reading someone closely examines the passage under discussion, every *nous* that is rough like Esau's, [that] is hairy with worldly matter and coarsened by forbidden thoughts, is hated by God. But every Jacob is loved, a smooth *nous*, plain and immaterial and solitary in its way. But also, in another way, every Isaac has two sons, of whom, before they are born, one is hated and one is loved. And these are "the law of the spirit"[141] and "the mind of the flesh,"[142] one of which is loved and the other of which is hated, even before they become active.

And in another way, Isaac is understood as a type of God. He had two sons, the written law and the spiritual law; and the one was hairy and rough, and the other was smooth. For the [written] law had many and countless observances and was hated according to [what] Isaiah [wrote]: "my soul hates your feasts and Sabbaths."[143] But the other [spiritual law] was loved for it was smooth. For the Gospel is smooth and concise, and it requires a sincere faith in God and a good conscience[144] towards one's neighbor.

[In another way, concerning the same passage]: According to the interpretation of the names, each one who is scornful and careless in piety has been hated by God. For this is how Esau is translated; but every vanquisher of evil is loved, which is the translation of Jacob.

Question 39
Why was it that Abraham saw three angels,[145] but Lot saw two?[146]

✛   Because Abraham was perfected and had transcended the visible things and was enlightened with the knowledge of the

Holy Triad and Monad[147]—for this reason he also receives the alpha as an addition to his name [his name is changed from Abram to Abraham] as one who alone has drawn close to the Alone in knowledge—fittingly he sees three angels. But Lot did not transcend the visible things by knowledge, but he worships the divine from the visible things and envisions nothing beyond them, and he did not move beyond the two, matter and form, from which the visible things come to exist, and he did not apprehend the word concerning the Monad and the Triad; as a result he sees two angels. For this reason, when the angels were urging him to go to the mountain to be saved, he hesitated to go up to the mountain[148] but asked to attain to Sigor, to the lesser knowledge. For Sigor is translated as 'small.' And the angels who expelled Lot are understood as the two testaments, the one of the written and the other of the Gospel law. Through these [two], one is chased out and escapes error regarding the perceptible things, and utterly escapes the burning that comes from them.[149] And he has sense perception ascending together with him, as a housemate. And so, if sense perception turns back "to the things behind" it becomes "a pillar of salt,"[150] an example set forth for all, bearing the unalterable habit of salt-like evil.

And since he also brought wine out of Sodomites, which signifies the mental pictures of impure thoughts, the two daughters get him drunk in order to conceive [by him].[151] The first daughter is desire; for when the *nous* awakens the first memories of the impressions of the mental pictures, desire, having intercourse, straightaway conceives consent.[152] And immediately the second daughter also comes; and she is pleasure, who, having intercourse with him, conceives activity[153] (*energian*). For this reason, such offspring are accursed and do not enter "into the congregation of the Lord until the third and fourth and even tenth generations."[154]

Question 40

Why is it that, when there exist many more serious insults, the Lord in the gospels stipulates that he who calls his brother a fool is liable to Gehenna, while he who says "*raka*,"[155] he says is subject to the council?[156]

✛   The name "fool" is said to be understood as "idiotic and unintelligent," and *raka* is interpreted to mean "despicable" in the language of the Hebrews. And so, since the name "fool" is said regarding the ungodly and unfaithful according to the saying, "the fool person has said in his heart, 'there is no God'"[157] and according to Moses, who says, "this people is foolish and not wise,"[158] whoever calls his brother of the same faith 'ungodly' and 'idolater' or 'heretic' and 'unfaithful,' this person says "fool," and, rightly, he becomes liable to Gehenna. But whoever says *raka*, which means, "you despicable, unclean one," he reproaches his brother's life and fittingly is subject to a lighter penalty.

Question 41
What does the story in Judges mean, that of the Levite and the abused concubine whom the tribe of Benjamin killed by sexually abusing her?[159]

✛   Since the sacred *nous*, which came existence from God in the beginning, put to death the natural law through its transgression, it received the concubine, that is, the legal worship, a worship which is not natural but brought in from outside. Then, the natural movements rose up against it, like wolves, and murdered it [the worship]. And the sacred *nous*, being angered, cuts this [the legal worship] into pieces and sends [them] to every border of Israel, to the twelve tribes; that is to say, it divides the commandments of the law and assigns each one to the relevant power of the soul, so that all are set in motion together for the destruction of disorderly thoughts. Now the powers of the soul are three: the rational, the desirous, and the irascible. And they are bound to the four principal virtues: for without these there is neither destruction of evil nor the successful accomplishment of virtue. Then in order that the right judgments might come to realization they are also in need of the five senses so that the number twelve, which symbolizes the entire Israel, might be fulfilled. Or the number twelve signifies both time and nature; for time is sevenfold and nature is fivefold.

The fact that during the war many of the Israelites fell and after these events few were victorious[160] indicates that it is necessary for the one who struggles with sin to cleanse every passion, since, while one is ruled either by conceit or vainglory or vanity or arrogance, or one condemns others or, whatever other passion it may be by which one is held captive, one in fact is found to be impotent in warring against the passions, and one falls. But one needs to cleanse oneself of all of them, and in this way be drawn into battle formation, and the Lord thus grants the victory. And Israel's being comforted for the remnants of Benjamin,[161] who fled for refuge in the rock of Remmon,[162] shows that it is not only necessary for the one who fights with the passions to wipe out, together with these passions, the natural power, but to acquire those things that are beyond natural power. For example, someone who struggles against the passion of gluttony should not completely deny the food essential for the maintenance of life but rather the luxurious and obsessive eating habits. The 'fleeing to the rock' represents the faith according to Christ,[163] or the solid habit of practical activity that easily puts to death without difficulty the disorder of the passions. For Remmon is translated as 'suspension of death.'

Question 42
What is that which the Apostle wrote in his letter to Timothy, "be urgent in season and out of season"?[164]

✤   He says that, if someone is entangled in evil, such that this person is "in season" for being taught, suggest to him, by your teaching, that he take flight from evil and choose what is good. If someone is not entangled in evil, which seems to be 'out of season,' you should suggest to such a person knowledge, he says, thereby protecting him from the future rebellion of the temptations.

Question 43
What does the parable of the ten virgins mean?[165]

✤   Since the human being has five spiritual senses susceptible to the spiritual perceptions and five bodily senses susceptible to the sense perceptions, the parable seems to hint at each human being. And so, whoever has the lamp of active virtue and also is irrigated with the oil of knowledge, that is, having his actions accompanied by knowledge, this one, having subdued the body and having joined the body's senses with the spiritual ones, has become the five wise [virgins]. And whoever appears to engage in the active life without having the oil of knowledge, but pursues this [life] mindlessly, whether as a result of an opinion or through gluttony or avarice, this one, having turned the spiritual senses towards perceptible and ephemeral things and rendered them earthly, has fittingly become the five foolish virgins, having knowledge only from sensible things.

Question 44

What does paradise being planted in the East[166] show according to the anagogic method?

✠ By "paradise" I think is indicated the human heart, which is planted in the East, i.e., in the dawning (*anatole*) of the knowledge of God. In the absolute center of it, God planted "the tree of life and the tree of the knowledge of good and evil."[167] And "the tree of life" is understood as the *logos* of intelligible things,[168] while "[the tree of] the knowledge of good and evil" is understood as the *logos* of perceptible things, since this has knowledge both of good and of evil. For to those who recognize the Creator from the beauty of the created things and through these are led up to their cause, there is knowledge of good; but to those who remain in the sense-perception alone and, being tricked by the superficiality of perceptible things, have turned every appetite of the soul toward matter, there is the knowledge of evil.

But if someone, being in doubt, should reply, 'how could this apply to one and the same person so that the knowledge concerning one thing might be at one time, good, and, at another time, evil?' one must say to him that since it was said that the two trees are the intelligible world and the perceptible world, and the human being as consisting of soul and body also shares in each, when the supreme power of the soul shall incline towards sense perception and the body then, behold, it has partaken of the tree and has known the experience of both good and evil—the good, on the one hand, since the body delights naturally in the enjoyment of the sensible things but, on the other hand, it has known the soul to be in evil[169] since it is governed by what is worse and its natural powers are utterly weakened.

Question 45

What is meant by the fish that, after the resurrection, was shown by the Lord, laid out upon the embers?[170]

✛   The fish indicates human nature swimming in the confusion of the passions, for which, the Lord, after going down into the sea of life because of his ineffable love for humankind, drew out again, and, by roasting it [human nature] in the fire of the Holy Spirit and dissolving away all stickiness of the passions, he prepared as food both for himself and for the apostles. For the *Logos* always hungers for our salvation as do those who agree with him. Wherefore, in imitation of him, they also chose to die for the sake of our salvation.

Question 46

What does Zacchaius, the tax collector, in the Gospel, signify and what are those things that are said about him?[171]

✛   Zacchaius, the tax collector, is the one who taxes God's creation for his own enjoyment. But he hears the *Logos* passing by and climbs up into the sycamore tree whenever the *logos* of repentance [comes to] exist in him. For it persuades him to go above "the mind of the flesh."[172] And this is the fig tree. From up there he will easily look upon the *Logos* and may hear him say, "make haste and come down,"[173] that is, 'if you desire to receive all of me, into your house, do not consider it enough to surpass carnal thoughts alone, but also make the journey through the virtues with me.' And "I restore it fourfold"[174] indicates either that he has furnished himself with each of the four principal virtues for a rectification of good works, or else it may mean that he keeps himself away from acting and consenting and preoccupations of memories and trivial daydreams—from acting, through self-control, from consenting, through attentiveness and the guarding of thoughts, from mental pictures, through chanted readings, and from daydreams, through intense prayer.

Or the passage speaks of the active and the natural and the theological, and of that which has to do with prayer. For prayer is higher than theology.[175] For the one [theology] theologizes about the divine based on past events, whereas prayer joins the soul, in an unknowable and ineffable way, to God himself.

Question 47

What does the passage in the song of Moses, "for their vine is from the vine of Sodom, and their vine-branch is from Gomorrah,"[176] mean, and what is the wine which the Nazarite must not drink,[177] and what is the vinegar, the strong drink,[178] the bunch of grapes, and the pressed remains?[179]

✛ "The vine of Sodom" is irrationality. "Sodom" is translated as looking into or, rather, blindness,[180] and Gomorrah is translated as 'embitterment.' For the embitterment of sin results from irrationality, and the manic drunkenness of evil is from wine. From that point, the passage commands the Nazarite to abstain from such wine; and "Nazarite" is translated as 'one who is fenced about.' For it is necessary for one who has become secure in the law of God to abstain from this wine of irrationality, but also from the grape, that is, from anger, and from the raisin of resentment,[181] for this is the aging of anger; but also from vinegar, from the sadness resulting from the failure to achieve things according to one's pleasure; and from the fortified drink, from the pleasure in taking vengeance against one's neighbor—for all fortified drinks are sweet; but also from the pressed remains, the intentional and concentrated (*sustatika*) forms of evil. But such a person does not cut off even his hair,[182] that is, the various concentrated thoughts of the *nous* that lend adornment to it. For this reason, Samson[183]— whose name, when he is shaven, is interpreted to mean 'likening a likeness,' and when he is hairy, to mean 'their sun'[184]—when he rested on the thigh of Dalida,[185] that is, when he threw himself upon the passionate part of pleasure, he was deprived of his hair, that is to say, his thoughts, those namely that supplied his strength [to fight] against the passions,[186] and became the plaything of the demons,[187] and was made blind in his two eyes,[188] namely, in the active and contemplative knowledge.

Question 48

What is, according to the Apostle, "having your loins girt about with truth"[189] and the rest of the weapons of spiritual resistance?[190]

✛ Gregory, the one given the name of Theologian, interpreted correctly the passage "having your loins girt about with truth," saying, "never in such a way that the contemplative strangles the desirous."[191] And "they who have put on the breastplate of righteousness"[192] is [written] because righteousness is a habitude that distributes what is equal, and it is necessary for the three powers of the soul in us to be of equal weight; and through these the four principal virtues should be set together with equal force—for this is righteousness—and by means of the intellect, the rational part, when it is set in motion toward the investigation of beings, securely links *logos* to *logos* like a chain-mail breastplate. And in like manner, prudence, joining the different *logoi* of the intellect and the rest together in the one [*Logos*], must secure itself so as not to be wounded by the arrows coming from the enemy. And, "the shield of faith"[193] must be understood as that "carrying about in the body the death of Jesus."[194] For the shield is constructed from wood and leather and thus suggests to us the mystery of the Cross and "the death [of Jesus] in the body."[195] For these become "the shield of faith"[196] for those who have acquired [them].

And one must understand "have your feet prepared in readiness [to preach] the Gospel of peace"[197] in this way: since we surmised the "Gospel of peace" to be the grace of detachment, the Apostle prescribes for the one who has not yet acquired it the binding of the lower parts of the soul by the mortification of the body in preparation for such grace. For in this way, one remains unwounded by the thorn of the passions and invulnerable to the serpents and scorpions, I mean, evil thoughts. And the "helmet of salvation"[198] is hope. Since the perceptive helmet is the headpiece, being constructed from bronze, and bronze is sturdy and glistens and does not disintegrate, and the head indicates faith, one must consider that it is hope that makes faith secure. Hope is steadfast and cannot be diminished, and it does not allow faith to be overlooked. For it hopes for all things[199] and does not cease from [having] confidence in God, but even if it supposes that it is despised, as Job did on account of his many woes, nevertheless, inwardly such a person is glistening and bright, being made glad by hope.

And the "sword of the spirit"[200] is discernment, "that which separates the better from the worse."[201] The Apostle orders that one always have this in hand, that is, [he commands that] keeping his sword always active by use, one should employ it. For just as the iron sword that is always ready is fearsome to enemies,[202] while if it is stowed away and remains inactive it is consumed by rust, so also with discernment, unless it is united to action, it is unprofitable and useless and consumed by evil.

Question 49

What does Doek the Syrian,[203] the one who murdered the 350 priests, signify[204]?

✛   "Doek the Syrian" is 'the proud thought' or 'the restlessness of the passions' according to the translation of the word. And naturally, such a one as Saul tends the mules,[205] the condition that produces no children for virtue. And he is set against David, I mean, the thought of humility. For David, according to one translation of his name, is translated as the one who is despised. This one [Doek] kills the priests of Nomba,[206] that is, the divine and propitiating thoughts seated in virtue—for Nomba is translated as 'seated'—and 350, since we, attending through the senses to the creation of God that has come into existence in six days, greatly admire its Creator of this and praise him through the scientific knowledge (*epistimonike*) regarding thoughts. And six multiplied by fifty produces the number 300. And again, fulfilling the ten commandments of the law through the [five] senses we complete the fifty. And so, the proud thought or also the restlessness of the passions occurs so as to kill the thoughts that are consecrated to God from among these and from among those that dwell in virtue.

Question 50

How should one understand what is said by the symbol of faith,[207] "becoming incarnate of the Holy Spirit and the Virgin Mary"?[208]

✛   Some among the saints say that the soul is sown by the Holy Spirit in the manner of the man's seed and that the flesh is formed from the virginal blood.

Question 51

What is the [passage] from Proverbs, "the one who strikes hand in hand shall not be unaccountable"?[209]

✛   The one who mixes a paltry action with a virtuous action "shall not be unaccountable."

Question 52

From the same, "do not make a promise to your friend";[210] for unless you have the ability to fulfill it, "the bed will be taken from under you[r ribs]."[211]

✠   The passage refers to the body as 'a friend' because of the relationship of the soul with it. It says, one should 'not make a promise' to it [the body], that is, one should not consider it worthy of sparing, and do not pay it back the things it is owed for the sake of virtue, if ever it should pursue relaxation. For if the *nous* concentrating on *askesis* begins to give way a little bit, when the *nous* finds itself unable to render and to account for what it has done for virtue's sake, then the demons also take away from it its ascetic labors on which it used to rest. For this is what the bed denotes.

Question 53

What does Isaiah's saying indicate, "who has measured the water in his hand and the heavens in a span and the entire earth in a handful"?[212]

✠   Since, according to the prophet Habbakum, "the virtue" of the Lord "covered the heavens,"[213] that is, his way of life in the flesh "covered" the virtue of the angels in heaven, he, by engaging in action—for this is the hand[214]—measured all knowledge, being named, figuratively, water.[215] For nature, being united to the *Logos*, comprehended all knowledge. And "the heavens in a span," calling "heaven" the higher *logos* of beings, and "span" the outstretched knowledge of the perceptible things, stretch out by action, because the hand has five fingers. Therefore, the Lord, "the one who summed up all things in himself,"[216] when he became incarnate, measured out these *logoi*. And "the entire earth in a handful" shows this, that the Lord restrained his own flesh, as it was earthly, in such a way so as not to allow the natural and blameless passions to function without his permission.

Question 54

Who is Ezekiel, and what is the weakness, and what is the cake of figs which healed the wound?[217]

✠   Ezekiel represents the face of humanity. And the trauma, that to his thigh, signifies the law of sin because of the proximity of the reproductive organs to the thigh. And the cake of figs is the life-giving flesh of the Lord that does not contain the sap of sin from which the healing of the wound of transgression takes place in us.

Question 55
What does the axe head signify, dropped by one of the sons of the prophets into the Jordan [River], which the prophet Elias, throwing the wood [into the river], caused to come to the surface?[218]

✛   Irenaeus says that the prophet showed by a work, through the lifting up of the axe head, that "we who negligently lost the solid *Logos* of God do not find it; we will receive it back again through the economy of the tree. And that the *Logos* of God is similar to an axe, John the Baptist teaches, saying, 'and even now the axe is put to the root of the trees'[219] and Jeremiah also who says, 'the word of the Lord is like a hatchet cutting a rock.'"[220]

Question 56
What does the number of the 153 fish in the Gospel signify?[221]

✛   By beginning at one and adding [all numbers consecutively] until [one reaches] seventeen, you will generate this number. Thus, this signifies that precisely through the fulfillment (*ekploreseos*) of the ten commandments and through the seven activities of the Holy Spirit, those who are being saved and will enter into the kingdom of heaven; or also, [it signifies] those who are being saved and made worthy of the kingdom through the faith of the Holy Trinity and by the hope of things to come—for the number fifty goes beyond the sevenfold [number] of weekly time—and by the operation of the commandments, which is signified by the number one hundred.

Question 57
Who are the men and women and snakes for the sake of whom the Lord, according to Gregory of Nyssa, spent the three days in Hades?[222]

✛   "Three" are the powers of the soul: the reasoning, the irascible, and the desirous. And so, the men represent the reasoning [power], and the women the desirous [power], and the snakes the irascible [power]. And so these three powers are restored to full knowledge in the coming age. And for their sake, the Lord also accepted his life-giving suffering[223] and his descent into Hades.

Question 58
How should we understand what is said in Proverbs, that "the man who is observant and sharp" in understanding ought to "stand before kings"?[224]

✛   The passage wishes to present the one who is sharp concerning the practical and contemplative concerning knowledge (*gnostikon*) according to the three laws (the natural and the written and that of grace) so that being led by them he might accomplish successfully the practical, natural, and theological philosophy.

Question 59
From the same, "a righteous person will fall seven times and rise again."[225]

✛   One must recognize that the righteous person here, the only truly righteous one, is our Lord Jesus Christ. And so, since he is said both to fall and to rise in us, by accepting all that belongs to us because of his love for humankind, and our nature fell seven times—first, the transgression of the ancestor;[226] second, the bloodthirsty murder undertaken by Cain[227] (the first one who introduced murder in nature); third, in the generation of Noah,[228] upon which the spirit of God did not remain "because it was flesh";[229] fourth, the construction of the tower;[230] fifth, the generation of Abraham, from which only he was truly acceptable to God; sixth, in that [time] of Moses, whose generation had fallen into such a degree of godlessness that he was sent from God as a defender against such impiety; seventh, the generation [in the time] of the prophets, which surpassed all previous generations in its capacity for evil—and so, since, as I said, our nature fell seven times, the Lord raised it, moved by his ineffable love for humankind, uniting nature itself to him in a hypostatic manner.

Question 60
Who is indicated by the Apostle when, writing to the Ephesians, he says, "those who had previously hoped in Christ"?[231]

✤   Every one of those saints [who lived] before the Lord's sojourning, whatever virtue each of them may have practiced, and even if they did not know the entire mystery of the economy, nevertheless, being moved naturally from a part [of the mystery], hoped and expected that he who had created nature would himself also restore it when it had been corrupted.

Question 61
From the same, "so that you might know what is the hope of his calling you, and what is the wealth of the glory of his inheritance in the saints, and what is the exceeding greatness of his power."[232]

✤   "The hope of his calling" is detachment in the midst of action, in keeping with the Lord's own way of life. And "the wealth of the glory of his inheritance in the saints" is the wealth of the knowledge of truth. And "the exceeding greatness of his power" is deification (*theosis*) that will be bestowed upon the worthy, since it is beyond nature and, by grace, will make gods of human beings.

Question 62
From the same Apostle, "for we were made by him, created for good works."[233]

✤   This is said by the Apostle, I believe, because in the beginning God made the human being; and when, through transgression, he went astray, God recreated him through his sojourning in the flesh[234] and restored him to his original [condition].

Question 63
From the same, "he made both one and tore down the middle wall of partition, the enmity in the flesh"[235] and the rest.

✤   This means either he joined together two people into one, or he joined earthly things and heavenly things—for he also joined these together because they were separated from each other— or you may take this to refer to each one of us: since he joined together the soul and the body, which are always at odds with one another. For he has subjected "the mind of the flesh" to "the law of the spirit."[236] "And he tore down the middle wall of partition."

He called "middle wall" either the flesh or the perceptible things or the worship according to the law, and the "partition" is sin. For, because we made use of these things neither with correct reason nor with spiritual knowledge, they walled us away from God and subjected [us] to sin. "The enmity with the flesh"—he calls sin "enmity." For it made us enemies of God. "He abolished the law of the commandments by the directives,"[237] the law of the commandments being "you shall not kill"[238] and the others. The one who naturally devotes oneself to the commandment and knows the reason for the commandment understands that not only must one abstain from physical murder but also from every passion that mars [one's] nature. For envy and slander and all the passions are destructive to nature. And so, the Lord came and "abolished the law by the directives" (instead of "he brought it to an end"), saying, "it was said to your ancestors, 'you shall not kill,' but I tell you, 'anyone who is angry with his brother, without cause, shall be held liable,'"[239] and not only did he teach so but also acted this way. And he abolished the sacrifices, the directives according to the law, preparing [us] to understand them spiritually. Rather, he put an end to many of them, showing that they were a prefiguring of the mystery regarding himself.

Question 64
From Proverbs, "Who ascended into heaven and descended? Who has gathered the winds in his breast? Who has crushed water in a garment? Who has held [in his hand] all the ends of the earth? What is his name?"[240]

✚ In the beginning, the human being was created for this purpose: to ascend in desire to the Cause (*aitia*) and then, accordingly, to descend to the created things that follow the Cause, and thus, having rightly investigates these things with knowledge, to raise them up to their Creator. But he [the human being] did not do this; before raising himself up to God he turned to material things. For this reason, our Lord Jesus Christ, the second Adam, came and "summed up all things in himself"[241] and showed for what purpose the first human being was brought into being. For in assuming human nature he first ascended, being moved towards the Cause; and then he descended according to his divine nature, being clothed with "the form of a servant,"[242] and he ascended again as both together, in the ascension after the resurrection from the dead. Thus, it is necessary, also for us, first to be raised up to God and to train the soul to direct its complete longing towards him, and once that occurs, to descend to the study of beings and to consider what is the nature of every being, then once again, through these things to be raised up in contemplative knowledge to their Creator.

Such a person gathers together "the winds in his breast." For he brings the different *logoi* of beings, which are figuratively called 'winds,' together in the breast of his own heart. And so, since "breast" is the navel[243] in which they say the first offspring receives its beginning, it is necessary to understand that, bringing together the different *logoi* in the productive and contemplative part of the heart, he brings forth one *Logos* of God. For the many *logoi* of beings are brought together into one. But he also strains "water through a garment." As you will find mentioned in many places in Scripture, the temptations are "water."[244] Patiently suffering these temptations, he crushes them in his own body or, also, by the ethical division of philosophy, sends them away unsuccessful. And again, he prevails over "the ends of the earth," not allowing the natural passions of the body to be expressed irrationally.

Question 65
From Isaiah, "and they who are left behind [as a remnant] will be" beyond "the gold not tested in the fire."[245]

✛   They who are tested through temptations and who undergo a fuller trial, as did Job, Joseph and those like them, are beyond "the gold not tested in the fire"; for example, they will be beyond Adam who was formed directly, the way gold is, and not fire tested by temptations; and he did not endure.

Question 66
What does "the coal and the green stone" in Genesis mean?[246]

✛   Both represent the Lord: the coal, as illuminating and flammable, because the Lord is the provider of knowledge and destroyer of depravity. And the green stone, since it strengthens the power of vision, also represents the Lord, as the maker of the contemplative intensity of the soul.

Question 67

What does the blinding of Samson mean with regard to contemplative interpretation?[247]

✠   Samson is interpreted as the sun and Dalida as an impoverishing woman. And so, Samson fell upon the thigh of Dalida, that is, upon the passionate part of pleasure, and she impoverished him of enlightening virtue. Then, she brought a barber and a razor "and he shaved his seven locks."[248] The "barber" is the devil, and the "razor" is deceit according to what has been written, "you have sharpened treachery like a razor."[249] And the seven locks are the seven activities of the Spirit according to the prophet Isaiah.[250] And so, when his hair began to grow, that is, when he came into repentance[251] with respect to what he had done, then the young child, that is, the law of God, takes him by the hand and leads him to the pillars "upon which stood the house" of the Philistines, which are anger and desire, by which every Philistine mind is conquered. And Samson, dying along with the Philistines,[252] signifies the destruction, or rather the mortification, of the carnal mind.[253]

Question 68

What does Samson himself indicate by slaying the Philistines with the jawbone of an ass?[254]

✠   Here, Samson bears the type of the true Nazarite (ascetic) of Christ.[255] For he received our flesh without any moisture of sin and destroyed the Philistine demons. And that Samson was bound by his own people and handed over to the Philistines obviously was fulfilled in the Lord. For the Jews, who appeared to be his own [people], bound him and handed him over to the Gentiles.[256] But from the body of the Lord flowed,[257] as from the jawbone, the water of knowledge that he thirsted for,[258] saying, "so that they know you as the only true God and Jesus Christ whom you have sent."[259] But, even each Samson, that is, the

Nazarite, by the jawbone (that is, by bodily self-control, which is of a different kind than that of the soul) just as the ass, in the law,[260] represents the Gentiles' position, kills the passions by the life of action. And then he thirsts after divine knowledge, and through the prayer that he sent forth from that same virtuous action, divine knowledge is sent down to him, quenching his thirst and refreshing him. And if he is found trapped inside the walls of Gaza,[261] that is, under perceptible things, he raises up the doors—that is the senses—on the shoulders of the active life and leads them up into the mountain of higher knowledge.

Question 69
For what reason did God order the children of Israel to destroy the seven nations[262] and not the five *satraps*?[263]

✛ God, hating all passions against nature, commands that they be utterly destroyed. However, he does not wish that the powers of the five senses according to nature be abolished. If, then, accordingly, they are ever set in motion against nature, their activities are to be killed.

Question 70
What does the Gospel indicate, saying, "wash your face and anoint your head"?[264]

✛ Our "face" is our life, which, just like a face, characterizes who we are "according to the inner self."[265] And so, the passage advises [us] to "wash" it, that is, to purify our life from every stain of sin.[266] And "head" is our *nous*, which the passage urges us to "anoint," that is, to make bright by divine knowledge.

Question 71
What is meant by the Lord's reply, when he said, "tell the fox" (referring Herod) "I accomplish healings today and tomorrow, and on the third day I am perfected"?[267]

✛ Herod is interpreted as "skin-like."[268] And so, one must despise the fleshly thoughts that wish to detach the *nous* from active virtue and say to them, "I accomplish healings today and tomorrow, and on the third day I am perfected," that is, I first heal, by the active life, my own members, and then I heal the senses in order to direct them towards perceptible things in a healthy way, "and on the third day I am perfected," receiving perfection by the contemplation of divine knowledge.

Question 72
What is meant by the Apostle's saying, that, "flesh and blood are not able to inherit the kingdom of God"?[269]

✠   "Flesh" is desire, and "blood" is anger.[270] And, naturally, the one who does not cleanse himself of these things "is not able to inherit the kingdom of God."

Question 73
What does Mount Sinai in Horeb show, and what are the mysteries that took place in it?[271]

✠   "Sinai" is translated as "temptation,"[272] and "Horeb" as "breaking up the ground."[273] And so, the one who desires the height of knowledge must first have patience with the temptations, and break up the ground, and sow the fruit of knowledge and righteousness, and be purified of all passions.[274] And for three days, representing the three powers of the soul, one must be cleansed of every fleshly pleasure and not bring along, as a companion, a woman or any animal, the text thus indicating that it is necessary for the one who desires to become worthy of the divine voice to approach the mountain of knowledge possessing nothing feminine or irrational but being clothed in the brilliant outer garments of virtue.[275] For, in this way, like the marvelous Moses, one who arrived at this state through natural contemplation and at the proper time[276]—which is depicted by the seventy elders[277]—and passing by voices and sounds which are the interpretations of appearances—takes with him only Aaron and his two sons, Nadab and Abiud, that is, Aaron, reason, and his two sons, anger and desire. But one must also, like smoke and storm, leave these behind as well[278] and have only Aaron, I mean, reason that is simple with regard to intellection, which is enlightened by the divine illuminations like lightening; then, also, to leave this [reason] outside and to enter into the darkness of unknowing, where every nonreason and nonintelligence exists. And I think the people who were purified at the foot of the mountain represent those who participate in the active life,[279] and the seventy elders represent those engaged in natural contemplation,[280] and the people in Aaron's company represent those who pursue theology, and the people who are like Moses represent those who are united to God by negation and unknowing.

Question 74
What is *diapsalma*?[281]

✛   I think that it is either a change from one meaning to another meaning or, if you will, a change from one method of teaching to another method.

Question 75
What is "it would have been better for him [to have] an ass's millstone" placed around his neck and be thrown into the sea "rather than he scandalize one of the little ones"?[282]

✛   "Little ones," I think, means those who are simple in mind and because of their smallness of mind are not able to discern the judgments of providence. And so, whoever might cause one such as these to fall into sin, it would be better for him to be of the position of the Gentiles, who, in the manner of an ass at the mill, have been held fast in only the movement of the world and to be cast out "into the depth of the sea," that is, into the confusion of life. And the Apostle Peter also confirmed this, saying, "it would have been better for them never to have known the way of righteousness than after knowing it to return back to what they had left behind."[283]

Question 76
For what reason does God order that hyacinth-colored threads be bound to the hems of their garments[284] after the stoning [that took place] by [his] directive of the one gathering the sticks on the Sabbath?[285]

✛   The one who spends the Sabbath engaged in action and in knowledge, and then becomes lazy, begins to collect for himself the clinging materials of the passions as if collecting sticks of wood; and the same thing applies in the case of the gnostic who turns toward the outward appearance of visible things; fittingly, such passions are put to death by the divine words as if by stones. But since God sees the carelessness and instability of human beings, in order that they should not be taken hold of by forgetfulness and fall from the commandment, he commands that the hyacinth-colored threads be bound to the hems of their garments, so that seeing the threads they may call to mind the command. This would appear to be the external purpose of the law. But the spiritual purpose which cleanses the depths [of the human being] is the following: since the hem is made up of the thread of the garment, this means it is necessary for faith—for this is the thread—to be hung upon the garment of practical, ethical philosophy, and simply for faith and action to be intertwined, and from these knowledge, that is wisdom, is to be entwined in the way the hyacinth [-colored thread has been]. For wisdom, according to those who give etymologies, is called "wisdom," which the color of hyacinth shows by darkening.

Question 77
What is the significance of Abel and Cain[286] according to the interpretive method of spiritual uplifting (*anagoge*)?

✛   Cain represents "the mind of the flesh,"[287] and Abel represents mourning or, rather, repentance. And so, whenever, having not yet perfectly corrected its active condition, the *nous* is mocked by "the mind of the flesh" and departs with it "into the plain,"[288] that is, into the expanse of natural contemplation, it is killed, being not strong enough to pass through the outward appearances of beings, but remaining within them. And so, whoever murders Cain, that is, "the mind of the flesh,"—which is the concern, for the one who kills mourning consents with evil— "cancels a sevenfold vengeance,"[289] that is, he does away with the seven spirits of wickedness or, if you will, [does away] with the seven passions of evil working beneath them. And the curse of the groaning of Cain[290] depicts the rebellion of the conscience that continually strikes and disquiets one's thinking.

Question 78 (I, 19; III, 14)
What does the story of Lamech show?[291]

✛ Some who have been educated in the divine things say that in the time of Lamech, when there was disorder and anarchy, the strong oppressed the weak. And so, this one, Lamech, met up with a man who was with his wife, then murdered him and took his wife. And encountering a brother with a sister, he also murdered him and took his sister. And Scripture called the one an adult man, and the other a young man. This is what it says according to the historical sense. But according to the contemplative interpretation, Lamech represents the working of evil. For it [the working of evil] murdered the adult man in us, the natural law, and took from him sense. It also murdered the young man, I mean, the spiritual law, and took from him thought, so that by consorting with these the sower of evil causes them to give birth to sin. Therefore, from this Lamech, one is punished seventy times seven [times], that is, one pays damages for one's consent with, and doing of, [evil]. When the Lord, being asked by Peter "how often" if "my brother" sins against me should I forgive him? "Up to seven times?"[292] The Lord answered, "not" only "up to seven times, but up to seventy times seven."[293] That is, you should forgive the one who repents, not only for small things that happen with his consent, but also for the actual deeds (*energias*).

Question 79
What do the molten image and the carved image and the *teraphim*[294] show, which were made in the time of Gideon,[295] and what do the earrings and the crescents show, which Gideon made into an *ephod*[296] and placed at the gate[297] and which became a stumbling stone for his household?

✛ That one, who makes a molten [image] according to Scripture, externalizes the models of evil [drawn] from mental pictures and molds them, and brings forth sin in an active way. And that one, who makes a carved image, creates passion from himself. And he makes a *teraphim* and has acquired the habit of [engaging in] the passions as if it is a storage place. For they say that the *teraphim* is the storage place of the blood of the sacrificial offerings. And that Gideon made the *ephod* from the earrings and the crescents signifies that whoever from each one [of these] teachers receives a word or a directive—for this is "earrings" and "crescents"—regarding something of the external images [found] in the creation, then assembles from all of these one mystical treatise of contemplation and makes this available or even compiles it together in a volume— for this is the "gate"—and whoever is incapable, having a childish mind, of comprehending the mystery and unity of the treatise is surely humiliated by the teacher who speaks.

Question 80
What does the story about the same Gideon mean, and the fleece and the war with the Madianites and the rest?[298]

Hagar, the maid of Sarah,[299] represents sense. It [sense] conceives through natural contemplation and begets the natural law. And if sense rises up against the *nous* just as that one [Hagar] did against Sarah[300]—and Sarah is translated as "one who rules"[301]—sense is rejected and the *nous* conceives Isaac,[302] the spiritual law, from whom comes Israel, that is "the *nous* that sees God." Whenever this one [Israel] is ruled by the Madianite,[303] that is, by sexual impurity, he is handed over by consent for seven years [as agreed], that is, to the temporal and temporary passions. "And the children of Israel made for themselves," it says, "dens and caves in the mountains, caves, and dens."[304] For the *nous*, being attacked, seems to think about sufferings and pains, but when it brings these about without knowledge it toils uselessly. For, it says, "the man of Israel planted seed, and Madian and Amalek and the sons of the East rose up and utterly destroyed" the fruits "of the earth."[305] And "Amalek" is gluttony, and "Madian" is sexual impurity, and the "sons of the East" are vainglory. All destroy the seed of the heart, which he [the man of Israel] seems to cultivate without knowledge. "And they did not leave behind the bare necessities of life in Israel,"[306] it says, from the flock to the calf to the ass, that is, from the rational to the irascible to the desirous. And "both their possessions and their tents went up," together with "their camels" which "were without number,"[307] that is, the various forms of the passions and their memories and the imaginings. "And Israel," it says, "was impoverished before Madian and the sons of Israel cried out to the Lord and the Lord sent them a man of prophecy."[308] When the *nous* is impoverished of every virtue and its thoughts cry out to the Lord from regret, the Lord will send forth a word that reminds [it] of the way up from Egypt, that is, of the rescue from the darkness of sins.

And the passage says, "and the angel of the Lord came and sat down under a terebinth"[309]—hinting at the mystery of the Cross—"and Gideon," it says, "was threshing the wheat in the trough,"[310] that is, he was engaging in the active life with knowledge. For this is the trough of the wine. "And the angel appeared to him and said" to him, "'the Lord, mighty in strength, is with you.'"[311] For as he had subordinated and enslaved the passions and possessed—as properly his own—lordship through action and knowledge, the angel addresses him out of his own proper qualities: "The Lord is with you" [because of these qualities]. And the humility of such a *nous* is shown by his reply. For he said, "and if the Lord is" with us, "why have such evils found us?" "And the angel said to him, 'go forward in your strength; by this you will save Israel,'"[312] that is, in the strength of action and knowledge. "And he said to" the angel, "'if I have found grace in your eyes, do not move from here until I come to you.' And Gideon went in and prepared a kid from among the goats and" took "an *ephah*"[313] of the finest wheat and "unleavened bread and he put meat in the basket and" put "the broth in a pot and carried them to him under the terebinth tree, and the angel said to him, 'Take the meat and the unleavened bread and put them on that rock and pour the broth'" on it. "And he did so."[314]

For whenever a spiritual thought is sent down to the *nous* and the *nous* is able to harmonize such knowledge through the appropriate actions according to what is necessary, that knowledge cannot be removed. And "to have brought forth the meat and the unleavened breads and the broth" signifies the action having been poured upon by knowledge free from arrogance. For this is what "broth" means. And he has commanded [Gideon] to place these things on the rock. For one must join knowledge as well as action together to faith in Christ. "And the angel stretched out the end of the rod that was in his hand and touched the meat and fire arose from the rock and consumed the meat and the unleavened breads, and the angel departed from his eyes."[315] For whenever such action and knowledge are perfected by faith, then the fire of the Spirit makes these things radiant and the *logos* of the beginning of knowledge at the same time takes flight (*sunaphiptatai*). For no longer is it there to remind as before. For since the *nous* is held by the whole light of the Spirit, no longer does it rest upon the things with which it began.

And the fleece means the Judaic worship, for the dew came upon it, since it had ordinances of worship. And "dryness" was on "all the ground."[316] For all the nations were dry of the knowledge of God. And "to squeeze the water into the bowl"[317] meant the future grace of baptism. For the old [worship] possessed in many places types of Holy Baptism. And so, those who are "squeezed into the bowl" of baptism suggested to us that mystery. And its repetition, in which, contrariwise, the fleece had the dryness,[318] and all the ground had dew signified the grace of the Gospel. For "all the earth" was filled with the dew of the Gospel. But the people of the Jews were left dry of every [bit of] faith. As to each detail: a "fleece" is the ethical philosophy, which is squeezed out into the bowl of knowledge. And all the earth having the dew means that after the proper ordering of ethical philosophy all the earth of the heart is full of divine knowledge. But if someone is puffed up solely on account of the right ordering of moral values, without the appropriate knowledge, such a person has in the earth of his heart no moisture, and appears to be beautifying the outer tent like a fleece.

And "turning back of 10,000"[319] allowing Gideon to marshal the troops means those who, because of cowardice, run away from the hard work of virtue, betraying their senses and their activities. And the 20,000, they who are bent down, lying on their stomachs and lapping the water,[320] are they who betrayed the perceptible things with the senses. For the four elements multiplied by the five senses makes the number twenty. These, rolling around in the earth, that is, being overcome by earthly attachment, attempt to drink the water of knowledge. The *Logos* dismisses them as having been rejected from the spiritual troops. And he singles out only the 300 who carried lanterns.[321] And they crucified themselves and kept safe the three powers of the soul by the 100 of perfection. For a hundred is the multiplication of the ten commandments by ten as each commandment includes the other and, to speak more clearly, each one equals ten; therefore, to Sarah, who was advanced [in age], the 100 was added, with the passage showing her perfection in virtue.[322] And they who carried lanterns drink the water with their hands.[323] For through the labors of action they draw the water of knowledge. And the commander of the spiritual troops orders them to hold in their left hand the water pitchers, with lamps inside [the pitchers], and in their right hand a horn, and to be interspersed in this manner among the enemies; through these things he signifies that someone who intends to marshal the troops against the invisible enemies must through action—for this is the left hand—rule over the body, having already through *askesis* thrown off every moistness of passions and become a dry order of earthenware, having the light of knowledge within, and that he must by the right hand, that is, by contemplation, maintain the teaching of the *Logos*. For this is the horn. And "to shatter the water pitchers" means that the complete mortification of the flesh and disdain for it uncovers the light of knowledge in us.

And the saying, "a sword for the Lord and for Gideon"[324] means that whoever brings the cutting word of the Lord,[325] along with his own personal willingness, nullifies the passions. And the dream which the Madianites saw[326] shows that when the *nous* begins to surrender itself to *askesis* and to mistreat the body, the demons of sexual impurity form a judgment, as by a dream, that, "if the *nous* is strong enough to apply itself to such *askesis*, then it kills us." For the rolling barley cake,[327] that is, an advancing *askesis*, tramples on the tents of the foreigners, which are clearly the productive passions of the demons.

Question 81 (III, 15)

What is the saying from the Lord to the apostles, "Behold, I am with you until the end of the ages"?[328]

✠   The Lord himself is said to be with us in the present age, and in the future [age] the saints will be with him, being united with God by grace.

Question 82

What does Jericho signify and who is Achar, the one "who stole" from "what is cursed,"[329] and why did God order him to be burned, but [instead] Joshua stoned him?[330]

✠   Whoever, being counted among the divine troops, encircles Jericho seven times sounding the trumpet,[331] that is, marching through the sevenfold age of this time period by the trumpet of the Gospel, is taught to entrust all things of this age to God. And whoever removes an ingot and hides it in the earth,[332] that is, hides the *logos* in the earthly wisdom of this world, or also, "a bare thing"—which is an outer garment—that is, practices morality for the sake of impressing onlookers, and steals "two hundred gold pieces,"[333] that is, all the things perceptible by the senses, and having concealed such gold pieces in the earth of his own carnal enjoyment, this one is killed, first by the commanding Word which boils upon him like a fire, and then also by the divine words, by which he is pelted as though by stones.

Question 83 (I, 20; III, 16)
Concerning God's different wills.

✤ It is necessary to identify three wills of God: according to good pleasure, according to economy, and according to permission. On the one hand, the will 'according to pleasure' is exemplified by that which relates to Abraham [when God] said to him to, "go forth from your land."[334] And then, the will 'according to economy' is shown by the things concerning Joseph[335] which happened to him by economy with a [his family's] view to their escaping what was going to happen later. And the things that happen in the case of Job show the will of God 'according to permission.'[336]

Question 84 (I, 54)
What is, "do not call a man blessed before his death"?[337]

✤ According to the *nous* accessible to most people, because of what is unknown and the unsteadiness of the human faculty of free choice (*proairesis*),[338] one must not pronounce someone blessed until, making his way through every virtue, he completes his life with an irreproachable end. But according to the higher *nous*, the one who begins, through repentance and *askesis*, to make the earthly mind (*phronema*) living within him humble and weak, is not pronounced blessed until through the intense labor of *askesis* he becomes dead and reaches perfection. For such a person is pronounced blessed since he dies together with Christ by not practicing evil and also is raised again by the height of virtues. This is what the psalmist means, saying, "blessed are they who are blameless in their ways,"[339] namely, they who are pure from evil, "who walk in the law of the Lord,"[340] those who make their way by [the practice] of good deeds.

Question 85
What does the psalmist mean, who says, concerning enemies, "they who are joined together in a circle to attack"?[341]

✠ The "circle" has the front, the back, the right, and the left. And so, the demons are placed in front of us whenever they entice us through superficialities (*epiphaneion*) of matter, and behind whenever they stir up the memory through the recollections of evil thoughts, and on the left whenever, through carnal and unbridled passions, they disturb[342] the soul, and on the right whenever they inflict the soul through vainglory and pride.

Question 86
What is "take up (*labete*) a song and sound (*dote*) the timbrel"?[343]

✠ Take up divinely inspired teaching and sound virtuous action through the mortification of the body.

Question 87
What is elemental matter (*stoicheiosis*)?

✠ They say that there are said to be three [types of] bodies: the first is that of the four basic elements, fire, water, earth, and air. Then, from these [come] the second bodies, all the trees that are brought forth as well as vegetation. And from these [is] the third body, the human and that of the animals. For by eating these, flesh is formed. And so, just as the source and elemental matter of our bodies are the four elements, thus also, for the soul, the elemental matter and source which is from the four cardinal virtues, produces the right ordering of morals. Then, from this emerges the habit of the virtues like a second body. Then knowledge, or rather, contemplation, is given bodily existence from this, "for action is the entryway (*epibasis*) to contemplation."

Question 88
What does the ladder seen by Jacob mean and who are the angels descending and ascending?[344]

✦ We take the ladder to be reverence for God. Regarding the angels who descend and ascend, those who ascend are the *logoi* of the virtues being elevated through us, and those who descend are the *logoi* of knowledge that come down because of the elevation of our virtues.[345]

Question 89
What does the *denarios*[346] mean, the one presented to the Lord by the Pharisees?[347]

✦ A *denarios* is the law given for the allowance (*sugchoresin*) of bodily need. And so, when the Pharisees, being a type of the demons, present this to us, one must hold and examine it closely through discernment and impart to nature the things pertaining to need—for this is to give, "the things of Caesar to Caesar"[348]— but impart the soul's entire appetite (*ephesin*) to God.

Question 90 (I, 55)
What does the passage show, "if they persecute you in one city, flee to another"?[349]

✦ Cities are for protection and security and the guarding of valuables. Therefore, a city is, according to the allegorical method of interpretation, the *askesis* (ascetic activity) devised out of various practices, such as self-control with regard to wine, abstention from foods, continuous vigil, and such things, which are protection and safety. And so, if the demons chase us from one of these, presenting conceit or vainglory through any form of *askesis*, it is better to withdraw from such a seemingly rigid discipline so that you might not fall into arrogance and to flee to another virtue without any vainglory, until the *logos* of detachment may come.

Or also, the passage may be interpreted in another way: cities mean human souls.[350] For the words sent from the Savior to these, as apostles, when received by those who are worthy, dwell in them; but when driven out by those who have judged themselves unworthy, settle in the souls of others who have become receptive to their teaching. And they will not be done with such cities of Israel, genuinely abiding in them, and in one place finding a home while elsewhere being driven away from them, "until the Son of Man comes"[351] fulfilling all things in his glorious [second] coming.

Question 91 (I, 23; III, 19)

What is, "he will not break a bruised reed and will not quench a smoldering wick"?[352]

✢   The one who employs a word of sympathy[353] in imitation of the Lord neither allows the one crushed by sin to be broken into pieces in the end by despair, nor quenches the one whose reasoning has been puffed up because of vainglory as a result of [the practice of] some virtues. But he lets him continue with eagerness until he comes into the perfection of full knowledge (*epignosis*). For this, I think, is what he meant by allowing the weeds "to increase together with the good seed,"[354] that is, allowing the passions of gaining popularity and vainglory to grow alongside with the virtues. Therefore, the cultivator of souls commands that these not be plucked out[355] until the virtues achieve some stability, lest someone desiring to remove such passions should also pluck out the eagerness for virtue.

Question 92

What is meant by the prophetic riddle that says, "sound the trumpet with the trumpet of the new month, on the auspicious day of our feast"?[356] What, then, is the auspicious feast?

✢   The passage orders the teachers of the church to sound the trumpet through the word of teaching.[357] And 'to sound the trumpet by the trumpet,' that is, by the mortification of the body. And [this takes place] 'at the new month,' namely, according to the moon. For the moon is called a month. "And the auspicious feast" according to the Jews is that of the trumpets which is celebrated in the seventh month.[358] And on the tenth day of the same month, they celebrate the fast of atonement,[359] and on the fifteenth day they celebrate the Feast of the Tents.[360] And we celebrate the feast spiritually this way: in the seventh month, that is, by the seventh law of grace we celebrate the auspicious feast of the Gospel. For the God of all, from the beginning, provided nature with seven laws: two to Adam (the one before the transgression, not to eat from the fruit of the tree,[361] and the one after the transgression, to eat the bread "in the sweat of his brow[362]"); third, the one in the time of Noah;[363] fourth, the one in the time of Abraham, that of circumcision;[364] fifth, the law of Moses;[365] sixth, the prophetic law; seventh, the Gospel law, in which we offer to God the beginnings of the fruits of virtue at the onset of illumination. For on the first of the month, those who keep to the law offer their first fruits. And on the tenth of the month, we who engage in the divine mystery observe the fast of atonement through the name of our Lord Jesus, who became our atonement,[366] and we fast from every evil. And on the fifteen [of the month] we take part in the Feast of the Tents. For adding to the mystery of our Lord Jesus the five receptive powers of the soul that are preoccupied with none of the perceptible things but are united to the Lord himself, we receive in him the stability of the virtues.

Question 93
From the *Ethica* (sermons) of St. Basil,[367] a difficulty in the text *Concerning Fasting*, "when" he says, "perfection was rejected, then enjoyment was allowed."

✛   Then "perfection was rejected," when a human being through disobedience turned aside the natural powers given to him. And so, it was impossible, since nature was entangled in passionate attachment to material things, to return to perfection until the creator of nature, becoming human beyond nature, brought nature back to that which is according to nature. And he says that "enjoyment is allowed" instead of "is handed over" to the self-law of error.

Question 94
From the same, regarding the First Psalm: for what reason at the beginning of the psalms, did he take as an example the foundation of a house and the keel of the ship and the heart of a living being?[368]

✛   Since a house composed of stones is a refuge from cold and burning heat and also a protection and defense for the human being, we learn from this, by following natural contemplation, that the *askesis* constructed of the *logoi* of virtue is a house, providing for us protection against the diabolical heat of temptations, and warmth against its chill of despair, and a defense against the scheming demons. And he understood the soul of each [person] as a ship having as a kind of keel, stability in understanding (*phronesis*), and whose well-fitted planks are the mortification of the body, which secures the joints of the soul with strict discipline as though with pitch and does not allow any salty evil to seep in, while it travels the sea of life and makes its voyage through this age, selling present things as would a merchant and buying in return the things of the future. And he understood faith as the heart of a living being, woven round on all sides with the virtues.

Question 95

From St. Gregory the Theologian's discourse, *On Baptism*,[369] a difficulty concerning a prophetic statement and prophecy [of Isaiah]: "Blessed is the one who sows upon every water and upon every soul that is to be ploughed and watered tomorrow, on which today the ox and ass tread."[370]

✛   The soul is ploughed and cleansed from the thorns of the passions through the active life, and it is watered through knowledge, "on which today the ox and ass tread"—he calls the Jewish law an ox, and the Gentile portion an ass. That soul, that is to say the soul that today remains at the literal level and is weighed down by irrationality, tomorrow through action and knowledge is transformed. The one who sows the seeds of virtue in the soul is blessed.

Question 96

From the same, "blessed is the one who though being in an overflowing river of rushes is watered from the house of the Lord."[371]

✛   "An overflowing river of rushes" is the flesh that sweeps away the powers of the soul by the storm of the passions and strikes like rushes by the roughness of sins. And one "is watered from the house of the Lord" whenever one is watered by the commandments of the Lord, the one who took up our flesh, from which, along the road of life, he drank the passion for our sake and has become for us, "a house of refuge."[372]

Question 97

From the same, "yesterday, you were dried up while flushing with a hemorrhage, for you were gushing forth crimson sin."[373]

✦ "Yesterday," he says, "you were dried up" of virtue and overflowing with sin. "Today, you have overflowed" with virtue, and are "dried up" of sin. "For you have grasped the hems of Christ"[374] (the hems of Christ are the different *askeses*), since just as the hems are fastened to the garment, thus, the *askeses* depend upon the ethical way of life. These virtues practiced with humility, cause the flow of the passions to stop.[375]

Question 98
From the same text, "yesterday, you were thrown onto the bed, paralyzed and exhausted"[376] and the rest.

✦ He calls a bed the refreshment of the body, and one is paralyzed by pleasures. "And you did not have," it says, "anyone," that is, a manly thought, "so that at such time as the water is troubled, he should put you in the pool";[377] so that at such time as a thought comes to you, troubling you with discernment of the good or the bad, he might place you in the water of purification. "Today you have found a human being who, at the same time, is God."[378] For whenever someone, making use of the teaching, cleanses himself, God is the one who effects this, and a human being is provided as some instrument for the salvation of the one who suffers. "You were raised from your bed, or rather, you took up the bed,"[379] that is, through the active life you raised up the body, no longer being taken down by it.

Question 99
From the same, "I know a fire that is not purifying but avenging, i.e., the fire of Sodom,[380] which he pours down on all sinners[381] mixed with brimstone and storms; or that which is prepared for the devil and his angels;[382] or also that which comes forth from the face of the Lord and shall burn up his enemies round about;[383] or more feared than these, that which is fused into one mass of sleepless worms, unable to be quenched but existing perpetually for the wicked."[384]

✦ "The fire of Sodom" is poured down upon those who trample on the law of nature by abusing it. And this is the reproof of the conscience, whenever, like fire, it completely burns it [nature or conscience, it is unclear]. And brimstone is the different circumstances (*peristatikai*), and storms are the sudden circumstances, which when mixed together injure in a more violent way. And they burn the conscience in imitation of "the devil and" his "angels" who through pride enviously slander (*diaballo*) the providence of God and employ treachery towards their neighbor. And the fire "which proceeds before the face of the Lord" burning "his enemies" is the energies (*energiai*) of God.[385] For they characterize the face of God, that is, his goodness, love of humankind, meekness, and things similar to these.[386] These energies enlighten those who are like them and burn up those who oppose and have been alienated from the likeness. And the passage did not say these, the forms of fire, are eternal, since according to Gregory of Nyssa nature must recover its own powers and be restored by full knowledge (*epignosei*) to what it was from the beginning, so that the Creator may be proven not to be the cause of sin.[387] And he called that the "more feared" fire, that "which is fused eternally into one mass with worms, not able to be quenched but existing perpetually for the wicked." For this reason, when the divinity appears and is offered to the worthy for their enjoyment, they who do not, through good works, illumine themselves, like a little worm which always uproots one's memory, are devoured, evaluated up by their failure and endless deprivation of the good, and are continually put to the test by a more violent fire.

Question 100

From the same author, on the passage from *Concerning Hail*, "I cannot allow the spring to be closed off and the swollen river to rush freely."[388]

✠ "A spring" is the Gospel teaching,[389] always gushing forth through faith, and a swollen river is the alien philosophy, having persuasiveness only in word. And in another way, a spring is the one who has a life in harmony with the *Logos*, and a swollen river is the word without action, seducing the hearing by mere utterance. Or also, in another way, a spring is the one who hands down the tradition to the learners according to the meaning of the contents, whereas a swollen river is the one who teaches according to the letter (*kata to gramma*).

Question 101
From the same work, "concerning God's righteous judgments, whether we comprehend them or are ignorant of their great depth."[390]

✛   "Depth" means the incomprehensible, which is from "to plug up" (*buein*) that is, from "to guard" (*phrassein*), according to what is said in the Psalm concerning the asp, "which plugs up the ears"[391] instead of "guarding [them]." And so, the judgments are incomprehensible to us who are unable to come to an understanding of the providence that pours them forth; but, yet, they are comprehensible in another way.

Question 102 (I, 56)
From the same, "how is it that mercy is also held in balance according to the holy Isaiah?[392] For neither does the good lack judgment, even if it seemed so to those in the vineyard."[393]

✛   While the mercy of God is balanced, it is also fittingly circumscribed. Rather, it is necessary to suppose this: that just as we have an optical, auditory, and respiratory ability (*dunamin*), and these things do not receive all the air or the light or the voice—since there will then be no partaking of these things left for anyone else—but in proportion to the power that is present in each, each partakes according to their ability; thus, also the mercy of God grants both forgiveness and grace according to the quality of the underlying dispositions (*diathesin*) of each one, e.g., when someone repented completely, he is also forgiven completely. One who repented partially also is forgiven partially. And the same thing also holds true for the one who loves.

Question 103
From the same, and "his wrath is in proportion to the sins" and it is also called "the cup in the hand of the Lord"[394] and "a chalice of falling fully quaffed,[395] even if he subtracts something from what is deserved, now he mingles the unmixed [wine] of his wrath with love of humanity, inclining away from severity towards what is yielding."[396]

✛   "Hand of the Lord" is the creative and preserving power that fashions what is good and unfashions what is bad.[397] And so, every sin, once it subsists, also has affixed to it the judgment coming to it from its end. And "it [the hand of the Lord] inclines away from the severity towards the yielding," through the saving commandments, placing in the soul the repentance that empties it of such a judgment.

Question 104

A question concerning a difficulty from St. Gregory the Theologian's discourse, *Concerning Good Discipline,*[398] "how is a word the offspring of a mind, and begets a word in another mind?" About which type of word does he speak, the internal or the uttered one?

✛   Our fathers say there is nothing free and simple in essence except the divine alone,[399] and that all other things, which have being after God and from God, are from essence and quality, or rather, potentiality, that is, from essence and accident. And if this is the case, then the soul, no doubt existing as mind according to its potential, possesses itself as unbegotten, as begetting begottenly in itself, so that there should be the word that is in the mind, and another begotten from the mind in it—that thing is the begetting mind—together with the identifying characteristic with respect to begetting, which in no way allows reversal. Therefore, this very word, which thus both is and is begotten, receiving the voice of the assisting nature, brings forth and begets a word in another mind, being sent to the mind through the hearing of him who receives it. But it "begets a word in another mind" not by creating a word in another but by giving forms, if I may so speak, and a power of shape so as to configure a thought in the hearer.

Question 105

From the writing of the same St. Gregory, *On Peace,* "a perfect Trinity out of three who are perfect, the Monad having been moved on account of multiplicity, and Dyad, which is through matter and form (from which bodies exist) having been transcended, being defined as Trinity on account of perfection: for it is the first that transcends the composition of the Dyad."[400]

✛   He does not give here the cause of being of the divine and blessed Trinity, which is beyond cause and reason, but [gives] the cause of our being led by the hand to the most truthful reverence of the Holy Trinity. For just as we understand the author of existence from the essence of beings, so, also, we are mystically taught the mode of existence of the most ineffable divinity from some symbols [found] in existing things, that is to say, the Holy Divinity itself moves us into an acknowledgement of itself and provides pious starting points [in order for us] to have the courage to examine closely the mode of its extraordinary existence. And so, it is said to be set in motion either because of us, who are set in motion towards it [the Trinity], or as the cause of our movement toward the knowledge of it. It moved itself in us toward the knowledge that some cause of all things exists. That is the "the Monad having been moved." "And the Dyad is transcended" has been said because the divine nature is perceived to exist outside composition (*syntheseos*). And "being defined as Trinity on account of perfection" is said because "being" itself is not without wisdom and life. Understanding this, we recognize wisdom as the Son and *Logos* of God and the Holy Spirit as life, therefore our soul also, which is created "in the image of God,"[401] is observed in these three things: *nous*, *logos*, and spirit.

Question 106

What is meant by that which is said in *Esdras*, "terrify them"[402] by the law of the Lord?

✠   "Terrify" is said instead of "amaze them," not because of the good things promised but because of the terrible things threatened. For this is appropriate to servants and fitting for the Jews.

Question 107

From the *Ethica* [semons][403] of St. Basil on the first Psalm, "so now, as though from a common medicine cabinet for souls, all of us humans might choose, each for himself, the remedy for his own passion. For a remedy," it says, "puts an end to great sins." For what reason did the teacher here not follow the Scripture? Because that [Scripture] interpreted that the remedy as 'letting alone the evil thought now comes into [one's head]' and not to accept it, whereas he interpreted the phrase as having to do with healing.[404]

✠   Since every beginning also has an end, and every statement
has a reply, and every activity has a result, often the strictest (*oi
akribesteroi*) of teachers compose the starting point of the same
argument's conclusions, and that is how the teacher here has
used [this text]. For the result of "letting the evil alone" and not
accepting it is healing and health.

Question 108
From the same, "therefore, prophets teach one thing and
historians teach another, and the law teaches something else, and
the form of proverbial advice teaches something different still."[405]

✠   Prophets teach the signs of the future, and historians teach
the recollection and display (*parathesin*) of good events, and
the law teaches knowledge of good and evil. And "the form of
proverbial advice" supplies counsel for deliberation, that is, it
suggests the ways in which things are to be done.

Question 109
From the same, "and when one of those people who are made
exceedingly savage by anger begins to become lulled by the psalm,
straightaway the fierceness of his soul departs, when his soul is
made calm by the melody."[406]

✠   The teacher spoke not with regard to the one who simply sings
but with regard to the one who knows how to sing. For, thus, Elisha,
too, from [the book of] Kings sought after a young man "who knew
how to sing,"[407] that is, one who understood and was able through
the mediation of the spoken word to transfer and inscribe [the]
indwelling meaning onto the soul. For such a person not only is able
to lull to sleep anger but also to banish demons, that is, not only to
quell the passions of the flesh but also to expel the demons who rouse
them up, as did the great David who banished the evil spirit of Saul.[408]

Question 110 (I, 58)
From the same, "a weapon for nightly fears, a rest from daily
troubles."[409]

✠   He called "night" the hidden deceitful attacks of the enemy,
and he called "day" the temptations that are acknowledged and

in plain sight. And so, the one who has received the state of divine knowledge and is in no way ignorant of the thoughts of the enemy does not fear any of the hidden attacks of the enemy. For fear is none other than anticipated evil.[410] Yet, truly, he also considers the labors endured on account of the acknowledged temptations to be a rest, because of the trustworthiness that comes to the soul from its struggle with them, and because of what is hoped for as a result of this, the blessed receiving of the crown of incorruption.

Question 111
From the Apostle, to the Romans, "for God has closed up all together in disobedience."[411]

✤   Just as a master chases his own flock that runs off and wanders away, and when, together with the pursuers, he closes off [its way of escape] and finds that it has been wounded, he cares for it; in this way, the *Logos* of God also became human and "closed all together" (instead of "apprehended") and found all to be disobedient and sinful, and, showing mercy, preserved them.

Question 112 (III, 24)
From the same, "and the weak one eats vegetables."[412]

✤   This is said by the Apostle, not concerning bodily sickness—for he always rejoiced in sicknesses of the body—but he orders the one who is weak in the soul to eat vegetables, that is, the ordinary and plain and easily digestible, and food that is not fattening. And this is the obvious (*procheiros*) meaning. But according to [the interpretive method of] contemplation, the one is weak and "eats vegetables" who is unable to ascend to the heights of knowledge and to approach, like Moses, the "darkness where God is,"[413] but still, whether he is among the laity or among the more advanced who belong to the seventy elders,[414] he is nourished by natural contemplation as by vegetables.

Question 113
From the same, "I say that Christ was a minister of circumcision for the sake of the truth."[415]

✤   Since, in the beginning, the human being was deceived and, being fond of transgression was "likened to the beasts,"[416] was condemned to be born and to die in the same manner as they do, the Lord, not allowing his own formation to be utterly destroyed, at various times, worked out his salvation; in the case of Abraham, he made quite plain the future salvation that would take place through his sojourn in the flesh, for which reason, after all the promises to him [Abraham], he gave to him circumcision,[417] which manifests the excision of the passionate part of the soul. And so, since all the saints circumcised the passionate part of the soul, although in fact they did not strip it off completely—for they remained under the condemnation of nature since they were born by sexual intercourse—when the Lord and master of nature came himself, the one who gave circumcision to Abraham, he became truly the minister and fulfiller of circumcision having made complete the stripping away of impassioned birth. For he was conceived without seed and was born without corruption.

Question 114
From the same, "and knowing that this is the time, that the hour has already come for you to be awakened from sleep."[418]

✛   He calls "time" that of the Gospel preaching (kerygma) and says that it is necessary for those who have believed and have been justified, in order to guard the justification which is by faith and grace, to adhere ardently to the virtues, and that it is necessary for those who are sleeping because of the inactivity of the commandments and who keep their mind inert towards spiritual and divine things, to be awakened in the heart and to keep their mind watchful for the heavenly and intelligible beauties, having put to sleep every sense towards the things of sense perception so that it should be true of us according to Solomon's saying, "I lie down to sleep but my heart is awake."[419]

Question 115
From the same, "if the dead are not raised completely, why are [some] also baptized on their behalf?"[420]

✛   Since he speaks about dead bodies—for they are the things that have fallen and have been raised up—and we are baptized for the sake of their resurrection—for baptism carries a type of the burial and the resurrection; and the immersion and emergence show this—the Apostle, silencing those who are in doubt concerning the resurrection, says, "why are [some] also baptized on their behalf?" For the one who, through baptism, performs here and now the type of the burial and the resurrection will expect that, in the appropriate time, the absolute true resurrection will also take place.

Question 116
What is signified by the linen sheet set before Peter in Acts and the beasts and the reptiles and quadrupeds that were on it?[421]

✣   Since, according to the vision by the prophet Ezekiel, "their work was like a wheel within a wheel,"[422] and through these a perceptible as well as an intelligible world are depicted as existing within one another—for the intelligible world is in the perceptible world by types, and the perceptible world is in the intelligible world by its *logos*—therefore, all of the perceptible world was shown to the Apostle. For the "letting down by its four corners"[423] signifies the world composed of four elements, existing as clean in the intelligible world according to the *logos* that exists inherently in these things. And he heard, "rise up, kill, and eat,"[424] that is, "by [your] *nous* raise yourself up from that which is according to sense, and 'kill and eat,' which means by the distinction of reason divides sense perception, and taking up these things spiritually make them your own."

Or, it also signifies the church that is supported by the four foundations of the gospels or, again, by the four cardinal virtues. And the beasts and reptiles depict the different human customs which, from the Gentiles, are going to [change over to] the faith in Christ. And the "kill and eat" shows "first, by the word of teaching, 'kill' the evil in them and then 'eat,' making their salvation your own just as the Lord also made it food for himself."

Question 117
What, in the same book of Acts, does the number of the five myriads of burned books indicate?[425]

✣   Since the number of a myriad is the perfection [or end] of every number, what is meant is that all magic and idle curiosity has no other end than the error of perceptible things, and recognizing this, they will burn it completely in the fire of apostolic teaching.

Question 118

What is the reason why the Lord breathed his last upon the Cross before the robbers,[426] and what do the robbers and the breaking of their legs signify?[427]

✠ Since our Lord, Jesus Christ, being God by nature, having taken on our flesh has truly become the only human being, the only one who preserved in himself God's intention, for the sake of which he said, "let us create a human being according to our image and likeness";[428] and just as the first human being was formed by divine hands, so also the first and only Lord, when he died the death for [the first man's] sake, committed his own soul into the paternal palms. And just as he was and became only-begotten and "first born among many siblings,"[429] so also he was the only and first to accept undergoing the death that does away with death, in order that he might both become the "first born of the dead" and "in everything be preeminent."[430]

And the robbers are understood as our nature being divided between the just and sinful. The breaking of the legs signifies that you find that no one dies without faults and [everyone] is crushed by sin, but only the Lord died intact and without any sin. But frequently the robbers are taken individually. For they are taken as representing both body and soul and the carnal and spiritual way of thinking (*phronematos*);[431] but also as anger and desire, as the perceptible and intelligible world, and as the written law and the law of grace. But since, whether we sin or act rightly, the *Logos* descending into our midst is always crucified, therefore, whenever through our evil acts and ignorance we render the *Logos* ineffective and cause it to sink down, immediately the invading demons break down the progressing and perambulatory powers of our soul.

Question 119

Why is there disagreement in the recorded passages in Acts, regarding Paul's vision? For regarding the vision on the road, Luke reports that those who were with him [Paul] heard the voice but no one saw [the vision].[432] But when Paul describes the same vision step by step, he says that those who were with him had seen the light but had not heard the voice of the one who speaks.[433]

✛   According to the historical interpretation, Chrysostom, interpreting the passage in an exceedingly skillful way, said that the first narrative, the one saying, 'they who were with [him] heard the voice,' means they heard the voice of Paul saying, "who are you, Lord?"[434] but no one saw anyone other than Paul. But the second narrative, which says that they had seen the light, but had not heard the voice of the one who speaks, says that they had not heard the Lord's voice which came to Paul, and the light alone had been seen. Now, according to [the interpretation by] contemplation, one must understand the passage in this way: the intelligent (*gnostikos*) *nous*, according to Paul, contains the thoughts (*logismous*) that accompany it. And so, in the first appearance of the *Logos* to the *nous*, the thoughts hear only echoes and images of knowledge, but they do not see (*theorousin*) anything that has been made clear. But as the *nous* advances and ascends by increasing intervals, that is, to the height of contemplation (*theoria*), the thoughts no longer participate in images but completely in the light of knowledge.

Question 120 (I, 32)
How should the regret of God that is found in the Scripture[435] be thought of piously?

✛   Those who have discerned how to think about divine things piously say it is impossible for God, who is by nature creator, not to be also by nature the provider (*pronoeten*) for the things that have been created. And if this is the case, and humanity is naturally provided for by God, it is entirely necessary for desire to be, with him, in need of the providence of God, [and] there are, with respect to him, many ways of salvation as regarding the nature for which God provides. For since the human being is a quickly changing animal, recklessly shifting with the seasons and events, it is also wholly necessary for divine providence, even while being one and the same, to shift with our dispositions, discovering a method through those things that suitably harmonize with the evils springing up in nature. And as in the case of medicine, there are many sicknesses which it [divine providence] treats, and the knowledgeable physician must, when the body he is treating undergoes change and experiences many and various sufferings, advance from weaker to stronger methods, so also, in God's case, the transition from one method of providence to another is called, by scriptural usage, God's regret.

Question 121
What does the short saying from the 104th Psalm show, "he turned his heart to hate his people."[436]

✦   God not only knows before the ages the things that exist, since they exist in him, in the Truth itself, and if all these same things, both the things that are and the things that shall be, did not receive simultaneously being known and actual being on their own, but each thing [receives being] at the proper time[437]—for it is impossible for the infinite to exist simultaneously with things finite[438]—nevertheless also the goal of the disposition of each thing [occurs] according to movement. For there is neither time nor age separating this [movement] from God. For nothing in him is recent, but the future things are as the present. And if the times and the aeons indicate the things that are in God, they do this not for God but for us. For we also must not think that, when God acts, it is then that his knowledge of a thing begins.[439]

And if this is correct, as it surely is, he definitely knew the future as though it were the present, not only the future wickedness of the Egyptians and their purpose to disobey every working of good and their ready disposition for vengeance or the evils that were done by the Israelites according to the custom of Egypt, but also the future disposition the Israelites to approach in an obedient way the word of piety by faith. Therefore, since he allowed such dispositions that had been hidden and had earlier been held back by him to become actualized, because of this he is said "to have turned around." For when a tightened valve holds back by force the pressure of the water, if something by chance should turn it, suddenly the water releases its hidden pressure; so also, when providence allows it, both wicked and good dispositions are brought through intervening events into manifestation.

Question 122
In the [book of] Exodus, Moses and Pharaoh are types of whom? And what is Egypt and how is it the plagues were for some and

not for others? And who is the destroyer and what is the death of the first-born, and why do the Scriptures, in some places, speak of leading up from Egypt and, in others, of leading out?[440]

✛   Moses is a type of the pious and their ends, and Pharaoh is a type of the impious and their ends.[441] For, to the extent that Moses was obedient and gentle, for [receiving] the impression of the divine instructions, to the same extent Pharaoh was disposed in the contrary way. And Egypt, according to one reading, is interpreted as darkness and is understood as this age.[442] And geographers say Egypt is lower lying than any other land. Because of this, the Scripture not only says, "he led out"[443] but also "he led up,"[444] indicating a "leading out" of those who were coming in from a passionate attachment of the flesh to the spirit, and a 'leading up' of those who were being lifted up from material things to things intelligible.

And "Egyptians" are all who love pleasure and love the world, even if they are well born in the body. And "Israelites" are all lovers of God and haters of the world. And so, for the former, the water is blood, and for the latter, water is natural. Since water is nourishing and life-giving, it shows that whoever directs the resources of this life toward injustice and greediness and manipulation, being a murderer of those who are wronged by him, has his water as blood. But whoever [directs] the resources of life from righteous labors, for this one the water is the water of life.

And the first-born of the Egyptians are killed because they did not have the doorjambs smeared with the blood of a lamb.[445] And the first-born are the first offspring and thoughts of the *nous*, and the doorjambs are the senses, and the destroyer is the devil, who fetters the soul with perceptible things through the intermediary of the senses and destroys its [the soul's] every divine movement. But the first-born of the Israelites are preserved by the anointing of the blood, that is, the divine movements of the *nous* [are preserved] by the mortification of the senses.

Question 123
What is the saying in the 75th Psalm, "the wrath of man will acknowledge you and the remnant part of the wrath will celebrate you"?[446]

✛   The celebration is for those who rejoice, and the acknowledgment is for those who examine [themselves]. And the one stems from grief and the other from joy. And so, the passage means this: that, in the judgment, when the transient and imperfect thought of the good is counterbalanced to a wicked and completed thought, it carries more weight. For the one is tested, and the other becomes a reason for celebration and joy.

Question 124

What does the Apostle mean, when he says, 'I would rather "speak five words in the church than a myriad of words with a tongue"'?[447]

✛ One speaks "five words," even if the 'one' is the one who is speaking, who speaks a word that is instructive for the five senses. And the one who brings about the intrusion of passions through one's own word speaks "a myriad of words in a tongue." And again, someone speaks five words if, through contemplation of being in the spirit, he shows forth the Creator. For nature is fivefold, existing out of form and the four elements.[448] And the one who speaks "a myriad of words" makes rhetorical comments and persuasive arguments regarding the activity of visible things for his own glory and enjoyment, deifying "the creation rather than the Creator."[449] For the creation was given not that it might be deified but that it might teach God.

Question 125

In the gospels, what do they who decline the invitation because of the field, and the wedding, and the yoke of oxen represent?[450]

✛ Through the wife, love of pleasure is depicted, and through the yoke of oxen, love of possessions, and through the field, love of food. Every person who is occupied with these is deprived of the divine promises.

Question 126 (I, 60; III, 26)

What is the etymology of gluttony (*gastrimargia*)?

✛ No one, neither the grammarians nor the rhetoricians, have made mention of it. But Aristotle, in his *Concerning the Animals*,[451] makes mention of an animal called lustful (*margou*), and says that it is born from the decomposition [that takes place] between the earth and water. From [the time] it is born, it [*margou*] does not stop eating the earth until, completely hollowing out the earth, it comes to the surface. And coming to the surface it dies for three days, and after three days a cloud of rain comes and soaks it from above and revives it, [and] no longer does it eternally eat. And it is from this, I think, the ancient philosophers began to call those who eat many foods 'gluttons' (*gastrimargous*). It is possible for someone who is knowledgeable to devote himself piously to the things that exist and to understand the things said by means of spiritual contemplation. For every passion, growing, is born from decomposition, and when it is born does not cease from eating the heart that gives it substance until, through its contentious habit, it becomes visible. And becoming [visible] it kills the three powers of the soul and thus, the grace of the Holy Spirit, as manifested through the clouds of teaching, allows drops of knowledge to fall, and it [the Holy Spirit] creates life, not like the former life in the passions but like that which is virtuous and familiar to God.

Question 127 (I, 61)
What is the parable, in the Gospel, of the hired workers in the vineyard and what is the seeming inequality?[452]

✛ The judgment of God is not according to time and body, because the soul, which is timeless and bodiless since it does not experience growth and limitation with regard to time, makes the movements of [its] will (*diatheseos*) apart from time. And it is good to clarify what has been said with an example: often, there is someone who has had seventy years in the monastic life and another who has had a single day. But since the aim of the profession is that having pulled away from the passionate attachment and attitude toward material things one may transfer one's entire soul to God, and the one who had seventy years died without having striven completely for such detachment, whereas the other, who had one day, because he drew away all his passionate thought (*dianoia*) from material things and placed it completely in the bosom of God, died perfected (*eteleiothe*). And so, in the disbursal [that occurs] during the judgment, one of them receives the wage worthily as he has completed the aim of the profession, while the other receives according to grace and only because he endured the toil of *askesis*.

Question 128
Did, in fact, sorrow become unbearable to Job, by the things that happened to him?[453]

✢   We say that Job had become impervious to sorrow. For the one who, once and for all, reverently made the examination of beings and confirmed in himself the hatred for the things that pass away and the love for the things that do not pass away, how, at the transient sufferings which things naturally are prone to suffer on account of their change of state, could he not feel sorrow?

Question 129
What, then? Did none of the saints experience sorrow? And why is it said, concerning many of the saints, that they did experience sorrow, as Paul also says, "I have continual sorrow,"[454] and the rest?

✢   One who concerns himself with practical things, until the time that the conscience, striking, stabs him by means of illusions based in memory, then completely engages in grief over the praiseworthy sorrow. But the one who has arrived at the measure of perfection exists beyond this. For one who has been enlightened through knowledge—having unfolded the intelligible [part] of the soul to God without division through a smoothness of movement, and having acquired the indescribable joy found in the continuous pleasure of the divine beauty—how can he accept the sorrow that is opposed to this?

But sometimes the saints are said to experience sorrow in imitation of their master. For both sorrow and joy are ascribed to God, with respect to his providence: sorrow, on the one hand, over those who are perishing, joy, on the other hand, for those who are being saved. And so, the word "sorrow," which is one, admits of multiple ways of being disposed. Therefore, that sorrow which is spoken of in the case of the saints is mercy and compassion and abundance of joy, a God-like perfection inwardly stored up and providentially bestowed upon things outside.

Question 130

Does contemplation precede action?

✣   The mode of contemplation is twofold: first, what is needful in things to be done, which, of course, precedes the things to be done; and the other, that which thinks about the things done, which reflects upon the action afterwards.

Question 131

From Isaiah, "I planted a vineyard and put a hedge around it,"[455] and the rest.

✣   The planting of the vineyard signifies the creation, and the hedge signifies the natural law,[456] and the enclosing with a fence signifies the written law, by these things the Creator strengthened nature. And so, whoever will genuinely cultivate by deliberate choice the naturally sown seed of the good by [his own] deliberate choice (*proairesin*), such a one produces fruit for the planter. But whoever is carried, against reason, towards nonbeing, such a person produces thorns, that is, the passions, and is trampled down beneath the demons that activate those things.

Question 132

From the Song of Songs, "come with me from Lebanon, my bride, come with me from Lebanon, from the dens of lions, from the mountains of leopards."[457]

✣   God, the *Logos*, tells the soul that is betrothed to him through good works, or, also, the entire nature of humanity, to come out from idolatry—for this is what Lebanon signifies[458]—and from evil habit—which is signified by the dens of the lions; for the lion always aims at the shoulders in attacking, that is, at one's practice—and "from the mountains of leopards," that is, from ignorance. For this animal naturally makes its assault against the eyes, and the eyes clearly are to be understood as knowledge.

Question 133

From Isaiah, "On the mountains and the hills I will be judged with you."[459]

✠   Since the angels are entrusted providentially with the life of the soul and of the body, and with this earthly place, ministering to us the divine words, and similarly, the prophets also conveyed to us the ways of salvation through their own words, therefore, regarding these it says, that they will be judged with us, calling the angels mountains and [calling] the patriarchs and prophets hills.

Question 134
What does this passage from the Psalm signify, "he will receive back the orphan and widow, and will bring the way of sinners to ruin"?[460]

✠   "Widow" is a soul that had died to the natural law, and "orphan" is the underhanded way, which is pursued for the sake of ostentation and richer profits, not having God as the father.[461] Therefore, when the Lord, by his suggested counsel, both gives life to the natural law and corrects the underhanded way so that it exists for the good itself and not for perishable glory, he receives these things back, doing away with "the ways of the sinners," that is, the former mindset in which they used to walk.

Question 135
From Job, "Because they do not have a roof, they embraced the rock."[462]

✠   The things that formerly did not have a roof, that is, faith, are the Gentiles. And "they embrace the rock," the faith in our Lord, Jesus Christ.[463]

Question 136
Is it possible to discover a natural proof concerning the Holy Trinity?

✠   All beings, are believed to exist in three modes: in essence, in difference, and in life. And we believe, on the one hand, that there is some essential being from the *logos* of the essence of beings who is the Father; and, on the other hand, there is some essential being from the difference of beings that is wisdom, that is, the Son—for from wisdom the imparting to each nature of an offered selfhood takes place, and it [wisdom] maintains each of the things that exist as both distinct and unconfused, both toward itself and the rest—

and there is some essential being from life that is the Holy Spirit. But in the case of God, these things are enhypostasized and called such, and in the case of the created things they are coincidental.

Question 137
From St. Gregory the Theologian, "all contributed that which had been preached to them, but," some were "self-motivated,"[464] and what is signified by the things that were offered?[465]

✦   The "self-motivated" are those who come to the good from the natural seeds that are in them, and "they who are preached to" are they who come to the good as a result of teaching. And gold is offered by someone who piously makes an argument concerning theology; and silver, by one who lives a spotless life and teaches a brilliant, transparent teaching; and precious stones, by one who adorns active sovereignty with divine words; and fine, threaded flax, by one who unwaveringly guards the habit of virtue in involuntary temptations and through these, as though by water, washes away and whitens thoughts that have come to dwell in the soul by sin; and spun red [fabric], by one who, with an abundance of reason, makes the passions that are upon us by pleasure and *** to disappear through the mortification of the members of the body; and purple [fabric], by one who embraces the knowledge of beings in an accurate way, without stumbling. For purple is understood as knowledge, according to one interpretation. And it is composed of many and diverse shades, just as knowledge also is composed of many and diverse theories. And red-dyed skins are offered by one who has died completely to sense perception; and hair, by one who has acquired complete indifference to present things.

Question 138
What is the [passage] from the Psalm, "serve the Lord with fear and rejoice exceedingly in him with trembling,"[466] and how is one able, at the same time, both to tremble and to rejoice exceedingly; and how, again, in Psalm 18, does it say, "fear of the Lord is pure, enduring forever,"[467] whereas John says, "love casts out fear,"[468] and if fear is cast out, how does it remain?[469]

✦   Fear is twofold: one kind is related to accusations; the other is in proportion to the worth of the one who is loved.[470] And so, love puts aside the fear that results from accusations, while it preserves that fear that is based upon the worth of the one who is loved. And "exceeding joy" is the disposition (*diathesis*) of feeling joy in the acquiring of some things, and gladness is the enjoyment of the things acquired.

Question 139

What do the cows and the ears of wheat shown to Pharaoh during his sleep signify?[471]

✣ Here, Pharaoh represents nature. The beautiful cows depict action, and the ears of wheat depict knowledge. For, in this [first] seven-year period, knowledge and action are functional (*energountai*). And the other cows and ears of wheat that are deformed and tossed by the wind depict ignorance and evil, which are strong enough to swallow down both the vigorous activity of the cows as well as the knowledge that is shown through the beautiful ears of wheat.[472] But our Lord, Jesus Christ, the true Joseph, the only one who foreknows and corrects such hunger, who receives faith as if it were gold, and radiant life as if it were silver, and ethical philosophy as if it were sheep, and effectiveness and eagerness of life according to God as if it were horses, supplies the grain, that is, true knowledge.

Question 140

What is "the unrighteous judge" in the Gospel, and who is the widow?[473]

✣ He calls "the unrighteous judge" the natural law hardened by the transgression, which "respected" neither God nor "man."[474] And a widow is the soul widowed from good works.[475] For if it should chance to come to a turning point, it overcomes the natural law, wearying it through *askesis* and self-control (*egkrateia*), forcing it to abstain from things contrary to nature. And if, he says, the *nous*, through dedicated and painstaking perseverance, is able to accomplish even things beyond nature, how much more, he says, will God give an ear to those "who cry aloud to him,"[476] through extensive prayer and unabashed perseverance.

Question 141

What is the scroll, the one given to Ezekiel the prophet, on which had been written "lamentation and melody and woes,"[477] and how was it sweetened in his mouth?[478]

✛   The scroll is the divine word. And lamentation has been inscribed on it, that is, the threats of punishments; and melody is the promises of good things; and woes are they who, because neither by fear of punishment nor by the encouragement of promises do they wise up and become better, will receive utterly the woe of eternal punishment. And the scroll's being sweetened in the mouth of the prophet depicts this: that the one who always bears in mind the things aforementioned and pays attention to both the threats and the promises is sweetened by hope.

Question 142
Why did the Spirit descend ten days after the ascension of the Lord?[479]

✛   Some who have been taught the divine things say that since the angelic powers are [composed of] nine orders, according to Dionysius the Areopagite, [480] when the Lord ascended in his humanity (for by his divinity he fills all things)[481] he assigned to each order one day from his last day [his ascension] until the final one [Pentecost]. For they were also in need of a visit from the Lord. For "in him," according to the Apostle, "are summed up" not only "the things on earth," but also "the things in heaven."[482] And after this he appeared "to God, the Father,"[483] and thereafter, the Spirit descends.

And one can consider the above also according to another method of contemplation. For, since the word of God has been concealed in his ten commandments, and is embodied in us, descending in us through the practice [of the commandments], then it leads us up, raising us through knowledge, until we come to the most lofty of all the commandments, which says, "the Lord is your God, the Lord is one."[484] For when it is released from all things, or rather, when it releases all, our *nous* will end in God himself, [and] then accepts the fiery tongues,[485] becoming God by grace.

Question 143
Why ever, when Luke, in Acts, says concerning Paul, that "he hastened, if it was possible for him," to arrange [on] "the day of

Pentecost [to be] in Jerusalem,"[486] is Paul manifestly shown to be kneeling, which is forbidden by the canons?[487]

✠ He does not speak about that very day of Pentecost on which the Spirit came down; but, since the fifty days [collectively] are called "the day of Pentecost," Paul hastened to arrange to be in Jerusalem on the first day after Pascha, so that it is clear that he kneeled during the period of the fasts.

Question 144
Why, ever, did the Apostle Paul call himself a Roman[488] and conversing with the tribunal, say, "but I was even born [a Roman]"?[489]

✠ People, in every land, because they actually considered it to be something important to be called "Romans," by supplying tribute were registered as Romans, and the name was passed down in the family. And so, since the parents of the Apostle, when they were in Tarsus, were registered in order 'to be called Romans,' the Apostle naturally as [one] born of them says, "but I was even born [a Roman]."

Question 145
From Amos the prophet, "and two or three cities will be gathered up into one city to drink water and they will not be satisfied."[490] What is meant by the cities?

✠ One must suppose that "cities" here are the souls,[491] because they are composed just like houses and are receptive to the virtues. And the two cities are the souls that have been built by action and contemplation, while three cities are the souls that keep a straight path in theology by means of an undoubting faith. And so, since the prophet put this in the form of a curse, it shows that when famine occurs, not of bread and water "but a famine of hearing the word of the Lord,"[492] if such souls achieve the extent of the virtues spoken of above, but become neglectful of them, they appear to seek knowledge. But since they do not pursue action, they fail. And even if they appear to gather together into one city, that is, into the teacher, they are not filled with knowledge. For, the grace of teaching is not given even to him, so that he should be able to give drink to those in need of divine knowledge.

Question 146

From the same, "the city from which one thousand soldiers marched out shall have one hundred left, and the city from which one hundred marched out shall have ten left."[493]

✤   Since everything[494] that is a number is included within four sets of ten—such as, the first one from the unit is ten,[495] then this is the unit of the hundred, then the hundred is the unit for the thousand, then the thousand is the unit for the myriad—and so, since the number for virtue is multiplied by accession and receives addition, what is shown by the number, I think, is this:[496] the one who performs (*katorthosas*) the ten commandments in such a way that each commandment is contained in the rest, multiplying them by ten, has come to the hundred and like Sarah,[497] i.e., she has had an "r" (which is 100) added to her name. And whoever has also achieved (*katorthosen*) knowledge in addition to these [virtues], multiplying these hundred by ten, reaches the thousand. But since this is also said by the prophet in the form of a curse, it shows that the one who has come into the realm of a thousand by virtuous behavior, if he acts in negligence, is lowered and returns to the hundred. And, in like manner, the one from the hundred acting in this way comes into the mere observances of the commandments out of social custom, and fulfills them in the Jewish way.

Question 147

From the same, "woe to those who desire the day of the Lord, for it is darkness and not light, in such way as when a person flees from the face of a lion and a bear meets him, or when he bursts into his house and rests his hands on the wall, and a snake bites him."[498]

✤   "The day of the Lord" is illumination and knowledge of the Lord. Therefore, whoever desires to seize the knowledge of God without engaging in action is struggling in vain. For troubled by the passions (by anger as well as by desire) and seeking to escape from the bite of the lion, that is, from anger, he falls in with the bear of desire.[499] Then, being distressed by them, he bursts into the house and settles his hands on the wall, and a snake bites him. A house is the soul,[500] and a wall is the body.[501] And so, whenever he directs the active powers of the soul toward the enjoyment of the body, pleasure comes forth—for this is the snake—and it bites him. For through each sense of the body, as through an opening, slithering pleasure bites the miserable soul. And so, for the one who is weak in the eyes of the soul, the sun of knowledge is darkness and causes blindness.

Question 148
From the Psalter, "the words of the Lord are pure words, silver that have been proved by fire, tested in the earth, having been refined sevenfold."[502]

✠ As the words purify us from every stain of sin, they are called "pure." And they are "silver that has been proved by fire" because of their transparency and brilliance as is the case with silver, and because of their sanctity and their ability thoroughly to scrutinize our hearts. For earth is interpreted as "the heart" in the Gospel.[503] And "they have been refined sevenfold" whenever we refine each commandment sevenfold. And it is good idea to articulate clearly what has been said with the example of one commandment. The law declares "you shall not murder." Therefore, those who want to refine this commandment sevenfold not only abstain from murdering physically, but, if he sees someone hungry, feeds him; and if he sees someone thirsty, gives him something to drink; and if he sees someone naked, clothes him; and if he sees a stranger, takes him in; and if he sees someone ill, does not overlook him; and if he sees someone in jail, runs to him. And, in short, whoever neglects one of these things, in that respect has committed murder. For to the extent that it was up to them, he let the other person die when it was in his power to restore him who was in need of him. And so, by adding the six commandments of the Lord to the commandment of the law, "you shall not murder," one refines the saying of the Lord sevenfold. And this is also applicable to each commandment.

Question 149
From Proverbs, "rarely put your foot into your friend's house, otherwise [he], having had enough, will hate you."[504]

✠   He calls "friend" here our body because of the natural union with it, as well as the affection for it. And so, the passage recommends that care of the body should not be provided in an anxious way but should be provided only by means of the footstep of the soul [a small amount] and, even that, only rarely; otherwise, by your providing it relaxation in many ways, it will exhibit in you the [desires] of your enemies and of those who hate you.

Question 150

What does the saying by the patriarch Jacob signify, "I repaid the loss of thefts by day and of thefts by night"?[505]

✠ One should understand "thefts by day" as the [losses that happen to us from the evil one] through the external senses and in repayment of which the patriarch bore the labors of *askesis*. And "thefts by night" are those things of which the enemy robs us through internal thoughts, in repayment of which we, like the patriarch, must endure labors and sleeplessness and the remaining forms of *askesis*.

Question 151 (I, 64)

What is signified by the heifer, which, according to the law concerning unsolved murder, had its sinews cut in the ravine?[506]

✠   The spiritual intention of the Scripture signifies through these things that not only must we fear the apparent sins for which we will pay in the future, but also, having taken fear for things done by us unwittingly, we should always cut the sinews of the heifer, that is, our flesh, in the ravine of self-control and *askesis*. And because of this, they left the heifer alive, so that we also might learn not to kill the body but, when pleasure rises up against us, to cut the sinews and tame them.

Question 152

What do Nadab and Abihu signify, they who "brought forth a strange fire" and because of this were completely burned?[507]

✠   They, who are priests of God forever and offer themselves to God as "a living sacrifice"[508] and have the fervor of the Holy Spirit in them as did Cleopas,[509] offer their own fire to God. And whenever, having become lazy, they find themselves removed from this condition (*katastaseos*) and gather in themselves the kindling of the passions, then they introduce the strange fire and are completely burned in their conscience by the fire of condemnations.

Question 153

Why is the finely ground flour always offered together with the sacrifices of the law, and is sometimes mixed with oil, sometimes put in an oven, and sometimes in a frying pan?[510]

✤   One should take the finely ground flour to mean reason, as it is nourishment for rational beings. And when it is mixed with oil, it indicates reason along with the illumination of knowledge. And whenever it is in a frying pan, it indicates reason that has been tested and safeguarded against the pleasurable temptations that have befallen us from within. And whenever it is in an oven, it indicates reason remaining steadfast by patience throughout the testing of the temptations that have befallen us from without.

Question 154

Why on the fifteenth day in the seventh month, during the seven-day celebration according to the law,[511] did they offer 14 calves on the first day and on each [following] day did they remove one calf until they arrived at the seven?[512]

✤   Since, according to the word of the Lord, it is necessary "to turn and become like children,"[513] and a child is deprived in every way of the movement of passion; but when he becomes fourteen years old, immediately the passionate movement begins to be aroused in him; for this reason, I think this mystical passage in the law hints at the need also for us to offer in sacrifice to God the lessening of natural movement, until we come into perfect passionlessness (*apatheia*).

Question 155

What do the 250 men who confronted Moses signify, and "they were offering the incense, fire came out from the Lord and consumed"[514] them, and the Lord commanded Eleazar "to take away" their "censers and hammer them into plates"[515] and fasten them to the altar?

✢   The number fifty always represents the divine things since it transcends what is subject to time. And the number two hundred represents perceptible things and the senses because of the combination of four with the number five. And so, they who understand the perceptible things by sense perception and pursue to the divine virtues through the perceptible things are confronted by the divine law and are completely burned in their conscience by the fire of condemnations.

And then the priestly *logos* of the teaching receives their censers, that is, the *nous*, in which they thought they were going to offer God "the zeal that is not according to full knowledge"[516] and through the teaching, the *Logos* drives off and thins out the fat that lies upon it, and brings it to the altar, to divine knowledge.

Question 156
For what reason does the law forbid, "a fee from a dog" and "wages of a prostitute"?[517]

✢   It indicates through these phrases that one must offer to God the virtues unmixed with anger and desire, calling anger the "dog" and "prostitute," the desire.

Question 157
Since, clearly, the 21st Psalm refers to the Lord, how should we think about "but I am a worm and not human"?[518]

✢   Our Lord, Jesus Christ, because of his inexpressible love for humankind, became and was called a worm for us.[519] For, just as the worm is brought forth without intercourse, thus, the Lord also is conceived without seed. But also, like a worm, he has become bait for the devil. For, opening wide his mouth as [he would] a worm's flesh, he was pierced through by the Godhead. But he is also a worm to enemies. For the wise one is immediately recognized by his wisdom, and the crooked one is recognized by his foolishness. But the worm also exists in us whenever we sin, utterly refuting and devouring our conscience.

Question 158
What has been written in Genesis, "and he placed the cherubim and the flaming sword, the one that turns in all directions, guarding the road to the Tree of Life"?[520]

✢ Just as the perceptible tree becomes nourishment for the flesh, so also the "Tree of Life," which is the Lord, has become nourishment and life for our souls. And the virtues are the road leading to him. And it is guarded by the cherubim and the flaming sword. And the cherubim is interpreted as 'the fullness of knowledge.'[521] Through knowledge, the longing for God comes to exist in us, and through the flaming sword, that is, through the discernment able to destroy hardships, fear attaches itself to us. And so, consequently, fear and longing are what guard the road to the Tree of Life. Now, the sword is said "to turn." For whenever we sin—[that sin] confuting us through our conscience—it [the sword] encounters us face to face. And whenever we repent, it provides a way of entry.

Question 159
From the Apostle, whoever "builds on this foundation with gold or silver, precious stones, wood, hay, straw, the fire will test them." Therefore, "if someone's work, built upon the foundation, survives, he will receive a reward; but if someone's work is consumed by fire, he will suffer loss, but he himself will be saved, but only as through a fire."[522]

✢ The "foundation" is the faith of Christ. And one person builds as if it were gold upon it, that is, instruction in mystical theology;[523] and as if silver, the transparent life; and precious stones, pious thoughts; and wood, attachment to perceptible things; and hay, what feeds its own unreason; and straw, what works destruction. And in the case of those who have [engaged in] good deeds, the day of knowledge shows that it is by a fire, that is, by the Spirit, that the revelation of these things has taken place. And in the case of the sinners, the works are completely consumed, while discernment renders the conscience righteous and diminishes the sins through repentance and saves the human being; and he is responsible for the loss of time that has passed as a result of the neglect of the virtues. But, also, in the future age, the works of sin give way to nothingness and nature saves its own powers by taking them through the fire of judgment.

Question 160 (I, 75)
What is that which David sings when he says, "give your strength to your children, and save the child of your maidservant"?[524]

✢   Since, by nature we are servants of God and children of his maidservant, wisdom, first he prays for strength to be given to us, that is, dominion over the passions, and then, because of this, there comes about salvation for us.

Question 161 (I, 76)
Since it is written in [the book of] Kings that God "stirred up David"[525] to count the [number of] people, and in Chronicles it says the devil did this,[526] therefore, how is divine Scripture shown to be in harmony with itself?[527]

✢   Since the Apostle calls the devil "god of this age,"[528] the passage from Kings must be understood in this way. Or in another way, since nothing occurs without the providence of God, but all things come into being either according to good pleasure (*kata eudokian*) or according to economy (*kat'oikonomian*), or according to permission,[529] what has been written in Kings, that God "stirred up," should be understood in a pious way, that is, instead of "allowed." And in the Chronicles, the devil has become the means and the cause. "Seventy thousand fell,"[530] [is interpreted as] either those who were with Absalom or those who possess the passion of conceit and pride. And according to [the interpretive method of] contemplation, this shows that every David, begetting a thought not by set propensity (*kata diathesin*) but by deception of pride, upon changing his mind, petitions God, and [then] thoughts about temporal and temporary things die. For the number seventy signifies temporal movement because of the seventh cycle. Because of this, it is better to entreat [God] than be pursued by hostile demons and [experience] "a famine of hearing the word of the Lord."[531]

Question 162 (I, 65)
What does the paralytic, the one who was lowered through the roof by the four [men], signify, and is it possible, according to the historical sense, that the house was uncovered?[532]

✢   According to the historical sense, the house was definitely uncovered since the eye witnesses from those places say the roofs of the houses are of pumice stone, which is extremely lightweight, and so, whoever wishes to uncover the roof is able to do so easily and quickly. And according to the anagogic method of interpretation (*anagoge*), a paralytic is every *nous* sick with sin and unable, through natural contemplation—for this is the door—to see the *Logos*. Through faith, which uncovers the thickest veil of the written law, he is lowered by the four virtues from the height of vanity towards the *Logos* who emptied himself,[533] and it [the *nous*] receives the healing by faith and [engaging in] action.

Question 163
What does the Babylonian furnace signify?[534]

✠   Temptations attach themselves to us in two ways: voluntarily, through the pleasure-seeking passions in us, and involuntarily, through external attacks. And when it happens voluntarily, then being encouraged by Nabuchodonosor, that is, by the devil, we kindle in ourselves the furnace of the passions, lighting anger from underneath as if it were brushwood, and desire as if it were pitch, and pleasure as if it were *naphtha*,[535] and the perversion of reason as if it were flax—for linen is understood as reason, whereby the priests who celebrate the mysteries also wear linen[536]—and so whenever reason becomes perverted, it becomes flax, and the remaining passions are easily enkindled by it. But if someone, as the blessed children did,[537] calls upon God through humility and fervent prayer, he is set free from the shackles on [his] hands and feet[538] (that is, his active journey according to God), and he is refreshed by the visitation of the Holy Spirit.[539] But when we are involuntarily tempted and the spiritual Nabuchodonosor ignites the furnace in us through external attacks, sicknesses, and the remaining undesired occurrences, even so, we are able through patience and gratitude to be refreshed by hope of good things to come.

Question 164 (I, 66)
For what reason did Elisha the prophet, when he was mocked by the children, curse [them] and "bears came out and mauled the forty-two children"?[540]

✠   Some say that the children were not Israelites but were from the Philistines, and not children in age but in intellect. And so, since they heard that the prophet was performing many signs and did not believe but mocked him, and there were some present who did not share in their vain inclination; therefore, in order that these would not be hurt and the blasphemy might return to God, God proceeded against them. And according to [the interpretive method of] contemplation, every bald-headed *nous* like Elisha, that is, cleansed of notions about material things, is mocked many times in the ascent to knowledge by thoughts of what concerns perceptible things and matter and form (where "forty" represents the perceptions).[541] And matter and form being added complete the number forty-two. Therefore, the *nous* is scoffed at by such thoughts so that it may become lazy with regard to virtue. And so, by prayer it destroys these through the two bears, that is, through pleasure and desire. For when such passions are used for the better, by reversal [of the passions' natural activities], they kill the mocking thoughts.

Question 165
What does the parable of the Gospel signify, the one describing the encounter of the kings of the 20,000 men and the 10,000 men?[542]

✤   The king who draws up for battle 10,000 [troops] signifies the kingly *nous*[543] in us as do the ten commandments, waging war on the "other king,"[544] the one having the 20,000 [troops], that is, the lord of the world who stands in formation with the perceptible things and the senses. For the five senses applied to the perceptible things, which are composed of the four elements, make the number twenty. For through these, the enemy prepares for battle in us. And "sit down and take counsel" signifies "whether it is possible"[545] to undergo every affliction (*kakopatheian*) and pain for the sake of virtue. "But if not," he says, those who are subject to the things of nature that have been imposed on us after the fall, [546] who are unable to pursue the life according to the Gospel, [should] "negotiate terms of peace."

Question 166
What does the mute demon in the Gospel signify?[547]

✤   A soul that does not listen to the commandments of the Lord is troubled by the mute demon. But when the word of God comes to exist in it through the doing of the commandments, then not only does it hear, but it also speaks by means of the knowledge of God.

Question 167

What does the tower indicate, according to the Lord's parable in the Gospel, according to which the one who is unable to complete [it] is mocked by those who pass by?[548]

✛   The tower indicates the perfection of the virtues,[549] which is constructed with knowledge. And so, whoever after [acquiring] detachment with respect to action has an aptness for the further acquisition of the natural and contemplative and theological *logoi*, through which perfect knowledge is completed, completes the construction of the tower. And [if] one of these is missing so that he is unable to bring the tower to completion, he is mocked by those who pass by *** .

Question 168

*** it will be shown by evangelists

✛   They say that universal terms are indicative of particulars and that particular terms are indicative of universals. And so, he who said, "I came to seek the lost,"[550] indicated the universal nature of Israel, which, according to the statement in Genesis,[551] is that which always sees God. And he who said that he was sent only to the sheep of the house of Israel, and "[to them] only was I sent"[552] also indicated the universal by the particular. For, since, in Abraham, the good of nature which slipped away as a result of the forefather's disobedience [Adam] has been recovered through full knowledge, God makes a promise to him that he should be "a father of many nations,"[553] of those who, through full knowledge, take part in the faith which is the same as his and are adopted as children by him. For it is clear that if they are adopted as children, they also are both joint heirs and of one body with the house of Israel.

And the request for the crumbs by the Canaanite woman[554] depicts the appropriate instruction for those who are entering from disbelief into the life according to virtue. For, the simple and most perfect word of knowledge is divided into many things in accordance with the disposition of those who receive [it]. Accordingly, for those who are just entering, what is appropriate is catechesis, which is compared to crumbs. And the dog, since it is a barking animal which, on the one hand, chases away strangers, and on the other hand, fawns over those who are familiar to it, is understood as the active state, which chases away the evils against nature and fawns over the natural virtues, strongly guarding these.

Question 169
What does the story regarding Joab[555] signify, when he chased after Sabee, the son of Bochori, "who lifted up his hand against David,"[556] and who is the woman who threw his head from the wall?[557]

✠ Joab, with a rough breathing mark [before the name], is interpreted as the one who is outside or who pursues, and, with a smooth breathing mark [before the name], as the one who gives or as a provider. And here Joab must be understood as courage, and Sabee as pride, in the manner of the primary room among the [bed] chambers, also includes the remaining passions. And so, whenever the virtuous *nous* perceives the uprising of pride, it sends Joab, that is, courage, to chase [it] away and to incite the powers of the soul to destroy it. And so pride flees and hides as if in some city—in one of the virtues. Courage pillages this, seeking to bring about the destruction of pride. But the wise woman, who is wisdom, by the discovery of the constitutive causes of virtue, brings about the destruction of the productive causes of the passions, through which every evil is constituted in the soul.

Question 170
What does the story of Amessae signify, when Joab killed him?[558]

✠ Amessae is interpreted as "one who has been anointed" or "who anoints." Therefore, he represents dispassion, as it easily escapes, through perfection, every grip of the opponents, and Joab represents courage. And so, whenever the soul, after attaining (by courage) a condition of perfect dispassion, forsakes prayer and becomes vainly preoccupied with some passion, it kills (makes inactive), that is, brings about the more perfect manner of contemplation because of its preoccupation with defeated enemies.

Question 171
What is signified by the story regarding the same Joab, when he killed Abner,[559] and what is the curse laid upon him?[560]

✠   Here Joab represents the resentful thought, and for this he receives the curse that he should, "lean upon a staff," "and fall on a sword,"[561] in which, I think, the text indicates, through the staff, the resentful person's hope concerning perceptible things. For every resentful thought, continually entrapped in material things, also has in them its point of leaning. While, again, through the words, "fall on a sword," it indicates the destruction of such a relationship by the sharpest word.[562]

Question 172

Whom does Housi represent[563] when David sent him, "to scatter the counsel of Ahithophel"?[564]

✠   Since Housi was the son of Iamini, he is interpreted, on the one hand, with regard to his own person as a spinner;[565] but, on the other hand, in relationship to his father, he is said to be a "right-hand son." And he is understood as discernment, for this, by its analytic power, refines or scatters the intentions of the adversaries.

Question 173

What does the saying by the Apostle signify, "the fullness of the one who fills all things in all"?[566]

✠   God, in an apophatic way, is separated from all beings with regard to essence. For he is neither spoken of, nor thought of, nor partaken of in any way, by anyone. But since, according to his providential emanation, he is partaken of by many, by them he is also filled. For each thing that has come to be according to its own *logos*, which exists in God, is said to be a member of God[567] and to have a place in God.[568] Without a doubt, surely, if someone is moved in accordance with this [*logos*], wisely as well as reasonably,[569] he will come to exist in God, fulfilling his own place and dignity within the body of Christ as a member who does useful work. But whoever, abandoning his own *logos*, is brought deceptively towards nonexistent things, he will justly pay the eternal penalty of whatever reproach has come upon him in the body of Christ.

Question 174

What is signified by Adonibezek, who was "hanged on a double tree"[570] by Joshua son of Nun?

✦   The "double tree" bears a type of the activity and relationship towards perceptible things, according to soul and body. And so, whoever, like Joshua of Nave, blazing the trail of virtue by observing the commandments, will make evil ineffective in the soul as well as in the body toward both sense and the things against nature, is "one who hanged the ruler of this world[571] on a double tree."

Question 175
What does the story about Ahab signify, when the prophet saw the angelic powers on the right hand and on the left hand [of God]?[572]

✦   The prophet here weaves [a narrative concerning] universal, providential reason knowing that the principal Reason[573] has been mixed in all. And by those on the right hand he introduces proposed reasons regarding proper actions, while by those on the left he introduces reasons for things that are not in our power. And if anyone is led towards what is upright neither by the teaching of the divine law, nor by the attack of afflictions that occur, such a person is handed over, abandoned to his self-love or rather to the sin that is in him, which propelling him into the utter depth of evils, does not cease until, by the court of judgment there to which it sends him, it kills him unrepentant.

Question 176
What does the woman in the Gospel signify, who was bent over for 18 years? [574]

✦   The woman who is bent over signifies a soul that, by its three powers, is entangled in perceptible things. For the number six, by which the perceptible world has been brought into being, when multiplied by three makes eighteen. And so, if, by repentance, the soul approaches God the Word, it becomes healthy, no longer bending down to the earthly things but beholding heavenly beauties.

Question 177
What does the song of Habbakum indicate, saying, "the sheep have ceased from their eating and the oxen are not at the manger"?[575]

✠ Sheep are the notions and motions of the *nous*, and oxen are the spiritual teaching. A manger is detachment with regard to action, which, if it does not take place, causes the spiritual teaching to cease. And when this has ceased, the notions and motions that, through his teaching, were established in the *nous* also disappear along with it; and the soul descends toward the matters of life because of the famine of the word that has overtaken it.[576]

Or [to interpret this] in another way: the rational sheep have ceased because they are not taking the spiritual food of the teaching, and because of the spiritual oxen, the teachers, "are not in the manger" of the church.

Question 178

What is signified by the Lord's instruction, "if someone compels you to go one mile, go two with him,"[577] according to anagogic method of interpretation (*anagoge*)?

✠ The one who compels us is the Lord, through his teaching, [which is] the "one mile" of his commandment. And so, it is good for us to listen to his bidding and to go two miles, that is, to obey the commandment and to add the other one mile through works.

Or [to interpret this] in another way: we are compelled to serve the mile of faith, and the works of faith are also demanded of us.

Question 179

What is if "someone strikes you on the right cheek, also turn to him the other"?[578]

✠ If, it says, the demons, through thoughts, should strike you "on the right cheek," exalting you by your right-hand works, "turn the other," that is, bring into sight all the works that have been done by us of a left-hand activity, leading [you] towards sight.

Question 180

What does the saying by the Lord to the disciples signify, "I will not drink from the fruit of the vine until the time when I drink it anew with you in the kingdom with my Father"?[579]

✤ Since our salvation, according to what has been written, is "God's food and drink"[580] and the Lord fulfilled this through the economy (*oikonomias*) in his flesh and brought to completion a way of life, his saving purpose, which has to do with our own selves, causes his disciples to exist beyond sense "no longer," [and] he says, "will I drink from the fruit of the vine," that is, from the salvation economically bestowed upon human beings through his sojourning. But in the future age, he drinks this [wine] anew, that is, renewed by the Holy Spirit, as, through the ecstatic and intoxicating participation of good things, he brings those who are worthy to perfection, gods by grace.

Question 181
What is "my spirit will not reside continually in these human beings, because they are flesh; and their days shall be one hundred twenty years"?[581]

✤ God, concerned about the salvation at that time of humanity, foretold that their life should be one hundred and twenty years. For, until the time Noah was warned to prepare the ark, twenty years had gone by. And he continued constructing the ark for one hundred years,[582] so as to bring them to correction through this exhibition. And after these things, he brought on the flood, and it carried off everyone. And Scripture rightly states that there should be one hundred twenty years in that generation, from the time he had warned them.

Question 182
What does Eutychus, in Acts, show, who fell "from the third story [of the building] when Paul was speaking"?[583]

✤ Every *nous* that has ascended the active [life] just as if it were the first story [of a building], and has engaged in natural contemplation as if it were the second story, and has established itself through undoubting faith to the height of theology just as if it were the third story, if it then neglects the divine word and falls asleep, falls from the aforesaid third story. But if the word (*logos*) of teaching, falling upon it, finds something alive in it and that is not completely dead by despair, it is given life again through repentance.

Question 183

Why is one [wage], the *denarius*,[584] said in the Gospel to be given by the landlord to those working in his vineyard, although their offering was not the same? And why are the summonses different?[585]

✠ Some of the holy fathers say the different summonses signify the different ages and others say the different purposes. And take the *denarius* to be self-control (*sophrosyne*); but there are many differences even of this. For one man, who has his own wife, in remaining hers maintains his self-control to that extent. And there is another man, better than the previous one, who does not continually make use of what is allowed by the law; and another one has intercourse with his wife only for procreation, the result being the succession of the family. And another, after having one or two children, refrains entirely from marital intercourse. And there is one, superior to all these, who does not marry at all, but, because of [his] love for the Lord, practices virginity. And so, the passage revealed five purposes, one higher than the next, in which the five summonses and the one *denarius* of self-control are shown. And you should recognize this also in the case of the other virtues.

Question 184

What is shown by the things that happen to the prophet Jonah, and what is the "Joppa" from which he flees?[586]

✠ Jonah, who flees "from the presence of the Lord,"[587] represents our nature. For it was at Joppa—interpreted as "searching for joy," which points to paradise—and, because of disobedience, it fled, and threw itself into the sea of life[588] and is storm-tossed and swallowed up by the spiritual whale[589] and [then] is vomited according to the three-day burial of the Lord in Hades. And it is received again even to the grace of prophecy, and it preaches in Ninevah,[590] that is, to the nations, and it is pitiably troubled on account of the gourd.[591] And the gourd is the bodily worship of the law, which the worm, the Lord Jesus Christ (the one who said, "I am like a worm and not a human being"[592]), caused to wither. For by his own presence he made null and void the temporary worship of the law.

And the fact that there were "twelve" thousand in the city "who did not know their right hand or their left"[593] signifies those who pursue virtue, neither by excess nor by deficiency but keeping to the middle position and to the royal way.[594]

Question 185
Why, ever, does a raven sustain Elias with bread in the morning and meat in the afternoon?[595]

✠   The raven represents nature blackened through disobedience, and Elias sitting in the gully represents the knowledgeable *nous* sitting in the gully of temptations and labors of *askesis*. He is nourished in the morning by bread from the blackened nature, that is, by gathering knowledge from the natural contemplation of the things that exist, and in the afternoon by meat. For he is initiated into the mystery of the incarnation of the Lord that will occur at the end times, because, certainly, the one who created nature out of nonbeing, will also restore it when it is corrupted.
Or [to interpret this] in another way: Elias represents a type of the Lord. For when a spiritual famine held all hearts in captivity, he went into the gully, that is, into life, voluntarily accepting temptations and sufferings; and "when he came into his own house, his own people did not accept him,"[596] nor did they nourish him. But the nations that had been blackened by idolatry welcomed and nourished him through knowledge and action, knowledge being signified by the bread and action by the meat.

Question 186 (II, 1)
What is the passage in the Psalm, "rejoice exceedingly as does the giant (*gigas*) who runs the course"?[597]

✠   The giant is interpreted as "one who attacks," and is understood as the Lord. For when he had undertaken our salvation, he rejoiced greatly in the course of the economy (*kata ten hodon tes oikonomias*), and he attacked demonic battle formations, invalidating their authority over us.

Question 187
From the 71st Psalm, "righteousness will flourish in his days, and abundance of peace, until the moon is taken away."[598]

✠   It is clear to everyone that the prophet foretold these things in the Spirit, regarding the Lord's incarnate course of life. And the "days of the Lord"[599] are not they which he spent in the body on the earth but the virtues, which, shining like days, cause righteousness to arise in us. What [kind of] righteousness, if not the distributive habitude that does not allow the worse to rebel against the better, that is, "the mind of the flesh against the law of the spirit"?[600] "The fullness of peace" exists in us whenever the passions, having been put to sleep, remain without causing disturbances for the soul. And "until the moon is taken away" signifies this: that such [peace] exists in the soul from the knowledge of God, which causes righteousness to arise in us, so that also the flimsy illusions (*phantasias*) of our changeable nature—for this is the moon—are destroyed completely.

"And may he have dominion," it says, "from sea to sea."[601] Here, a sea indicates action; beginning from this, he rules over those who are subject to his law "to the sea," the sea, that is, of boundless knowledge, in which those who partake in this knowledge swim by means of the contemplation of beings. Or else, understand, by the sea, baptism, in which, according to the prophet, "the face" of the adversary vanishes "in the first sea and his back parts in the last sea";[602] he calls the first sea, as it has been said, baptism,[603] and the last [sea], the resurrection, in which the back parts of the enemy are abolished. Then our nature completely puts aside the law of sin that was placed in us through the transgression.

Or also, [to interpret this] in another way: the face of the devil vanishes, that is, wicked actions, by the active life. For this is, as it has been said, the first sea. And the back parts also vanish, that is, preconceptions of the evil things and illusions, through the second sea, that is, through knowledge.

Question 188

In the conversation that took place between the Lord and Nicodimus, in which he says, "the spirit blows wherever it wills, and you hear its sound,"[604] about which spirit is he speaking?

✠   Some think that the Lord speaks of the wind, but it seems to me that he speaks rather of the Holy Spirit. For this authoritatively "blows wherever it wills," and it wills [to be] in those capable of receiving it and those who are pure in their thinking.[605] For they, breathing in the divine graces, do not know from where or why such a grace was given to them, nor to what end the gift of grace comes, but they only hear the sound, that is, the very activity of grace that is revealed through their purity of life and which, as it were, utters a voice, whether it be a gift of teaching or of healing, or, again, *** .

Question 189

What is "the blasphemy against the Spirit," and how is it that "every sin will be forgiven for all people, but for those who blaspheme against it, they will not be forgiven, neither in this age nor in the age to come"?[606]

✤   The difficulty regarding blasphemy against the Spirit has a resolution from that same passage. For when the Lord performed different types of healing, the Jews attributed these, the activities (*energeias*) of the Spirit, "to the ruler of the demons."[607] And the statement that neither here nor in the future age is given to those who blaspheme is explained by the following: some who, through the Spirit, have closely examined such things say that there are four ways by which forgiveness of sins occurs, two here and two in the future. Since the memory of all time is insufficient for remembering one's faults, so that the human being might now repent of them, the master of nature who is a lover of humankind provided ways of repentance, even in our lack of repentance. And in the future, it has been said there are two. Whenever someone indiscriminately sins here, and again, indiscriminately does good works, whether he is moved to pity and to empathy for his neighbor or to any other activity that is connected with love for humanity (*philanthropias*), when in the future these are weighed at the time of judgment, if the balance turns toward them, forgiveness occurs. This then is one way. And the second is this: whenever someone who is entangled by sins and who hears the Lord say "do not judge so you will not be judged"[608] fears this and judges no one, in the investigation of the things done in his life he is not judged since he kept the commandment. For the one who is supremely free from deceit will not be forgetful of his own commandment. And the other two ways of forgiveness are as follows: whenever someone engaging in sins is, by providence, dealt with misfortunes, with necessities, with sicknesses—for he does not know that God is purifying him through such things—if he offers thanks when he is tempted, he receives the payment for his thanksgiving. But, if he is thankless, he is cleansed of whichever sins for which he may have been punished but is penalized for his ingratitude.

And so, as the passage has shown, one has many possibilities for forgiveness of his sins toward human beings—for if someone sins toward one person but does good toward another person, then the one nature against which he sinned is the nature also to which he renders an account. But as for blasphemy with regard to the Spirit—and faithlessness does not have another chance for forgiveness unless it becomes faithful—it stands to reason that, for someone who enclosed his life in faithlessness, the sin of faithlessness and disbelief in God will not be forgiven now or in the future.

Question 190
From the Gospel, "Amen, I say to you, there are some standing here who will not taste death until they see that the kingdom of God has come with power."[609] This is what Mark said, whereas Matthew said, "until they see the Son of man coming in his glory."[610] [Which one is the correct passage?]

✠   Since the *Logos* of God is not circumscribed by the events that occur in history, but, being active everywhere, shines forth its own light like the sun, he said to the disciples, "there are some standing here," not only in the historical sense, but also concerning all those who, like them, would be illustrious in [acts of] virtue, instead of saying, "those who have a place close to me on the basis of their virtues." And "they will not taste death" is said also regarding the apostles, because "they will not taste" of the physical "death until they see" through the transfiguration[611] the image of the future splendor that will be [available] for the saints. But, since the *Logos* is aware of the different deaths—for the mortification of the passions is also called death. But also, when someone who engages in action (*praktikos*) leaves the battle with the passions and engages in natural contemplation, he dies to his former state, becoming occupied with the contemplation of the things that exist, and the contentious battle concerning action becomes 'inactive.' But, again, the one who passes through natural contemplation and leaves behind all things that are caused and comes to the Cause through theological negation (*apophasis*) has also died to his former state, no longer moving among the created things but has transferred movement to the Creator of all things. Concerning, therefore, the death that takes place by the removal of all things, he says that "they will not taste" it, that is, these who are the apostles' equals in virtue will never experience this until the Lord, being transfigured, shall present himself, no longer making a positive statement from the affirmation of what exists but exhibiting by theological negation (*apophasin*) the inaccessible secret of the divinity.

And that one of the gospels says, "the Son of Man (*anthropou*) coming in his glory" and the other, "until they see the kingdom of God having come with power" signifies this: since in his divinity he is a Son of God, and in his humanity he has become, because of us, a Son of Man, therefore, with respect to the fact that he is the Son of God, he possesses glory eternally; whereas, because he became the Son of Man it is said, "he comes in his glory." For in this way he glorified the assumed humanity because just as he was seen transfigured on the mountain[612] in the body that is subject to suffering, so also we shall be in the resurrection when we receive an incorruptible body. For when he said "has come with power [or, in potentiality]" he showed that the incorruptible and eternal kingdom, hoped for by the saints, not yet present in its full actuality (*energeia*).

Question 191

"And after six days, Jesus took Peter and James and John and led them up a high mountain by themselves. And he was transfigured before them and his face shone like the sun, and his clothes became white as the light."[613]

✠   "After six days" signifies that since God brought the visible creation into existence in six days, those who, by the wealth of their virtues and knowledge, have moved beyond all the visible things, [these] ascend together with the *Logos* onto the mountain of theology. But since Luke mentions eight days[614] and seems to point out a contradiction among the evangelists, I think the difficulty finds its resolution in the manner that follows, in which the historical account concurs closely with the contemplative interpretation.

Just as according to the historical account, the one who said "six days" spoke of the [days] in the middle, and the other who said eight days meant both the beginning [day] in which the Lord spoke and the final [day] on which the transfiguration took place, so also this holds true according to contemplation. For since the human being, through the transgression, slipped away into that which is against nature, it is necessary for the one who desires to ascend together with the *Logos* up the mountain of theology first to pass through the things that are against nature, as though this were one day, and, according to six days, to pass through nature and come to that which is above nature, which is the eighth day. For this [the eighth day] is beyond the state of time and characterizes the future condition.

But why did he take only Peter and James and John with him? Since the *Logos* always avoids the state that is turbulent and full of trouble, and since Peter, according to his first name of Simon, is translated as "obedience,"[615] and according to the name Peter denotes immutability, what is shown through these things is [that] faith in God which, by obedience to the commandments, is immutable and unchanging. Now James is translated as "supplanter," and hope is shown through this— for unless someone hopes to receive from these passing and corruptible things that which is inaccessible and incorruptible instead, he would not be able to supplant the devil who always finds deception in the perceptible things. And John is translated as "dove," and love is shown through this. Since meekness is nothing other than the nonmovement of anger and desire toward the things against nature, and someone who falls into anger neither because of desires nor because of failure to obtain things desired clearly loves everyone, therefore, the *Logos* ascends to the mountain of theology together with those who have acquired faith, hope, and love and "is transfigured before them" no longer being referred to by [words of] affirmation, as

God and holy and king and such things, but being referred to by negation as beyond God and beyond holy and all such things as are spoken according to preeminence.

And the face of the *Logos*, which radiated like the sun, is the inaccessibility that characterizes his essence, upon which it is impossible to gaze by an interpretation of thoughts, just as neither can one gaze upon the brightness of the sun even if someone has entirely purified his optical ability. But since Scripture mentions a robe,[616] one must, in keeping with the sequential order also of the body makes mention. The body of the *Logos*, therefore, is the essence of the virtues, such as goodness, meekness, and such things. And the robes of the *Logos* are the words of Scripture and the creation of the world that has been put forward and received being from God. They are seen as white by those who strip off the thickness that lies on the letter of divine Scripture and who, by the contemplation of the Spirit, behold the radiant beauty of the meaning. And they behold in a brilliant way the perceptible creation by the removal of deception by sense, and from the greatness of its beauty, they reason analogously about its Creator.

Question 192

"And behold, Moses and Elias were seen talking with him, and Peter, answering, said to Jesus, 'Lord, it is good for us to be here; if you wish, we will make three tents, one for you, one for Moses and one for Elias.'"[617]

✢   For they who cross over from the letter to the spirit see that both the law and the prophets join together with the Logos and proclaim his coming with a penetrating voice. And why did Peter mention the tents? Because every knowledge and every virtue, being compared to the future condition, in no way differs from an easily disassembled tent, according to the Apostle who says, "either prophecies will come to an end or knowledge will be abolished." And there are three tents: active, natural, and theological. And he attributed the theological to the Lord as God, the natural contemplation to Moses as having recorded the beginning of all things [author of the book of Genesis] and the active to Elias since he was a virgin and a zealot and an ascetic.

Question 193

What is the reason why Moses and Elias fasted for forty days,[618] and why, ever, does the Lord, as if confirming the things done by his servants, also, himself, undertake his consent to remain without food for the same 40 days?[619] And what does the number forty signify?

✛   The number forty has been found in the divinely inspired Scriptures in many places referring to something distressful, such as, the Israelites who suffered forty years in the desert[620] and again in Egypt [where they suffered] four hundred years.[621] But this world in which we endure affliction is also constituted from four elements. And so, Moses, as the first one to legislate and hand down the law to the Jews (who were infants), fasts forty days signifying that his handing down of the law legislates the abstinence from sins committed by action. For every sin is constituted from perceptible things and from the senses. And Elias, bearing the type of prophetic grace (as one who has transcended the precepts of the law), fasts for forty days, signifying that prophetic grace legislates abstinence from things done with one's consent. And the Lord, as the fulfillment of the law[622] and the only one who "took away the sin of the world,"[623] having fasted the forty days, has given power to us not only to abstain from the sins of action and consent but also to be above the simple mental images themselves.

Question 194

What does the Gospel signify, where after the Lord repelled every temptation of the devil the evangelist indicates that, "the devil departed from him until an opportune time"? Until what time?

✛   The temptations are twofold, voluntary as well as involuntary, that is, pleasurable as well as painful. At first, the devil tempted the Lord through pleasurable things, through gluttony as well as avarice and vainglory—for all these are causes of pleasure—and since he [the devil] was repelled, "he departed until an opportune time." Until what time? Until the suffering on the Cross, so that by attacking the Lord also by involuntary and painful temptations[624] he would be able (so he thought) to discover in him something of the human passions. But he was driven away also by means of these things, and being defeated on the Cross he was brought to nothing.

Question 195
Since John [the Baptist] was declared by the Lord himself to be greater than all who were born, for his life was pure and separated from every sin, *** .

❖ ❖ ❖

[Translator's Note: The following heading is from the critical edition.]

By Saint Maximus, Various Questions and Selections from Various Passages that Are Perplexing.

Question I, 1
Which virtues belong to the soul and which to the body?[625]

 Virtues that belong to the soul are these: love, humility, meekness, long-suffering, forbearance, lack of resentment, lack of rage, lack of anger, lack of envy, lack of judgmental behavior, freedom from vainglory, mercy, discretion, lack of covetousness for money, kindliness, not being puffed up, freedom from pride, and compunction. And virtues that belong to the body are these: fasting, sleeping on the ground, wakefulness, self-control, lack of possessions, attentiveness.

Question I, 2
What is the saying in [the writings of] the Apostle, "I shall sing with the spirit, and I shall sing with the mind"?[626]

Someone "sings with the spirit" whenever he or she conveys only the sound of things sung with the tongue, and "sings with the mind" whenever he or she is delighted, understanding by contemplation the power of the things that are sung.

Question I, 3
What is, "I was conceived in iniquity, and in sin did my mother bear me"?[627]

Since the original intention of God was not for us to be born through [intercourse that takes place in a] marriage and corruption (it was the transgression of the commandment [that] introduced marriage because Adam disobeyed, that is, rejected the law given to him from God), therefore, then all who are born of Adam are "conceived in iniquity" and fall under the forefather's sentence of condemnation. And "and in sin did my mother bear me" signifies that Eve, the mother of us all, first conceived sin by becoming wanton for pleasure. Because of this, we, too, falling under the sentence of the mother, are said to be conceived in sin.

Question I, 4 (II, 12)
What is the saying by the Apostle, "to be accursed from Christ for the sake of my kinsmen"?[628]

✠ "I would pray,"[629] he says, to be handed over from Christ to the devil to be whipped and undergo for Israel's sake the punishments which, according to what is just, they deserved because of their faithlessness to God, only so that they might be saved. In the same manner, the Lord also "handed himself over"[630] and "has become a curse for our sakes."[631]

Question I, 5
In how many ways does the human being sin?

✠ I think the human being sins according to four ways: by impulse, by deception, by ignorance, and by inclination (*diathesin*).[632] And the first three easily come to full awareness (*epignosin*) and repentance, but the one who sins from inclination and [who] is brought to repentance neither by experience nor over time, has an incurable punishment.

Question I, 6
What does the Lord in the Gospel indicate when he says, "two sparrows are sold for an *assarion*"?[633]

✠ They say the *assarion* is ten *noumi*. Through [the number] ten the [Greek] letter *iota* is signified. And this is the initial [letter] of the name of our Lord, Jesus Christ. And so, the old and the new people, both "the inner"[634] and "the outer" person[635] are redeemed through the name of the Lord.

Question I, 7
What does the pronouncement from Elisha mean, when Elias was taken up,[636] "where is God, *appho*?"[637]

✛   The passage is interpreted according to three points of view:
either "where is the God of my father?" or "where is the God of
my great one?" or "where is the God of the hidden one?"

Question I, 8
In how many ways are there allegories, and what is tropology?

✛   Allegory is that which pertains to inanimate things, such as
mountains, hills, trees, and the rest. And tropology is that which
pertains to the parts of our body, such as the head, the eyes, and
the rest. For tropology is referred to instead of "to be turned [in a
certain direction]."

Question I, 9
What is the saying in the Psalm, "sitting, you spoke against your
brother and placed an obstacle against the son of your mother"?[638]

✛   Whoever slanders the action of a fellow believer, as if lying in
wait [to utter] abuse against him, this one rightly is said "to speak
against his brother." And the one who harbors ill will against the
son adorned with wisdom who maligns him and gives offense to
all, it is he who places an obstacle against [his] mother's son.

Question I, 10
Since in [the text of] St. Diadochus, in the 100th chapter, it has
been written, "some will be judged through fires and purified in
the future age," I ask [that] the father's aim [St. Diadochus] be
revealed to me by clarification.[639]

✛   They who have acquired the perfection of love for God and
have elevated the wing of the soul through the virtues, according to
the Apostle "are caught up in the clouds"[640] and do not come into
judgment.[641] And they who did not completely acquire perfection
but have acquired both sins and good works, come into the court of
judgment; there, they are scorched as by a fire by the comparison
of their good and evil deeds, and if, in fact, the scale of their good
deeds weighs downwards, they are cleansed of punishment.

Question I, 11
Concerning different kinds of righteousness.

✣   Those who are wise in divine things say there are three kinds of righteousness: human, angelic, and divine. And human [righteousness], they say, is both distributive equity and right judgment with regard to the perceptible things of this world; and angelic [righteousness] is the unstinted sharing of divine knowledge; and they define divine righteousness as suffering for the sake of sinners.

Question I, 12
For what reason did the Lord, rebuking Peter, call him Satan?[642]

✣   The Lord does not call Peter "Satan," as some might think, as a curse but because the Lord's "states of being deprived" have become our own "states of having": for example, his death has become life for us, and his disgrace has become glory for us. And so, when the Lord said that he was destined to suffer, the Apostle Peter assumed, in keeping with the nature of things, that it is not possible for life to experience death or for so great a glory to be dishonored. And so, the Lord, doing away with this thought, since one must not expect to find a sequential order of nature in things that are beyond nature (for it was his plan to bring about these things through their opposites, life by death, glory by disgrace), and since this thought was in opposition to his purpose, he says, "get behind me" instead of saying, "follow my advice and make no presuppositions, looking for [the normal] sequence of things." And they say the name of Satan is interpreted as "adversary," which the Lord states not as a curse but as if saying "opposed to my purpose."

Question I, 25
How ought we to understand, in a pious way, the [passage] of the Gospel, "the Father judges no one but has given every judgment to the Son,"[643] and how, in another place, does it say, "I judge no one"[644] but "the word that I have spoken, that will judge him"?[645]

✣   As God, neither the Father nor the Son "will judge anyone." For neither does the human being become a judge of irrational beings but of human beings. And the Father "has given the judgment to the Son," not because he is God but because he is human. And he [the Son] will judge all things, comparing his own conduct as a human being with ours. And again, his word will judge, that is, his teaching, which is revealed through his deeds according to what has been written, "that which Jesus began to do as well as teach."[646]

Question I, 27
What does the paradox from Proverbs reveal, "if your enemy is hungry, give him bread to eat; if he is thirsty, give him a drink. For by doing this you heap coals of fire on his head"?[647]

✠   We have an enemy against our soul—our body—always waging war on us by the uprising of the passions. And so, if "the mind of the flesh,"[648] being weighed down by the conscience, is hungry, that is, has an appetite for salvation or thirsts for divine knowledge, one must nourish it through self-control and labors and water it by the study of the divine words. For in this way "you heap on his head," that is, on the *nous*, "coals of fire," which are divine and spiritual thoughts.

Question I, 28
What is indicated by the statement in the 101st Psalm, "I am like a lonely pelican"?[649]

✠   This pelican is a bird. And the snake is very much an enemy of its newborn. What then does the pelican contrive? In a high place he fixes his nest, fencing it off on every side because of the snake. And so, what does the mischievous snake do? Looking for the direction from where the wind blows, it breathes its poison on the young ones, and they die. Then the pelican comes, realizing that his children are dead, gazes up to the clouds, and flies to the highest point; and with his wings he beats his sides and blood comes forth, and it drips through the cloud onto these [newborn birds], and they are revived. The pelican is to be understood as the Lord. And his children are Adam and Eve, our nature, and his nest is paradise, and the snake is the apostate devil. Therefore, the originator of evil,[650] the snake, breathed onto the first-formed [human] beings by [encouraging] disobedience, and they have become "dead to sin."[651] Our Lord and God, then, because of his love for us, is raised on the precious Cross and, being pierced on his side,[652] through the cloud of the Holy Spirit, grants us eternal life.

Question I, 29
What is, "there they build their nests"?[653]

✠   He calls "sparrows" either souls or the different virtues.

Question I, 30
What is the meaning of, "the dwelling of the heron leads them"?[654]

✠   They say that a "heron" is a bird, and it lives with such chastity that whenever it is about to come together for sexual intercourse it mourns for forty days, and after these, again, another forty days. It sets its nest within the trees where it will not be obstructed overhead by anything but has open space. And, on account of these things, it indicates chastity; for this takes the lead of all the virtues. And it has a distaste for perceptible things, preferring not to be overshadowed by anything temporal. For the number forty contains the perfection of each of the four elements.

Question I, 31
What is "I pass down the sins of the parents onto the children until the third or fourth generation for those who hate me"?[655]

✠   We have interpreted "first generation" to be the seed of evil, that is, the attack, and "second" to be the desire [for evil], and "third" to be the habit of evil, that is the consent, and "fourth" to be the activity, that is, the deed. And so, he passes [sins] down "until the third and fourth generations," that is, on account of the consent and the deed. For the attack and the desire are free from any culpability since the evil did not yet reach its end [during those stages].

Question I, 33
What is meant by "for the three or four transgressions of Tyre, I will not turn back"?[656]

✠   I think by "four transgressions" the word [of the prophet Amos] hints at these: the attack, the desire, the habit of evil, and the activity. And so, during the first and second [transgressions], that is, during the attack and the desire, God shows forbearance, because evil does not progress to its completion. And "for the third and fourth transgressions," that is, [for] habit and activity, or rather, [for] the consent and the hardening, the passage rightly offers the rebuke.

Question I, 34
That it is not possible to say that Christ is "of the Spirit" as, in the case of the Father and of the Son, it is said indifferently "the Spirit of God" and "the Spirit of Christ."

✠   Just as the *nous* is the cause of a word, so, also [the Father is the cause] of the Spirit through the mediation of the *Logos*. And just as we are not able to say that the word is of the voice, neither can we say that the Son is of the Spirit.

Question I, 35
What does the saying by the Lord show, "if the eye or hand or foot is an obstacle for you, cut them off, and throw them away from you"?[657]

✠   One could easily suspect the parable to be hinting at friends as eyes,[658] and relatives as hands that are indispensable to us, and companions as feet that serve us, which, if they are an obstacle and greatly injure the soul, the *Logos* ordered to be cut off. But it is also possible to understand the commandment according to the anagogic method of interpretation (*anagoge*). If you have contemplative knowledge in the same way you have an eye, and it elevates you with conceit and arrogance, cut it out. And if you also [engage in] a courteous act and it becomes for you a cause for self-aggrandizement, cut it off. And in the same way, if you also have some proficiency with regard to service towards others, which is the foot, and you are puffed up from this, separate yourself from it. For it is better for you to be apart from these seemingly virtuous traits and avoid complete destruction through haughtiness and arrogance.

Question I, 36
What does it mean by, "the sun was elevated and the moon stood in its orbit"?[659]

✦ Whenever the "sun" of "righteousness"[660] is lifted up in us through good deeds and true knowledge, then "the moon stands in its orbit," that is, our nature, which is subject to turning and alteration, occupies a fixed orbit.

Question I, 37

What does the passage in the universal [letter] of Peter denote, "so that they might be judged, on the one hand, in the flesh like human beings, and, on the other hand, they might live according to God in the Spirit"?[661]

✦ Since he refers to those [caught] in the flood,[662] and they had complete ignorance of God and lived together in wicked pursuits, whatever sins they committed against each other as a result of the temptations that befell them, wars, allurements, and miscellaneous occurrences, he forgave them. But he did not forgive their sins that were related to their ignorance when, because of his love for humankind, he came into the place of Hades, all those who were to believe in him would, by faith [in him], be forgiven the sin of impiety and "might live according to God in the Spirit," that is, being judged in the flesh, as is stated, for the sake of their misdeeds against human beings.

Question I, 45

What is this that is said in the psalms, "be still and know that I am God"?[663]

✦ There are six stillnesses by which, if we achieve them, we are able to know God fully: first, from sinful activity; second, from an exciting way of life; third, from a place of mingling with those who live in an unguarded way; fourth, from pursuits unsuitable for the life according to God; fifth, from an existence subject to slander and to many distractions of the *nous* by many things; sixth, the [state of] not having one's own will—completely. And this is both a renunciation and a subordination, both true and according to God.

Question I, 67

How ought we to think about the Son's ignorance concerning the end (*sunteleias*)?[664]

✚   Ignorance is, in a way, double: one kind is reproachable, and the other is irreproachable.[665] One depends upon us, and the other does not. That which is reproachable and depends upon us is ignorance of virtue and piety. And that which is irreproachable and not dependent upon us is whatever we are ignorant of (although we wish to know), such as, things distant and in the future. And so, if, in the case of the holy prophets, distant things that are not dependent upon us were discerned by grace, how much more was the Son of God not cognizant of all things and thereby his humanity, too, not by nature but by union with the *Logos*? For just as iron having been heated in the fire has all the properties of fire—for it shines and burns—although, to be sure, it is not fire by nature but iron,[666] so also the humanity of the Lord, inasmuch as it was united to the *Logos*, knew everything, and in it, clearly, everything worthy of God was revealed. But insofar as the nature united with human things, he is said not to know.

Question I, 68 (II, 27)
What does the monastic habit signify, and before this, what is the clipping of the hairs?[667]

✚   As the head governs all the parts of the body, thus, also, the *nous* holds the place of the head in the soul.[668] And so, it is necessary to clip off from this all worldly thoughts. And the inner robe, since it protects the entire body and leaves only the hands exposed, signifies that we should put on the ethical way of life, having separated ourselves from the practical activities of sin (for the hands, by general agreement, are a symbol of action and operation).

And the belt, because it is made from dead skins and binds the loins and the navel, signifies mortification through self-control, and it is necessary for self-control to have authority over the power and activity of evil. For "the power" of the opposing authority of the wicked one is, according to Job, "in the navel of the belly,"[669] and "the loins" according to the blessed David are filled with demonic "mockings."[670] And "mockings" are the different activities of sexual impurity.

And the scapular, since it has the cross both on the front and the back, symbolizes, according to the Apostle, that we must not only be crucified to the world but also the world [must be crucified] to us,[671] so that fleeing the world we may not have anything hindering us, and may neither, by a relationship with the world, be held in its power through obvious deceit, nor again in being pursued by it from behind, that we should lessen the intensity of devotion because of involuntary temptations, but so that we should remain, towards both involuntary and voluntary passions, insensible and dead.

And the hood shows the grace of God guarding and protecting our *nous*. For the one who has clipped off the notions of the world receives "the helmet of salvation."[672]

And the sandals have this meaning: since they are from dead skins, and they are situated beneath a small part of the body, in the same way that the whole body is related to the soles of its sandal, so the soul must make use of the body, and the body with this is dead to the unnatural passions.

And the cloak, since it is square and the world is made of four elements, signifies that we must be cloaked with natural contemplation so as not to see the visible things in respect to sense perception and passion but, through the *logos* that is in them, to be led up toward their Creator. And the exposing of the left hand means that the good deeds in us must be brought to light, according to the teaching of our Savior, "so that people may see your good works and give glory to your Father in heaven."[673] And the garments being black signifies that it is necessary for us to be invisible in the world since we have "our citizenship in heaven."[674] And if someone were to understand the cloak, since it is square, as also signifying also the four cardinal virtues, he will not mistake what is fitting.

Question I, 69[675]

The priest pronounces "Peace" from the highest chair to the church, imitating the Lord who assumed that seat, both sending forth and giving[676] his own peace. And, "and with your spirit,"[677] the response by the people, shows this: you granted us peace, O Lord, and unanimity with each other; but give that peace also to us, the indivisible union with you, so that living by peace with your Spirit, which you placed in us at the beginning of the creation, we may remain inseparable[678] from your love.

Question I, 70[679]

"If the dead are not completely raised, why are there some who also are baptized for their sake?"[680] the divine Apostle said. If, he said, our bodies were not completely raised, why do we also believe that, by being baptized, they are to be transformed into incorruption?

Question I, 71[681]

If you are looking for a clarification of the music found in Scripture, understand it in the following way. "Praise the Lord with the sound of the trumpet":[682] at the commemoration of the resurrection the earth is jolted by a trumpet, as it has been written. "Praise him with stringed instrument and harp":[683] with our tongue and our mouth as though we were being plucked by the Spirit, as by a plectrum. "Praise him with timbrel and dance":[684] with flesh and soul, from which our petitions, like dancers, step across to God. "Praise him with strings and pipes":[685] with the heart and with all the internal organs and nerves, which he has called pipes. "Praise him with clanging cymbals":[686] with the lips through which the harmonious songs of psalmody are composed.

Question I, 72, (II, 11)

Since, according to some of the manuscripts of the Apostle, the reading is given, "we will all fall asleep, but not all will be changed,"[687] and according to others, "we will not all fall asleep, but we will all be changed,"[688] I entreat [you] to explain which of the editions one must accept, and what is indicated by these things?

✠   I think that since the ancient copies also contain correct readings, someone who understands either edition in a pious way will not deviate from the apostolic aim. With regard to "we will all fall asleep, but not all will be changed," one must understand the passage in this way: that we all undergo the sleep through death, but not all of us will receive, in exchange, glory and confidence [to approach God]. The same Apostle posits this [more clearly] in another place saying, "if in fact, by being clothed, we will not be found naked."[689] And as for [the reading], "we will not all will fall asleep, but we will all be changed," one must take it in this way: "we will not all sleep" the temporal sleep so as to require burial and a decomposition into corruption. But they who are found at that time will undergo a brief death and will be in no need of temporal sleep because of the resurrection that will immediately occur. "But all will be changed," that is, they will be clothed in incorruption.

And one can also interpret this by another theory: "we will not all fall asleep," bringing about cessation and inactivity to our sins, nor will we put our own passions to sleep according to the passage, "I sleep and my heart is awake."[690] For the one who has written the Songs of divine loves signifies that whoever has become completely inactive with regard to all the perceptible as well as to the intelligible things is awake only in his heart, rejoicing solely in the contemplation of God. And "but we will all be changed" shows the common change into incorruption.

Question I, 77
What is the saying [in the letter] of the Apostle, "would that they also cut themselves off"?[691]

✢ This is said instead of "they will lament and beat their breasts," when they come to repent for their sinful behavior in unsettling the faithful.

Question I, 78
For what reason are the Moabites and Ammanites forbidden to enter into the temple of the Lord, "until the third and fourth and tenth generations and until forever"?[692]

✢ Since Moabite is translated as "the internal part of the father" and Ammanites as "the father of [his] mother," it is indicated through these [passages] that whoever inherits from another an example of evil has is revealed "the internal part of the father." And whoever brings forth sin from [within] himself, is "a father of a mother," that is, of his own sin. And so, such people "do not enter into the" house "of the Lord until the third and fourth and tenth generations, and until eternity," that is, the one who makes himself at home with God, neither through good habit and [good] action—for this is the third and fourth generation of virtues—nor through the name and faith of the Lord Jesus, nor through the ten commandments of the law, nor through the regeneration that will occur in the age to come—such a person will not enter into the house of God, that is, into the heavenly city, in which is the dwelling place of all who rejoice.[693]

Question I, 79

Why, ever, is the one who is leprous on a part [of the body] considered unclean according to the law, whereas the one who is completely leprous is considered to be clean?[694]

✢   For someone who is a leper with respect to some part, the part in which his leprosy exists is dead. As the life-giving blood withdraws, the site becomes ulcerated; and when by the touch of the priest the leprous ulcer ceased from growing, it defiled that one [the priest]. So, also, the one who is leprous on some part of the soul, by having an ulcerated soul, that is, by is being humbled by the retreat of the life-giving power of virtue, becomes unclean. The one who is completely leprous however, although he has the color of a leper, has the life-giving blood circulating completely throughout the periphery of the body. Accordingly, this indicates that the one coming to the ultimate limit of evil, if he then becomes repentant, takes up again the life-giving power of virtue and has only his conscience stained by the earlier predispositions (for he is unable not to think of the things he did, as if he did not do them). And so, because of this, the law declares such a person 'clean.'

Question I, 81

Why is it that Ham erred and Canaan was cursed?[695]

✢   And if someone should take the sense of this Scripture according to the letter, the righteous Noah is shown to be unrighteous in this case, bringing forth the curse upon the one when the other erred. And, in any case, even if Canaan was cursed, it was surely necessary also for his tribe to be cursed, but we find that his tribe, more than the others, advanced toward faith of Christ.

Everywhere we find God and all the saints struggling against evil and cursing it (*kataromenous*). Therefore, since evil first receives its beginning as a habit in the human being, and sin, as an action, emerges from this, naturally Canaan, characterizing the sin that is an action, has received the curse. And if you also desire to consider this solely with respect to the movement of the soul—that which, in the amalgam (I mean of body and soul), is a habit that does not advance to its end, is, in the soul, an activity.

Question I, 82
"Furthermore, providence is attention from God bestowed upon things that exist. Providence is the will of God, through which all beings receive their suitable administration."[696]

Question I, 83
He was seen by Abraham by means of an angel, by Moses by means of fire in the bush, by Isaiah by means of the seraphim, by Ezekiel by means of the cherubim. These all have witnessed to having seen [God] in different ways.

From the writings of our holy father, Maximus the Confessor

Question II, 6
What is, "Behold how good and pleasant it is for brothers to dwell together"?[697]

✚   With regard to the obvious meaning, whenever [brothers] possess the same faith, behold the "good." And whenever they are also harmonious in their deeds, behold the "pleasant." [The phrase] "brothers who dwell together" is understood as the three powers of the soul or of the soul and the body, whenever they are in agreement with regard to the knowledge of divine things and with regard to good deeds. For whenever they act rightly, behold the "good." And, when knowledge also is in agreement, behold the "pleasant."

Question II, 7
"As myrrh on the head that runs down onto the beard, the beard of Aaron, and runs down onto the stole of his vestments."[698]

✣   "Myrrh" is the Holy Spirit, and "head" is the *nous*, and "beard" is the word. For the word encompasses the heart. And "the beard of Aaron" is the word that slaughters the passions and consecrates the virtues to God. And the grace of the Spirit runs down, also, "onto the stole of the vestment," that is, it is transmitted through the active life and [drips down] upon the ethical philosophy. For the "stole of the vestment" is the end.

Question II, 8
"As dew of Hermon, it runs down onto the mountains of Sion."[699]

✣   "Mountains of Sion" are the saints[700] who aim for the higher things. "The dew of Hermon" runs down onto them [the saints], and "Hermon" is translated as "rejection of the beasts." They also say that the Jordan river is sprung from there. And it indicates, through these things, the grace of Holy Baptism. For it [grace] eternally runs down onto the saints, and it is through this that the rejection of the spiritual beasts takes place.

Question II, 9
"There the Lord proclaimed the blessing, life eternal."[701]

✣   For a pledge, both of all good things and of eternal life, is the grace given through Holy Baptism, in which we may partake by the grace of our Lord Jesus Christ.

Question II, 14
How should we understand the writing of St. Dionysius, "nonbeing also longs for God"?[702]

✣   Since God is not one from among the beings but is beyond all beings, according to this, nonbeing also has a place. For nonbeing is properly meant with regard to him since he is not among beings.

Question II, 18
What is, "it is easier for a camel to go through the eye of a needle than for a rich person to enter into the kingdom of heaven"?[703]

✣   "It is easier," it says, for the crookedness of the Gentiles—for this is "the camel"—to go through the "straight and narrow,"[704] which is "the eye," "into the kingdom of heaven" than for the people of the Jews who have the law and the prophets. And just as the needle is applied to two rent pieces [of fabric] and produces one, thus also our Lord Jesus Christ, who is the needle, united the two peoples [Jews and Gentiles] according to the Apostle "making both one."[705] But the one who refined and spun himself through self-control enters more easily through the narrow gate into the kingdom of heaven than a rich person who always makes himself broad by [sitting at] the table and by human glory.

Question II, 23 (III, 2)
Why did human beings, in the past, live for many years but the most recent [generations] for a few [years]?

✣ Because the people of the past were completely sick from disbelief, God deigned that they be detained for a long period of time in this life so that through cumulative misfortunes he might lead them into the realization that there is some providence that directs the various turns of events. But "the most recent generation," since it has received knowledge both of the written law and of the spiritual law, is not detained by a life of many years.

Question III, 1
What is "let us make the human being according to the image and likeness of God,"[706] and a little further down he says, "and God made the human being, he made him according to the image of God"[707] and omits the "according to the likeness"?

✣ Because the first objective of God was for the human being to come to be "according to the image and likeness of God," and what is "according to the image" is incorruption,[708] immortality, invisibility, which image the divine; and he has bestowed these on the soul for it to possess, having bestowed along with them both self-governance and self-determination, which are all imagings of the essence of God. And "according to the likeness" is detachment, meekness, long-suffering, and the remaining marks of the great goodness of God, which are all indications of God's energy. Therefore, those things that are of his essence, the things that manifest the "according to the image," he has given to the soul by nature. And those things that belong to God's energy, characterizing the "according to the likeness," he left for our voluntary deliberation (*autexousio gnome*), anticipating the perfection of the human being, in the case that someone might establish him or herself "like" God through imitation of the godly characteristics of virtue. And so, because of this, the divine Scripture omitted in the things said after this, the "according to the likeness."

ABBREVIATIONS

ACW	Ancient Christian Writers
AnBoll	Analecta Bollandiana
BHG	*Bibliotheca hagiographica Graece*
CCSG	Corpus Christianorum Series graeca
CS	*Cistercian Studies*
CSCO	Corpus scriptorum christianorum orientalium
CWS	Classics of Western Spirituality
DOP	*Dumbarton Oaks Papers*
GCS	Die griechische christliche Schriftsteller der ersten [drei] Jahrhunderte
GNO	Gregorii Nysseni Opera
JECS	Journal of Early Christian Studies
Lampe	G. W. H. Lampe (ed.), *A Patristic Greek Lexicon*
LCL	Loeb Classical Library
LS	H. Liddell and R. Scott (eds.), *An Intermediate Greek-English*
LSJ	H. Liddell, R. Scott and H.S. Jones (eds.), *A Greek-English Lexicon*
Mansi	J. D. Mansi (ed.), *Sacrorum Conciliorum Nova et Amplissima Collectio*

Morani	M. Morani (ed.), *Nemesii Emeseni De Natura Hominis*
ODB	*Oxford Dictionary of Byzantium*
OLA	Orientalia lovaniensia analecta
OrChrAn	*Orientalia christiana analecta*
PG	Patrologia cursus completus Series Graeca
PO	Patrologia orientalis
PTS	Patristische Texte und Studien
Pusey	P.E. Pusey (ed.), *Cyrilli Archiepiscopi Alexandrini In xii prophetas*
RB	Revue biblique
RevScRel	Revue des sciences religieuses
RSPT	Revue des sciences philosophiques et théologiques
SA	Studia anselmiana
SBL	Society of Biblical Literature
SC	Sources chrétiennes
SP	Sacra pagina
StPatr	Studia patristica
TU	Texte und Untersuchungen zur Geschichte der altchristlichen Literatur
ThH	Théologie historique

ABBREVIATIONS OF MAXIMUS'S WORKS AND EDITIONS USED FOR THIS TRANSLATION

Amb.Io.	*Ambigua ad Iohannem* (PG 91.1061–1417)
Amb.Th.	*Ambigua ad Thomam* (PG 91.1032–1060)
CC	*Centuries on Charity* (Ceresa-Gastaldo)
DP	*Disputatio cum Pyrrho* (PG 91.288–353)

EOD	*Expositio orationis dominicae* (CCSG 23)
Ep.	*Epistles* (PG 91.364–649)
EP	*Expositio in Psalmum 59* (CCSG 23)
GC	*Capita theologica et oeconomica* (PG 90.1084–1173)
LA	*Liber Asceticus* (CCSG 40)
Myst.	*Mystagogia* (PG 91.657–717)
OD	*Orationis dominicae* (PG 90.872–909)
Op.	*Opuscula theologica et polemica* (PG 91.9–285)
QD	*Quaestiones et dubia* (CCSG 10)
QT	*Quaestiones ad Thalassium* (CCSG 7 and 22)

OTHER ANCIENT AUTHORS AND WORKS

Aristotle

De part. an.	De partibus animalium
Nich. Eth.	Nichomachean Ethics
Rhet.	Rhetorica

Athanasius

Ex. Ps.	Expositiones in Psalmos
Ser. ann.	Sermo in annuntiationem deiparae

Basil of Caesarea

Epist.	Epistulae
Hom.	Homiliae

Cassius Dio

Hist. Rom.	Historiae Romanae

Clement of Alexandria

Paed.	Paedagogus
Strom.	Stromatata

Cyril of Alexandria

De ador.	De adoratione et culte in spiritu et veritate
De incar.	De incarnatione domini
Ex. Ps.	Expositio in Psalmos
Col. vet. test.	Collectio dictorum veteris testamenti
Com. xii proph.	Commentarios in xii prophetas minores
Com. Is.	Commentarios in Isaiam prophetam
Com. Luc.	Commentarii in Lucam
Glaph. Pent.	Glaphyra in Pentateuchum
In Reg.	In Regum

Diadochus of Photike

Cap. char.	Capita de charitate

Didymus the Blind

Com. Ps.	Commentarii in Psalmos
Com. Zac.	Commentarii in Zacchariam
Frag. Ps.	Fragmenta in Psalmos
In Gen.	In Genesim

Dionysius the Areopagite

De cael. hier.	De caelesti hierarchia
De div. nom.	De divinis nominibus
De eccl. hier.	De ecclesiastica hierarchia

Epiphanius

Pan.	Panarion

Eusebius of Caesarea

Com. Ps.	Commentaria in Psalmos
Praep. ev.	Praeparatio evangelica

Evagrius of Pontus

De ora.	De oratione
Keph. gnost.	Kephalia gnostica
Prak.	Praktikos

Galen

De symp.	De symptomatum causis
De temp.	De temperamentis

Gregory Nazianzus

Apol.	Apologetica
Carm. dog.	Carmina dogmatica
In patr. tac.	In patrem tacetem
Or.	Orationes

Gregory of Nyssa

Contra Eun.	Contra Eunomium
De inst.	De instituto Christiano
De op. hom.	De opificio hominis
Hom.	Homiliae
In Cant.	In Canticum canticorum
In ins. Ps.	In inscriptions Psalmorum
Or.	Orationes

Heliodorus

Aeth.	Aethiopica

Herodotus

Hist.	Historiae

Hesychius

Com. brevis	Commentarios brevis
In s. Steph.	In sanctum Stephanum

Irenaeus
Adv. Haer.	Adversus Haereses

John Chrysostom
De jej.	De jejunio
Frag. Job	Fragmenta in Job
Frag. Prov.	Fragmenta in Proverbia
Hom.	Homiliae
In asc.	In ascensionem
In ep. Eph.	In epistulam ad Ephesios
In ep. Heb.	In epistulam ad Hebraeos
In ep. I Cor.	In epistulam I ad Corinthios
In ep. I Thes.	In epistulam I ad Thessalonicenses
In ep. Tit.	In epistulam ad Titum
In. sanc. Jul. martyr.	In sanctum Julianum martyrem
In Gen.	In Genesim (homiliae 1-67)

John Moschus
Spir. Pratrum	Spritual Pratrum

Josephus
Ant. Jud.	Antiquitates Judaicae

Lives and stories
Apoph.	Apophthegmata Patrum

Apophthegmata Patrum
V. Euty.	Vita Eutychii
V. Sab.	Vita Sabae
V. Theo.	Vita Theodosii

Macarius
Hom.	Homiliae spirituals

Nemesius of Emesa
De nat. hom.   De natura hominis

Nilus
Com. Cant.   Commentarii in Canticum Canticorum

Olympiodorus
Com. Job   Commentarii in Job

Origen

Com. Johan.	Commentarii in evangelium Johannem
Com. Matt.	Commentarii in evangelium Matthaei
De Prin.	De Principiis
Ex. Ps.	Excerpta in Psalmos
Ex. Prov.	Expositio in Proverbia
Frag. Lam.	Fragmentum in Lamentationes
Hom.	Homiliae
In Jer.	In Jeremiam
In Jesu	In Jesu Nave
Sch. Cant.	Scholia in Canticum canticorum
Sel. Gen.	Selecta in Genesim
Sel. Ps.	Selecta in Psalmos

Philo

De Abra.	De Abrahamo
De cher.	De cherubim
De ebr.	De ebrietate
De mut. nom.	De mutatione nominum
De som.	De somniis
Leg. alleg.	Legum allegoriarum
Quod deus imm.	Quod deus sit immutabilis

Plato
Reg.	Regula
Rep.	Republica

Plotinus
Enn.	Enneades

Posidonius
Frag.	Fragmenta

Pseudo-Galen
Def. med.	Definitiones medicae

Proclus
In Plat. Alc.	In Platonis Alcibiademi
In Plat. Parm.	In Platonis Parmenidem

Procopius
Com. Is.	Commentarii in Isaiam

Romanus the Melodist
Cant.	*Cantica*

Theodoret
Int. xii proph.	Interpretatio in xii prophetas minores
Int. Ez.	Interpretatio in Ezechielem
Int. Jer.	Interpretatio in Jeremiam
Int. Ps.	Interpretatio in Psalmos
Quae. Reg.	Quaestiones in libros Regorum et Paralipomenon

NOTES

INTRODUCTION

1. For a more in-depth look at the research and its contribution to the study of Maximus, see Aidan Nichols, OP, *Byzantine Gospel: Maximus the Confessor in Modern Scholarship* (Edinburgh: T&T Clark, 1993), appendix A. Fr. Nichols's work ends with the scholarship of the early 1990s.

2. Notes two through eighteen provide examples of the types of scholarship discussed; these are not necessarily exhaustive references. Peter van Deun et. al., *Maximi Confessoris liber asceticus*, CCSG 40 (Turnhout: Brepols, 2000).

3. Bronwen Neil and Pauline Allen, eds. and trans., *The Life of Maximus the Confessor Recension 3*. Early Christian Studies 6 (Strathfield, NSW, Australia: Pauls, 2003), with translation.

4. Bart Janssens, ed., *Maximi Confessoris Ambigua ad Thomam una cum Epistula secunda ad eundem*, CCSG 48 (Turnhout: Brepols, 2002).

5. Stephanos Sargologos, *Florilege sacro-profance du Pseudo-Maxime* (Hermopolis, Greece: Syros Typokykladike, 2001).

6. Maximus the Confessor, *On the Cosmic Mystery of Jesus Christ: Selected Writings of Maximus the Confessor*, trans. Paul Blowers and Robert Wilken (Crestwood, N.Y.: Vladimir's Seminary Press, 2003).

7. Pauline Allen and Bronwen Neil, eds. and trans., *Maximus the Confessor and his Companions: Documents from Exile* (Oxford: Oxford University Press, 2002).

8. Maximus Confessor, *La Mystagogie*, trans. Marie-Lucie Charpin-Ploix (Paris: Migne, 2005).

9. Maximus Confessor, *Centuries sur la charite*, trans. Joseph Pegon (Paris: Cerf, 2006). For the purposes of my translation, I will be using the critical edition of Aldo Ceresa-Gestaldo, *Capitoli sulla carita, editi criticamente con introduzione, versione e note* (Rome: Editrice Studium, 1963).

10. Demetrios Batharellos, *The Byzantine Christ: Person, Nature and Will*

in the Christology of Saint Maximus the Confessor (New York: Oxford University Press, 2004); and Melchisedec Toronen, *Union and Distinction in the Thought of Maximus the Confessor* (New York: Oxford University Press, 2007).

11. Adam G. Cooper, *The Body in Maximus the Confessor: Holy Flesh, Wholly Deified* (New York: Oxford University Press, 2005).

12. Pascal Mueller-Jourdan, *Typologies patio-temporelle de l'ecclesia byzantine: la Mystagogie de Maxime le Confesseur dans la culte philosophique de l'antiquite tardive* (Leiden: Brill, 2005); and Vasileios Betsakos, *Stasis aeikinetos: he anakrainise tes aristotelikes kineseos ste theologia tou hagiou Maximou tou Homologetou* (Athens: Ekdoseis Harmos, 2006).

13. Assaad Elias Kattan, *Veleiblichung und synergie: Grundzuge der Bibelhermeneutik bei Maximus Confessor* (Leiden: Brill, 2003); and Edouard Jeauneau, *La figure de Melchisedech chez Maxime le Confesseur* (Chartres: Association des Amis du Centre Medieval de Chartres, 2000).

14. Torstein Tollefsen, *The Christocentric Cosmology of Maximus the Confessor* (Oxford: Oxford University Press, 2008).

15. D. A. Pospelov, *Disput s Pirrom: prp. Maksim Ispovednik I khristologischeskie spory VII stoletiia* (Moscow: Khram Sofii Premudrosti Bozhiei, 2004).

16. Philipp Gabriel Renczes, *Agir de Dieu et liberte de l'homme: recherches sur l'anthropologie theologiqu de saint Maxime le confesseur* (Paris: Cerf, 2003); Bernardo De Angelis, *Nature, persona, liberta: l'antropologia di Massimo il Confessore* (Roma: Armando, 2002); and Michael Weeks, *Maximus the Confessor: Re-ascending to God through his Anthropology* (MA thesis, 2002).

17. Antione Levy, *Le cree et l'incree: Maxime le confesseur et Thomas d'Aquin: Aux sources de la querelle palamienne* (Paris: Vrin, 2006); Luigi Manca, *Il primate della volonta in Agostino e Massimo il Confessore* (Rome: Armando, 2002); Edward Moore, *Origen of Alexandria and Maximus the Confessor: An Analysis and Critical Evaluation of Their Eschatological Doctrines* (PhD diss., 2005); and, interestingly, Georgios Varvatsoulias, *Neurose kata ten Karen Horney kai hoi anthropologikes theoreseis tou Hag. Maximou tou Homologetou: synkritike melete* (Athens: Ekdoseis Akritas, 2004).

18. Benjamin Blackwell, *The Two Natures of Christ and the Deification in Maximus the Confessor* (ThM thesis, Dallas Theological Seminary, 2002); Michael Jin Choi, *Spiritual Theology of the Lord's Prayer according to Maximus the Confessor* (PhD diss., Dallas Theological Seminary, 2002); Tamara Grdzelidze, *The Concept of Place/Space in the Writings of Maximus the Confessor: Liturgical Space according to the Mystagogia* (DPhil diss., University of Oxford, 1998); Edward Siecienski, *The Use of Maximus the Confessor's Writing on the Filioque at the Council of Ferrara-Florence (1438–1439)* (PhD diss., Fordham University, 2005); Elena Vishnevskaya, *Perichoresis in the Context of Divinization in Maximus the Confessor's Vision of a Blessed and Most Holy Embrace* (PhD diss., Drew University, 2004); and mine, Despina D. Prassas, *Maximus the Confessor's Questions and Doubts: Translation and Commentary* (PhD diss., The Catholic University of America, 2003). This does not include the numerous theses that have emerged from the European universities, especially the works produced under the direction of +Prof. Nikos Matsoukas at Aristotle University, Thessalonica, Greece.

19. A. N. S. Lane, *A Concise History of Christian Thought* (Grand Rapids, Mich.: Baker Academic, 2006); G. R. Evans, *The First Christian Theologians: An*

Introduction to Theology in the Early Church (Malden, Mass.: Blackwell, 2004); and Normal Russell, *The Doctrine of Deification in the Greek Patristic Tradition* (New York: Oxford University Press, 2004), to name a few.

20. José H. Declerck, *Quaestiones et dubia*, CCSG 10 (Louvain: Brepols, 1982). Hereafter in notes, this work will be referred to simply as "Declerck."

21. Emmanuel Ponsoye, trans., *Maxime le Confesseur: Questions et difficultés*, intro. Jean-Claude Larchet (Paris: Cerf, 1999).

22. Michael Exaboulites, *In vitam ac certamen*, PG 90.68-109, hereafter, simply *In vitam ac certamen*. For a full discussion of the available sources on Maximus's life, see Neil and Allen, *Life of Maximus*; and Pauline Allen and Bronwen Neil, *Scripta Saeculi VII: Vitam Maximi Confessoris Illustrantia una cum latina interpretatione Anastasii Bibliothecarii iuxta posita*, CCSG 39 (Turnhout: Brepols, 1999). For a translation of several of the texts found in the CCSG volume, see Allen and Neil, *Documents from Exile*.

23. Regarding the Exaboulites *Vita*, see Wolfgang Lackner, "Zu Quellen und Datierung der Maximosvita (*BHG*3 1234)," AnBoll 85 (1967), 285–316. Not everyone agrees with Lackner's position. For a discussion of the various views, see Pauline Allen, "Blue-print for the Edition of *Documenta ad vitam Maximi Confessoris spectantia*," in *After Chalcedon: Studies in Theology and Church History offered to Professor A. Van Roey for his Seventieth Birthday*, OLA 18 (1985), 14–17.

24. Published in 1973 by Sebastian Brock, "An Early Syriac Life of Maximus the Confessor," AnBoll 91, 299–346.

25. Both Brock, in "An Early Syriac Life," 336, and Robert G. Hoyland, in *Seeing Islam as Others Saw It: A Survey and Evaluation of Christian, Jewish and Zoorastrian Writings on Early Islam*, vol. 13 (Princeton: Darwin, 1997), 139, suggest that the *Vita* was probably written close to the time of the Sixth Ecumenical Council (680). However, it is possible the text could have been written several decades later, either in the seventh or the eighth century. See William Wright, *Catalogue of Syriac Manuscripts in the British Museum Acquired Since the Year 1838*, vol. 3 (London: Cambridge University Press, 1872), 1206.

26. Jean-Claude Larchet provides an excellent overview and criticism of the discussion of the two vitae in *La divinisation de l'homme selon saint Maxime le Confesseur* (Paris: Cerf, 1996), 8–12. The latest decision regarding the more accurate account of Maximus's early life is found in Bronwen Neil's introduction in Neil and Allen, *Life of Maximus*, 11–12, where she sides with the Greek *Vita*.

27. Brock, "An Early Syriac Life," sec. 1, 314.

28. Ibid., sec. 3 and 4, 314–15.

29. *In vitam ac certamen*, PG.128C.

30. Ibid., 69A and C.

31. Nichols, *Byzantine Gospel*, 15. See also, Ihor Sevcenko, "The Definition of Philosophy in the *Life of Saint Constantine*," For Roman Jakobson (The Hague: Mouton, 1956), 449–57.

32. Μήτε μὴν πεῖραν ἔχειν τῆς πρὸς λέγειν δυνάμεώς τε καὶ τριβῆς ἰδιωτεῖ συντεθραμμένος (*Myst.*, 660B6–8). Andrew Louth does not take this statement seriously; see *Maximus the Confessor*, Early Church Fathers (London: Routledge, 1996), 4n4.

33. For more on this position, see *asekretis*, ODB, 1, 204.

34. For questions regarding the date and significance of Maximus's appointment, see Wolfgang Lackner, "Der Amtstitel Maximos des Bekenners," *Jahrbuch der Oesterreichischen Byzantinistik* 20 (1971), 64–65.

35. *In vitam ac certamen,* PG 90.72C. According to Pauline Allen, the description of Maximus's early years in the first recension "conforms strictly to the conventions of the genre, with the usual account of noble origins, a perfect boyhood, and an adolescence committed solely to the study of theology and philosophy." Neil and Allen, *Life of Maximus,* 6.

36. Letter 12, PG 91.505B.

37. Maximus's extant letters (epistles) number forty-five. See the following letters for references to John the Cubicularius: *Ep.* 2 (PG 91.392D–408B), *Ep.* 3 (PG 91.408C–412C), *Ep.* 4 (PG 91.413A–420C), *Ep.* 10 (PG 91.449A–453A), *Ep.* 12 (PG 91.460A–509B), *Ep.* 27 (PG 91.617B–620C), *Ep.* 44 (PG 91.641D–648C), and *Ep.* 45 (PG 91.648D–649C).

38. PG 91.393A, 408C, 413A, 420B. It is unclear whether Maximus and John saw each other face to face after Maximus entered the monastery. There is mention of a meeting in the first few lines of Letter 2 (PG 91.393A), καὶ ἤ δη μὲν μαθὼν παρ 'ἐμαυτοῦ παρὼν . . . , which Larchet seems to interpret as a recent meeting. See *Maxime le Confesseur: Lettres,* trans. Emmanuel Ponsoye, intro. Jean-Claude Larchet (Paris: Cerf, 1998), 36. However, the phrase could also refer to their time together at court.

39. Letters 2, 3, and 4. See Polycarp Sherwood, *An Annotated Date-List of the Works of Maximus the Confessor,* SA, fasc. 30 (Rome: Herder, 1952), 25.

40. Venance Grumel, "Notes d'histoire et de chronologie sur la vie de saint Maxime le Confesseur," *Echos d'Orient* 26 (1927), 25.

41. The monastery of Philippikos at Chrysopolis was constructed in 594 by Philippikos, a general who had a less-than-stellar career during the reigns of both Maurice and Phokas. He was brother-in-law to Maurice. The monastery was dedicated to the Mother of God, and during the reign of Phokas, Philippikos was tonsured and exiled to the monastery. Brought back to work by Heraclius in the winter of 612–13, the general died soon after and was buried at the monastery. See *Philippikos* in *ODB* 3, 1654.

42. *In vitam ac certamen,* PG 90.72D. For more on the monasteries in the suburbs of Constantinople, see Michel Kaplan, "L'hinterland religieux de Constantinople: moines et saints de banlieue d'après l'hagiographie" in *Constantinople and its Hinterland,* ed. Cyril Mango and Gilbert Dagron (Hampshire, Great Britain: Variorum, 1995), 191–205. On why a person would turn from the world and become a monk, see Peter Charanis, "The Monk as an Element of Byzantine Society," *DOP* 25, 79–80. The Emperor Maurice, finding so many of his soldiers leaving military service to take up the monastic life, would not allow soldiers to become monks. See Andreas N. Stratos, *Byzantium in the Seventh Century,* trans. M. Ogilvie-Grant. (Amsterdam: Adolf M. Hakkert, I: 602 CE–634 CE, 1968; II: 634 CE–641 CE, 1972; III: 642 CE–668 CE, 1975; V: 668 CE–685 CE, 1978; V: 686 CE–711 CE, 1980), I:8.

43. *Ep.* 12, PG 91.505B.

44. *In vitam ac certamen,* PG 90.72.

45. Sherwood, *Date-List,* 9; Georges Florovsky, *The Byzantine Fathers of the Sixth to Eighth Century,* The Collected Works of Georges Florovsky 9, trans. Raymon Miller, Anne-Marie Döllinger-Labriolle and Helmut Schmiedel

(Vaduz, Liechtenstein: Büchervertriebsanstalt, 1987), 208; Lars Thunberg, *Microcosm and Mediator: The Theological Anthropology of Maximus the Confessor* (Lund, Sweden: Gleerup, 1965; repr., Chicago: Open Court, 1995), 2; Joseph Farrell, *Free Choice in St. Maximus the Confessor* (South Canaan, Pa.: Tikhon's, 1989), 20.

46. *Ep.* 6, PG 91.424C–433A. Sherwood dates this letter to before 624 but states that it could be before or after Maximus's stay at Cyzikos. He concludes it must be before.

47. Maximus attended many official meetings, and he was always referred to as a monk rather than an abbot. Had he been a *hegoumenos*, he would have been addressed by his title, Grumel, "Notes d'histoire," 32.

48. Florovsky, *Byzantine Fathers*, 209.

49. Ibid.

50. Mansi, X, 910D. For a discussion on Maximus's role in the drafting of the decisions of the Lateran Council, see Rudolf Riedinger, "Die Lateran Synode von 649 und Maximos der Bekenner," in *Maximus Confessor: Actes du Symposium sur Maxime le Confesseur, Fribourg, 2–5 septembre 1980*, Felix Heinzer and Christoph von Schönborn, eds. Paradosis 27. (Fribourg: Éditions Universitaires, 1982), 111–21.

51. Pauline Allen mentions two manuscripts, *BHG* 1233m (10, 5–6) and *BHG* 1236 (22, 32–33), that suggest Maximus stayed at the monastery of Arsenius. Allen, "Blue-Print," 18n49.

52. George Ostrogorsky, *History of the Byzantine State*, rev. ed., trans. Joan Hussey (New Brunswick, N.J.: Rutgers University Press, 1969), 95.

53. Sherwood, *Date-List*, 25. Larchet disagrees; see page 42 in his introduction in *Lettres*.

54. *In vitam ac certamen*, PG 90.168A. Anastasius, who had been the secretary to Heraclius's second wife, Martina, became Maximus's disciple in 618. Cyzikos (Κύζικος) became the metropolis of the province of the Hellespont under the reign of Diocletian (284–305), who established there the headquarters of a legion and an imperial mint. Though half the city was destroyed by an earthquake in 539, it would remain a strategic base for any military activity, whether by the Byzantines, the Arabs, the Turks, or the Latins. Cyzikos was the episcopal seat of the region of the Hellespont and therefore would have been surrounded by many monasteries. See *Kyzikos*, *ODB*, 2, 1164–5.

55. Robert Devreesse, "La fin inédite d'une lettre de saint Maxime: Un baptême forcé de juifs et de samaritains à Carthage en 632," *Revue des sciences religieuses* 17 (1937), 31.

56. *Ep.* 12, PG 91.461A.

57. There is no direct statement describing a stopover in Cyprus, but Maximus's relationship with Marinos, a Cypriot monk, would suggest a face-to-face meeting at one time. See *Ep.* 20, PG 91. The stop on Crete is reported in Opuscule 3 (PG 91.49C). Maximus took part in a discussion with Severian bishops there. He also met the bishop of Cydonia, to whom he wrote; see *Ep.* 21, PG 91.604.

58. *DP*, PG 91.288–353.

59. Mansi XI, 536E–537A.

60. Nichols, *Byzantine Gospel*, 18.

61. For a thorough discussion on the monothelite controversy and the development of monenergism which led to monothelitism, see Allen and Neil, *Documents from Exile*, 2–21.

62. Larchet, *La divinisation*, 18–19.

63. For a transcript of his trial, see *Relatio Motionis*, PG 91.109–129; for the critical edition of the Greek and Latin texts, see Allen and Neil, *Scripta Saeculi*, 12–51.

64. *Disputatio Bizyae*, PG 90.136–169; for the critical edition of the Greek and Latin texts, see Allen and Neil, *Scripta Saeculi*, 72–151.

65. Larchet, *La divinisation*, 20.

66. According to Wright (*Catalogue of Syriac Manuscripts*), the Syriac *vita* was written in either the seventh or eighth century. Brock also concedes that the *vita* is to be dated, "at the latest to the eighth century . . ." See Brock, "An Early Syriac Life," 336.

67. Jean Daniélou and Henri Marrou, *The Christian Centuries: The First Six Hundred Years*, vol. 1, trans. Vincent Cronin (Paramus, N.J.: Paulist Press, 1964), 377. For a discussion of early monasticism in Constantinople, see Gilbert Dagron, "Les moines et la ville. Le monachisme à Constantinople jusqu'au concile de Chalcédoine," *Travaux et Mémoires* 4 (1976), 229–76.

68. Kaplan, "L'hinterland religieux," 191.

69. Hippolyte Delehaye, "Byzantine Monasticism," chap. 5, *Byzantium: An Introduction to East Roman Civilization*, ed. Norman Baynes and Henry St. Lawrence Beaufort Moss. (Oxford: Clarendon, 1949).

70. Ibid., 145. On the Stylite saints in general, see Delehaye, "Les Saints stylites," Subsidia Hagiographica 14 (Brussels: Bollandistes, 1923).

71. *Theodosiani Libri*, ed. Theodor Mommsen and Paul Meyer (Berlin: Weidmannos, 1905), xvi, 3.1, vol. 1, part 2, 853.3.1, "Quicumque sub professione monachi repperiuntur, deserta loca et vastas solitudines sequi adque habitare iubeantur" and 3.2, "Monachos, quibus interdictae fuerant civitates, dum iudiciariis aluntur iniuriis, in pristinum statum submota hac lege esse praecipimus; antiquata si quidem nostrae clementiae iossione liberos in oppidis largimur eis ingressus." Canon 23 of Chalcedon (451) does not allow monks to be roaming the capital (*ΠΗΔΑΛΙΟΝ*, 202).

72. Cyril Mango, *Byzantium, The Empire of Rome* (New York: Scribner, 1980), 112.

73. Kaplan, "L'hinterland religiuex," 191.

74. Delehaye, "Byzantine Monasticism," 145.

75. Justinian issued the *Corpus Iuris Civilis* in three parts from 529 to 534; the three parts are the *Code of Law*, the *Digest*, and the *Institutes*. A number of other laws, called the *Novellae*, were issued later.

76. *Novella* v.ii.0, v.ii.2, and v.i.28, *Corpus Iuris Civilis*, vol. 3, eds. Rudolf Schoell and Guilelmus Kroll (Berlin: Weidmannos, 1928).

77. Canon 13, Mansi, II, col. 1101D.

78. Canon 14, col. 1101D–1104A.

79. Canon 15, col. 1104A.

80. Canon 16, col. 1104A.

81. Canon 17, col. 1104B.

82. Canon 19, col. 1104BC.

83. Mansi, XI, col. 959A.

84. Mansi, XI, col. 964E. It is unknown whether this canon superseded the third canon of Gangra (Mansi, II, 1101A) or the fourth canon of Chalcedon (Mansi, VII, col. 359CDE), both of which state that slaves are not allowed to enter monastic life without the permission of their owners.

85. Mansi, XI, col. 965A.

86. Mansi, XI, col. 965ABC.

87. Mansi, XI, col. 977CD.

88. John F. Haldon, *Byzantium in the Seventh Century: The Transformation of a Culture*, rev. ed. (Cambridge: Cambridge University Press, 1997), 366; see also, Peter Brown, "Rise and Function of the Holy Man in Late Antiquity," in *Society and the Holy in Late Antiquity* (Berkeley: University of California Press, 1982), 109.

89. Mansi, XI, cols. 969E–972A.

90. Anastasius of Sinai (d. after 700) addresses questions about false prophets and miracle workers in question 20 (PG 89.517C–532B), question 62 (PG 89.648A–652D), question 94 (PG 89.732B–733C), and question 108 (PG 89.761A–B).

91. Mansi, XI, col. 952CD.

92. For the "six successive moments" in Origenism, see *Enclycopedia of the Early Church*, ed. Angelo DiBerardino, trans. Adrian Walford (New York: Oxford University Press, 1992), 623–24; for more on the Origenist controversy, see Elizabeth Clark, *The Origenist Controversy: The Cultural Construction of an Early Christian Debate* (Princeton, N.J.: Princeton University Press, 1992).

93. Polycarp Sherwood, trans., *Maximus the Confessor: The Ascetic Life and Four Centuries on Charity*, ACW 21 (Westminster, Md.: Newman, 1957), 8. Sherwood, in *The Earlier Ambigua* [*The Earlier Ambigua of St. Maximus the Confessor and His Refutation of Origenism*, SA, fasc. 36 (Rome: Herder, 1955), 8] devotes a section to Maximus's adversaries: Ambigua 10 (PG 91.1180A2) and 39 (PG 91.1301B8) describe actual difficulties experienced among the monks at Cyzikos, while Ambigua 7 (PG 91.1089BC), 42 (PG 91.1336C, 1337B), and 15 (PG 91.1216C13) describe contemporary adversaries. Sherwood himself questions whether all the adversaries may have been contemporaries. See *The Earlier Ambigua*, 8n17.

94. Derwas Chitty, *The Desert as City: An Introduction to the Study of Egyptian and Palestinian Monasticism under the Christian Empire* (Oxford: Basil Blackwell, 1966), 123.

95. See note 132 in *Cyril of Scythopolis: The Lives of the Monks of Palestine*, trans. Richard M. Price, annotated John Binns, CS 114 (Kalamazoo, Mich.: Cistercian Publications, 1991), 219, tracing the development of Origenist thought from Justinian's Edict of 543 against Origenism to the Council of Constantinople in 553.

96. Tribes attacked the Lavra of Sabas, torturing and killing forty-four monks. Stratos, *Byzantium* I.108. Chitty, *The Desert as City*, 155.

97. *Vita Euthymii*, 11.10–15, TU 49:2.

98. Charanis, "The Monk," 81.

99. From the time of Pachomius, monasteries were required to have libraries; see ibid.

100. Ibid., 80. If a monk did not know how to read he learned by "studying three times a day with the one who was capable of teaching him."

101. Theodore Studite, *Constitutiones Studitanae*, PG 99.1713.

102. In the sixth century, Justinian did not support pagan learning. He closed the academy at Athens though it did continue to function in a diminished way, he withdrew state subsidies for teachers; promulgated laws forbidding pagans, heretics, and Jews to teach; and, in general, weakened the educational system of the empire.

103. In the seventh century, there was a variety of monastic literature being produced: stories, such as those found in John Moschus's *Spiritual Meadow* (PG 87.2852–3112); John Climacus's instructional text for spiritual fathers, *Ad Pastorem* (PG 88.1165–1208); and *quaestiones*. These writings also provided spiritual guidance of the type found in Evagrius's *Chapters on Prayer*.

104. For a discussion of the different monastic genres, see Jean Leclercq, *The Love of Learning and the Desire for God: A Study of Monastic Culture*, 3rd ed., trans. Catherine Misrahi (New York: Fordham University Press, 1982), chap. 8.

105. Examples include the *Apophthegmata Patrum* (PG 65.71–440); *Historia monachorum in Aegypto* (Brussels: Festugiere, 1961); and Palladios's *Historia Lausiaca* (Cambridge, England: Dom Cuthbert Butler, 1904).

106. Examples include Evagrius's *Praktikos* [trans. Antoine and Claire Guillaumont, SC 170–71 (Paris: Cerf, 1971)] and his *Kephalaia gnostica* [trans. Antoine Guillaumont, PO 28, 1 (Paris: 1958)]; the *Capita centum de perfectione spirituali* of Diadochus of Photike (SC 5ter, ed. Edouard des Places, 163); and the *Capita Hortatoria ad monachos in India* (PG 85.1837–60).

107. Miracle stories were recorded in the histories of the lives of monks. See the following: Theodoret's *Histoire des Moines de Syrie*, SC 234, 2.19,20; 9.5,7; 13.9,13; 14.3, trans. Pierre Canivet and Alice Leroy-Molinghen (Paris: Cerf, 1977) [English translation, *A History of the Monks of Syria*, CS 88, trans. Richard M. Price (Kalamazoo, Mich.: Cistercian Publications, 1985)]; Paphnutius's *Histories of the Monks of Upper Egypt*, CS 140, trans. Tom Vivian (Kalamazoo, Mich.: Cistercian Publications, 1993), 98–107; and Benedicta Ward, "'Signs and Wonders' Miracles in the Desert Tradition," StPatr 18 (Oxford: Pergamon, 1982), 539–42.

108. Examples include Cyril of Scythopolis's *vitae* of Euthymius, Sabas, John the Hesychast, Kyriacus, Theodosius, Theognius, and Abraamius [Eduardus Schwartz, ed., *Kyrillos von Skythopolis*, TU 49 (Leipzig: 1939), 2.]

109. Perhaps the most well known are the homilies of Pseudo-Makarius (PG 34.449–822). For the critical edition, see *Die 50 Geistlichen Homilien des Makarios*, ed. Hermann Dörries, Erich Klostermann, and Matthias Kroeger, PTS 6. (Berlin: De Gruyter, 1964).

110. For example, Barsanuphius and John [see *Questions and Answers*, ed. Derwas Chitty, PO, vol. 31, fasc. 3 (Paris: Firmin-Didot, 1966), 449–616] and Theodoret's *Octateuch* (PG 80.76–528).

111. With the possible exception of Letter 6 (PG 91.424C–433A) to Archbishop John of Cyzikos (see Sherwood, *Date-List*, 2 and 25). There seems to be a general dependence upon Sherwood for the dating of many of Maximus's writings. Van Deun raises the question of dating when he asks whether the *LA*, believed to have been written c. 626, could have been produced later and considered "comme un testament spirituel" [*Maximi Confessoris Liber Asceticus*, CCSG 40 (Turnhout: Brepols, 2000), xvii]. Maximus states that he worked out some of the more difficult passages of the *Orations*

of Gregory Nazianzus that contributed to the content of the *Amb.Io.* while at Cyzikos (PG 91.1064B8).

112. For the critical edition, see *Maximi Confessoris Opuscula Exegetica duo*, CCSG 23, ed. Peter van Deun (Turnhout: Brepols, 1991). Van Deun suggests this text may have been written in response to the Persian incursions of 626 since Psalm 59 speaks of being freed from the miseries of war. See page xxi.

113. Letters 2, 3, and 4, Sherwood, *Date-List*, 25. Nichols, *Byzantine Gospel*, 20 includes Letter 1.

114. *Amb.Io.*, PG 91.1064B8.

115. Larchet, *La divinisation*, 13

116. For dates and works, see Sherwood, *Date-List*, Part II, 23–56.

117. PG 91.212CD; Larchet, "Introduction" *in Maxime le Confesseur: Opuscules théologiques et polémiques*, trans. Emmanuel Ponsoye (Paris: Cerf, 1998), 19.

118. Larchet, "Introduction" in *Opuscules*, 8. Stephen Shoemaker believes it was probably written before 626 [see *Ancient Traditions of the Virgin Mary's Dormition and Assumption* (Oxford: Oxford University Press, 2002), 73]. For the critical edition, see Maximus the Confessor, *Life of the Virgin* [Michel van Esbroeck, ed., *Maxime le Confesseur, Vie de la Vierge*, 2 vols., CSCO 478–79 (Louvain: Peeters, 1986)].

119. Larchet, "Introduction" in *Opuscules*, 8. Brian Daley has also questioned its authenticity [see Hans Urs von Balthasar, *Cosmic Liturgy: The Universe According to Maximus the Confessor*, trans. Brian Daley (San Francisco: Ignatius, 2003), 77n94]. See also, van Esbroeck, *Vie de la Virge*, xxxi, where the author argues in favor of the text's authenticity. See also, Shoemaker, *Ancient Traditions*, 73–74, where he recognizes scholars who have acknowledged the authenticity, n160.

120. For the critical edition, see Declerck.

121. Sherwood, *Date-List*, 26.

122. Sergei L. Epifanovich, *Materials to serve in the study of the life and works of Maximus the Confessor* (in Russian) (Kiev: 1917), 7. For criticism of the criteria of Epifanovich, see Declerck, XV.

123. M.-Th. Disdier, "Une oeuvre douteuse de saint Maxime le Confesseur," *Echos d'Orient* 30 (1931), 102n1.

124. Hans Urs von Balthasar, *Die "Gnostichen Centurien" des Maximus Confessor*, Frieburger Theologische Studen, Heft 61 (Freiburg in Breisgau: 1941), 149–56. For criticism of these criteria, see Irénée-Henri Dalmais, "L'oeuvre spirituele de saint Maxime le Confesseur. Notes sur son developement et sa signification," *La Vie Spirituelle*, suppl. 6 (1952), 219.

125. Paul M. Blowers, *Exegesis and Spiritual Pedagogy in the "Quaestiones ad Thalassium" of St. Maximus the Confessor*, An Investigation of the *Quaestiones ad Thalassium*. Christianity and Judaism in Antiquity 7 (Notre Dame: University of Notre Dame Press, 1991), chap. 1.

126. Blowers, *Exegesis*, 28. He states: "The *quaestio-responsio* was never destined to be a pure literary genre *per se* but primarily a teaching device adaptable to a wide variety of literary formats." For the history of the genre within the Christian tradition, see Gustave Bardy, "La littérature patristique des 'Quaestiones et Responsiones' sur l'Écriture sainte," *RB* 41

(1932): 210–36, 341–69, 516–37; and *RB* 42 (1933): 14–30, 211–29, 328–52. See also Blowers, *Exegesis*, chap. 1. For Maximus, in particular, see Bardy, "La litterature patristique," *RB 42*, 332–39. Also called zetematic literature with titles referring to ζητήματα, λύσεις, πεύσεις, ἐρωτήσεις, ἀποκρίσεις, this literary form had apologetic, public, and educative properties. See Sze-kar Wan, "Philo's *Quaestiones et solutiones in Genesim*: A Synoptic Approach," SBL 1993 Seminar Papers, 36–37. For a criticism of what constitutes zetematic literature, see Hermann Dörries, "Erotapokriseia," (B. christlich), *Reallexikon für Antike und Christentum*, vol. 6, cols. 347–70.

127. *Ep.* 13, PG 91.533A.

128. *QD* 32. Diadochus is also mentioned by name in *DP* (PG 91.301C). Irénée Hausherr states that Maximus had studied the works of Diadochus very carefully: *Philautie: De la tendresse pour soi à la charité selon saint Maxime le Confesseur*, OCA 137 (Rome: Pontificale Institutum Orientalium Studiorum, 1952), 42.

129. *QD* 142 and II, 14.

130. For the question of whether Maximus read Origen, see Daley, *Cosmic Liturgy*, 127–36, who has proven from Maximus's *GC* (PG 90.1084–1173) that Maximus had read Origen's work. For his refutation of the Origenism of his time, see Sherwood, *The Earlier Ambigua*, part 2.

131. Sherwood sees the possibility of Maximus having Origen's *De Principiis* before him while writing the *Ambigua*. See *The Earlier Ambigua*, 88–92.

132. For example, see *paralipomena*, chap. 4 in *Pachomian Koinonia II*, CS 46, trans. Armand Veilleux (Kalamazoo, Mich.: Cistercian Publications, 1981), 28–29.

133. Han Urs von Balthasar has suggested that Maximus had been heavily influenced by Origen in his earlier writings but seems to have cooled to him by the time he writes *Ambiguum 7*. See von Balthasar, *Die "Gnostichen Centurien*," 42. Sherwood also speaks of Maximus's refutation of Origen in *The Ascetic Life*, 8–9.

134. Origen, *Selecta in Psalmos*, PG 12.1220A.

135. Origen, *De Principiis*, 1.6.2.

136. Marcel Viller, "Aux sources de la spiritualité de saint Maxime: Les oeuvres d'Évagre le Pontique" *Revue d'ascetique et de mystique* 11 (1930), 156–84, 239–68, 331–36.

137. PG 40.1220C–1221C.

138. *On the Ecclesiastical Hierarchy*, 6, 3, 3 (PG 3.536A).

139. *On Renunciation*, PG 88.1617B–1640D, and Lucien Regnault and J. de Préville, trans., SC 92, 146–84. The English translation is found in *Dorotheus of Gaza: Discourses and Sayings*, trans. Eric P. Wheeler, CS 33 (Kalamazoo, Mich.: Cistercian Publications, 1977), 86–88.

140. *Institutes* 1, trans. J. C. Guy, SC 109, 34–54.

141. Manlio Simonetti, *Biblical Interpretation in the Early Church: An Historical Introduction to Patristic Exegesis*, trans. John A. Hughes, ed. Anders Bergquist and Markus Bockmuehl (Edinburgh: T&T Clark, 1994), 1.

142. Philo, *De somniis*, 2, 47, 2.

143. Didymus the Blind, *Fragmentum in Psalmos*, 802, 11 and 825, 4.

144. "*Logos* of discretion" is found in Philo, *Legum allegoriarum* II, 78; II, 98; II, 99.

145. Commentary on "hand as action" is found in *Legum allegoriarum*, III, 43, 8; III, 45; *Quod dues sitimmutabilis*, 135, 4; and in *De congressu eruditionis gratia* 113, 8.

146. The name of Origen is only mentioned once in connection with Maximus: in *Relatio motionis* (PG 90.120AB), Maximus is accused of Origenism and of leading others to this teaching. Maximus proclaims an anathema on Origen. See Neil and Allen, *Life of Maximus*, 16.

147. There is a story of an encounter between Antony and Didymus where the great monk praises Didymus's spiritual sight. See Richard Layton, *Didymus the Blind and his Circle in Late-Antique Alexandria* (Urbana: University of Illinois Press, 2004), 25.

148. Ibid., 31. For an example of Maximus's use of an interpretation also found in Didymus, see *QD* 73, where the word "Sinai" is interpreted as "temptation" (Didymus, *Fragmentum in Psalmos* 14, PG 69.694A). In all, there are nine interpretations in the *QD* that are found exclusively in both Maximus and Didymus.

149. Simonetti, *Biblical Interpretation*, 78. For Didymus, the term *anagoge* was used more often than "allegory." Simonetti says that "allegory seems to indicate the interpretative procedure in a broad sense, while *anagoge* indicates the Christian content of the allegory" (85n31).

150. The *QT* (CCSG 7 and 22), *Amb.Io.* (in Greek, PG 91.1061–1417; in Latin, CCSG 22), and the *Opuscula* (PG 91.9–285). The word θέλημα appears three times in the *QD* (*QD* 21: τὸ αὐτεξούσιον θέλημα; *QD* 83: the entire question addresses διαφόρων θελημάτων θεου[n]; and *QD* I 45, where the author speaks of the importance of not having one's own will.) There is never a direct reference made in the *QD* to either one or two wills in Christ.

151. Ceresa-Gastaldo lists forty manuscripts from which he compiles the critical edition of the *CC*, and van Deun lists sixty-two for the *LA*. Declerck lists thirteen manuscripts for the *QD*.

152. *CC* and *LA*, both of which Sherwood dates to before 626 (*Date-List*, 26), were written at approximately the same time as the *QD*. These works were thought to have been composed while Maximus was either at Chrysopolis or Cyzikos. This time of literary activity would only be surpassed by Maximus's work at Carthage, where he arrived sometime before 632 (Sherwood, *The Ascetic Life*, 10).

153. José H. Declerck, "La tradition des 'Quaestiones et dubia' de S. Maxime le Confesseur" in *Maximus Confessor: Actes du Symposium sur Maxime le Confesseur, Fribourg, 2–5 septembre 1980*, Felix Heinzer and Christoph von Schönborn, eds. Paradosis 27. (Fribourg: Éditions Universitaires, 1982), 85–96; Utto Riedinger, "Die 'Quaestiones et Dubia' (Erotapokriseis) des Maximos Homologetes im Codex Vaticanus graecus 1703 (s.10)," in *Byzantinischneugriechische Jahrbucher* 19 (1966), 260–76; Giannelli, "Una 'editio maior,'" 100–111 (this article has been reproduced in Carlo Giannelli, *Scripta minora* (*Studi bizantini e neoellenici* 10 [1963], 215–24, and all references are to this last publication); Jean-Claude Larchet, "Introduction," *Maxime le Confesseur: Questiones et difficultés*. (Paris: Cerf, 1999), 7–26; Ἰγνάτιος Μ. Σακαλής, Εἰσαγωγή", *ΜΑΞΙΜΟΣ Ο ΟΜΟΛΟΓΗΤΗΣ*, Φιλοκαλία τῶν Νηπτικῶν καὶ Ἀσκητικῶν᾿Α, Παναγιώτης Κ. Χρήστου, Θεσσαλονικη· Πατερικαὶ Ἐκδόσεις "Γρηγόριος Ὁ Παλαμᾶς", 1992, 7–8; Bardy, "La litterature patristique," 337–

39; see also, Blowers, *Exegesis*, 53–56. Translations of the *QD* are in French in *Questiones et difficultes*, trans. Emmanuel Ponsoye (Paris: Cerf, 1999), 29–187, and in Greek, in Σακαλῆς, *ΜΑΞΙΜΟΣ Ο ΟΜΟΛΟΓΗΤΗΣ*, 10–347; there are translations of specific questions of the *QD* in Blowers, *Exegesis*, 54, 55, 231n36, 236n75; Larchet, *La divinisation*, 105n79, 122n150, 175n313, 209–10, 279, 387; Alain Riou, *Le monde et l'eglise selon Maxime le Confesseur*, ThH 22 (Paris: Beauchesne, 1973), 211; and Juan Miguel Garrigues, *Maxime le Confesseur: La charité, avenir divin de l'homme*, ThH 38 (Paris: Beauchesne, 1976), 111, 130n13, 144n20, 160–61, 190.

154. Sherwood, *The Earlier Ambigua*, vii.

155. Blowers, *Exegesis*, 255. According to Bardy's categories, which he admits are not exact, it is difficult to determine into which of his two categories (artificial/authentic) an interrogation may fall; see Bardy, "La littérature patristique," 351.

156. Blowers, *Exegesis*, 54. In comparing the *QT* to the *QD*, Blowers says both texts have "clear affinities . . . except for the obvious difference that these [the interrogations of the *QD*] are his [Maximus's] own queries."

157. "On ne trouve dans les questions et dans leurs reponses aucune allusion a des interlocuteurs ou a des correspondants qui viendrait justifier cette derniere hypothese (correspondants estrangers), mais celle-ci n'est pas imporbable si l'on considere que Maxime fut toute sa vie durant, et des les premieres anees de sa vie monastique, frequemment consulte sur des questions spirituelles et theologiques par de nombreuses personnes . . ." Larchet, "Introduction" in *Questiones et difficultes*, 8.

158. There are two letters to the abbot, Thalassius [numbers 40 (CCSG 7, 267–77) and 41 (CCSG 7, 279–83)] referring to the request that Maximus answer certain questions. The *QT* would comprise these responses. Although Letter 40 is addressed to Thalassius, Paul Canart claims that it was sent to Stephen. See Paul Canart, "La deuxieme lettre a Thomas de S. Maxime le Confesseur," *Byzantion* 34 (1964), 425–26. There is no record of a request from Theopemptus; the introductory letter of the *Amb.Io.* hints that Archbishop John had commanded Maximus to record the substance of their discussions on some of the difficult passages of Gregory the Theologian (PG 91.1064B); in the Prologue to the *Amb.Th.*, Maximus states that the task of answering the questions has been demanded of him (PG 91.1032B-33A).

159. The first (and last) pages of the most complete witness, *Vat.gr. 1703*, are mutilated, and all the other manuscripts containing the *QD* lack any reference to a recipient. See Declerck, X. Declerck also states that seventeen quires precede the beginning of the *QD*, though they have disappeared, and that all would not have contained questions of the *QD* (Declerck, XVIII).

160. Larchet, "Introduction" in *Opuscules*, 8.

161. Possible recipients of the *QD* from among those with whom Maximus corresponded before 626 include the following: Archbishop John of Cyzikos, [Letter 6 is dated to before 626 according to Sherwood (*Date-List*, 25), and Maximus continued his relationship with the archbishop after he was forced to leave Cyzikos (Letters 8 and 28–31)]; Archbishop John, to whom the *Amb.Io.* is directed; Auxentius (*Ep.* 22, PG 91.636C–638B), though there is no way of determining when Maximus wrote to him (Sherwood, *Date-List*, 25; Larchet agrees, see "Introduction," *Letters*, 41); the *hegoumenos*,

Polychronios (*Ep.* 32–39, PG 91.625D–33B), who provided Maximus's community with food and was something of a spiritual child to Maximus (Sherwood, *Date-List*, 43); the priest and *hegoumenos*, Stephan (*Ep.* 23 and 40, PG 91.605D–606B, and 633C–636A), and even though Sherwood dates Letter 23 to the time after Maximus left Cyzikos, he hints at the possibility of Maximus knowing the abbot during his stay at Chrysopolis (*Date-List*, 33); the priest and *hegoumenos*, Conon (*Ep.* 25, PG 91.613A–D), whom Sherwood believes to have been the abbot of a monastery in Africa, (*Date-List*, 40) while Larchet disagrees with that assessment: "Elle peut être écrite . . . depuis le monastère de Cyzique a l'higoumène d'un monastère de la même région ou de la région de Constantinople" ("Introduction," *Lettres*, 48); and, though unlikely, the *hegoumene*, Jania (*Ep.* 11, PG 91.453A–457D). Although this letter is anonymous, Photios believed Jania to be the recipient. See Codex 192 (PG 103.648D). Sherwood, who does not give a date to the letter, puts it during Maximus's stay in Africa (*Date-List*, 43). Nuns did read the works of Maximus; "(Neilos) Damilas especially recommended to the nuns the works of Maximus the Confessor, specifically the *Logos Ascetikos* and the *Kephalaia peri agapes* . . . ," according to Alice-Mary Talbot in "Bluestocking Nuns: Intellectual Life in the Convents of Late Byzantium," *Okeanos: Essays presented to I. Sevcenko on his Sixtieth Birthday by his Colleagues and Students*, Harvard Ukranian Studies 7, ed. Cyril Mango and Omeljan Pritsak (Cambridge: Ukrainian Research Institute, 1983), 608.

162. For the oral tradition in monasticism, see Douglas Burton-Christie, "Oral Culture, Biblical Interpretation, and Spirituality in Early Christian Monasticism" in *The Bible in Greek Christian Antiquity*, Paul Blowers, ed. and trans. (Notre Dame: University of Notre Dame Press, 1977), 415–40, especially 417–22.

163. *QD* I, 69; I, 70; I, 71.

164. In the *Amb.Io.*, even though Maximus twice refers to John directly using the singular form of address (*Amb.Io.* 6, PG 91.1065B and *Amb.Io.* 38, PG.91.1300C6), more often he uses the plural form of the noun. Perhaps he uses the more formal plural for Archbishop John as a sign of reverence. But in *Amb.Io.* 45 (PG 91.1352C12) there is a reference to "my good fathers," which would indicate a group of priests or elder monks. See Sherwood, *The Earlier Ambigua*, 7.

165. *QD* 15, 49, 71, 80, and 184. See Antoon Schoors, "Biblical Onomastics in Maximus Confessor's '*Quaestiones ad Thalassium*'" in *Philohistor, Miscellanea in honorem Caroli Laga septuagenarii*, Antoon Schoors and Peter van Deun, eds. OLA 69 (1994), 257–72.

166. *QD* 49, 56, 80, 117, 164, and 165.

167. There are 122 references to the soul, ψυχή, in the *QD*.

168. *QD* 116, 121, 173, and 175. For a discussion of the *logoi* in Maximus, see Irénée-Henri Dalmais, "La théorie des 'logoi' des créatures chez saint Maxime le Confesseur," *Revue des sciences philosophiques et théologiques* 36 (1952), 244–49; and Eric Perl, *Methexis: Creation, Incarnation, Deification in Saint Maximus Confessor* (PhD diss., Yale, 1991), 147–59, 166–79.

169. Found in the *QT*, Thunberg, *Microcosm*, 144n311.

170. Specifically, *Amb.Io.* 7, PG 91.1069A. See Thunberg, *Microcosm*, 81–83, especially n217.

171. *Ep.* 12–18, PG 91.460–589B.

172. *Op.* 3 (PG 91.45B–56D) and 7 (69B–89B), and the *DP* (PG 91.287–353).

173. Giannelli, *Scripta minora*, 218.

174. Larchet lists sixty-seven questions that provide an allegorical exegesis. See "Introduction," *Questiones et difficultés*, 12–13.

175. Τρόπος and its various forms appear forty-seven times, while ἀναγωγὴ and its forms appear twenty times.

176. Θεωρία appears fifty times, πρᾶξις appears ninety-seven times, and ἀρετὴ appears over one hundred times.

177. PG 91.1352C.

178. The first recension consists exclusively of *Vat.gr. 1703*, 195 questions dating from the tenth century; the 83 questions of the second recension (Selection I) are represented in *Vat.gr. 2020* (c.); *Par. gr. 174* (10th/11th c.); *Scor.Y.III.3* (10th/11th c.); *Coislin. 267* (12th c.); *Par. gr. 1277* (13th c.); *Vat.gr. 435* (ff. 9v-13v, 13th c.); *Par., suppl.gr. 256* (ff. 301v-304v, 14th c.); *Sinait.gr. 1609* (15th c.); *Vat.gr. 1744* (15th c,); Bellun., Bibl.Sem., 8 (15th/16th c.); *Dresd. A 187* (16th c.); *Taur. c.II.15* (16th c.); *Bucure, Bibl. Acad. Dacoromanae, gr. 691* (18th c.), and though containing a smaller number of questions, *Vat.gr. 2064* (12th c.); *Scor. e.IV.18* (15th c.); *Monac.gr. 277* (15th c.); the 27 questions of the third recension (Selection II) are found in *Vat.gr. 435, Par.suppl.gr. 256*, and another representative, *Ambros. H 22 sup.* (16th c.); the single question of the fourth recension (Selection III) is contained in *Vindobonensis philologicus graecus 149*, from the fourteenth century. For more detailed information about the manuscripts of the direct tradition, see Declerck, XXV–LXXVIII.

179. Ibid., IX.

180. Ibid.

181. Ibid., CCXXXVI.

182. Ibid., XCV.

183. Ibid., CCXL–CCXLI.

184. Ibid., CCXLIV. Specifically, *QD* 5, 17, 29, 31, 58, 71, 145, 190, 193.

185. Ibid., CCXLIV.

186. *QD* I, 7; I, 42; I, 44; and I, 16.

187. *QD* I, 28; I, 30; and I, 80.

188. Ibid., CCXLV.

189. Ibid., CCXLVI.

190. Ibid., CCXLVIII.

191. Ibid., LXXVIII.

192. The "errant" questions come from *Athonensis, Cutlumusii 9* (*QD* I, 68, 14th c.); *Athonensis, Iberorum 382* (*QD* 19, 15th c.); *Florentinus, Med.-Laur., plut.LXXXVI, 13* (*QD* 19, 14th c.); *Londinensis, British Library, Additional 17472* (*QD* I, 68, 14th c.); *Neapolitanus, Bibliothecae Nationalis, III AA 6* (*QD* 189, 13th c.); *Oxoniensis, Bodlieanus Cromwellianus 10* (*QD* 189, 15th/16th c.); *Parisinus graecus 1163* (*QD* I, 68, unknown date); *Parisinus graecus 1268* (*QD* 19, 12th c.); *Scorialensis R.I.8* (*QD* 19, 15th c., *QD* I, 68, 11th c.); *Laur.plut.IX.16* (four questions, 10th/11th c.); *Monacensis graecus 10* (2 questions, 16th c.); *Monacensis graecus 225* (two questions, 13th c.); *Oxoniensis, Bodlieanus Baroccianus 85* (four questions, 15th c.); *Scorialensis Y.III.2* (four questions, 13th c.); *Scorialensis Y.III.19* (five questions, 14th c.); *Vaticanus graecus 1700* (two questions, 14th c.);

Vaticanus graecus 1778 (two questions, 16th c.). For more on these manuscripts, see Declerck, LXXVIII–XCII.

193. Declerck, X. Declerck also acknowledges the existence of other witnesses through researching the catalogues that he was unable to obtain. He insists that the witnesses are very partial, and the majority do contain the same "errant" questions described above. A listing of these manuscripts: *Athonensis, Stavronikita 62* (*QD* 19, 14th/15th c.); *Cryptoferratensis B.a.VII* (*QD* I, 1, 12th/13th c.); *Florentios, Med.-Laur.,plut. VIII, 20* (*QD* 19, 10th/11th c.); *Mosquensis, Bibliothecae synodalis gr. 363* (information incomplete, 15th c.); *Oxoniensis, Bodlieanus Cromwellianus 7* (*QD* I, 68, 13th c.); *Petropolitanus, Bibliothecase publicae Saltykov-Scedrin, gr. 108* (two questions, 12th/13th c.); *Sinaiticus gr. 1864* (information incomplete, 17th c.); *Venetus Marcianus graecus 570* (*QD* I, 1, 11th c.); *Venetus Marianus graecus II, 85 (olim Nanianus CVII)* (*QD* 159, 14th c.). See Declerck, XCIII–XCIV.

194. Declerck, CCXLVI.

195. Ibid., CCXLVII.

196. Ibid., CXCIII.

197. Ibid.

198. Ibid., XII. The oldest witness of Selection I is *Vat.gr. 2020*.

199. For more details on how the order and priorities of the questions were determined, see Declerck, XI–XII.

200. Giannelli cites specific examples, "Una 'Editio Maior,'" 219–21.

201. Declerck, CLXXI. There was an increase in both *catenae* and *florilegia* in the seventh century, as a result of the decline of biblical exegesis. Karl Krumbacher, *Geschichte der Byzantinischen Litterator von Justinian bis zum Ende de ostromischen Reiches (572–1453)* (1897).

202. There are single fragments found in *catenae* on Matthew (type A), Luke (type I), John (type E), on the Acts of the Apostle by Andrew, on the Epistle to the Romans, and from *Vat.gr.349*. See Declerck, CXCVI–CCIII.

203. Declerck, CLXXII.

204. Ibid., CLXXIV. Declerck acknowledges problems regarding the authenticity of the questions found in the *catenae*; see CLXXIIn6. Manuscripts are categorized under the form distinguished by Georg Karo and I. Lietzmann in *Catenarum graecorum catalogus*, in Nachrichten von der Konigl, Gesellschaft der Wissenschaften zu Gottingen, Philologische-historische Klasse aus dem Jahre 1902, I, 20–66. The *catenae* on the Psalter, type I (*Oxon.,Bodl. Auct.D.4.1 (Misc.5)*, 9th c.), type II (*Vat.gr. 2057*, 10th/11th c.), type IV (*Mosq.,Bibl.Synod. gr. 194*, 10th/11th c.; *Vat.Ottob.gr. 398*, 11th/12th c.), type VIII (*Vat.Pal.gr.247*, 11th/12th c.; *Sinait.gr.23*, 12th/13th c.), type IX (*Vat.Reg.gr.40*, 13th c.), type X (*Oxon.,Bodl.Barocc.223*, 15th/16th c.; *Hierosol.,S.Crucis* I; *Vat.Borgian.gr.2–4*), type XIV (*Ambros.B.106 sup.*, 10th c.), type XV (*Par.gr.146*, 10th c.; *Vat.gr.1422*, 10th c.), type XVI (*Florent., Med.-Laur., plut.VI,3*, 11th c.), type XVII (*Vat.gr.744*, 10th c.), type XIX (*Vat.gr.754*, 10th c.), type XXIV (*Par.gr.169*, 14th c.), type XXVII (*Oxon.,Col.Trin.gr.78*, 10th c.). See Declerck, CLXXIII–CXCV, and Marcel Richard, "Les premieres chaines sur le Psalter" in *Bulletin d'information de l'Institut de Recherche et d'Histoire des Textes* 5 (1956), 87–98.

205. Declerck, CCXVII. The main *florilegia* examined include *flor. Coislin.I* (*Coislin.294*, 12th c.), *flor.Coislin.II* (*Par.gr.924*, 10th c.), and *flor. Coislin.III* (*Ambros.Q 74 sup.*, 10th c.; *Athon.,Iber. 38*, 13th c.; *Vat.gr.491*, 13th

c.; *Strasburg.gr. 12*, 13th c.), but also minor contributions are found in *Vat. gr.504*, 12th c.; *Neapolit.,Bibl.Nat., II B 18*, 13th c.; *Monac.gr.56; Leidens., BPG 67 A*, 17th c.; *Oxon., Bodl.Barocc.141, Floilegium Hierosolymitanum (Hierosol.,S. Sepulchri 15*, 10th/11th c. is the main codex), the *florilegia* of Ps.-Anastasios of Sinai (questions from the *QD* found in PG 89.616A), the *Evergetinon* of Paul, the "Thesaurus" of Theognostos, and other manuscripts (*Vind.phil. gr.149, Oxon.,Bodl.can.gr.15, Athon., Dionysii 180, Athon., Esphig. 29*). See Declerck, CCIV–CCXXII. Also see Marcel Richard, *Florileges spirituels grecs*, in Dictionnaire de Spiritualité 5, coll. 475–512 (Paris, 1962–64).

206. *Vat.gr. 504.*

207. Declerck, CCX–CCXI. *QD* I, 1.

208. Declerck, CLXXXIV.

209. Ibid., XIVn12.

210. With one exception; see Declerck, CLXXIIn7.

211. Ibid., CLXXII.

212. Ibid., XV.

213. The same question is raised by Bardy in *RB* 42 (1933), 337n3, and by Disdier, "Une oeuvre douteuse," 101n3, who believe there are interpolations, but neither offers concrete examples. Giannelli maintains that the burden of proof of interpolation rests in the hands of the critic. See "Un 'Editio Maior,'" 222.

214. Declerck, XV.

215. *QD* I, 29.

216. *QD* 80.

217. Citations from Gen number 82; Exod, 38; Lev, 23; Num, 20; Deut, 16; Josh, 15; Judg, 62; Kdgms (all four books), 34; Chr, 2; Ezra, 1; Job, 4; Ps, 56; Prov, 13; Eccl, 3; Song, 4; Sir, 1; Isa, 14; Jer, 3; Ezek, 5; Dan, 5; Sus, 1; Bel, 1; Hos, 1; Joel, 1; Amos, 9; Jonah, 8; Mic, 1; Hab, 5; Mal, 4.

218. Eighty-two, with nine references to Gen 1:26.

219. Citations from Matt number 74; Mark, 32; Luke, 50; John, 34; Acts, 29; Rom, 36 (with nine references to 8:6); 1 Cor, 34 (with eight references to 15:51); 2 Cor, 10; Gal, 4; Eph, 34; Phil, 3; Col, 1; 1 Thess, 1; 2 Tim, 1; Heb, 5; 1 Pet, 2; 2 Pet, 1; 1 John, 3.

220. Seventy-four, with seven references to Matt 16:28 and seven references to Mark 9:1, in question 190, where the two passages are compared.

221. Referenced in seven questions by name (*QD* 5, 9, 48, 95, 104, 105, and 137) and unnamed references in eight questions (*QD* 87, 96–103).

222. Three citations, two in *QD* 19, and one in *QD* 57.

223. Two named references, questions 142 and II, 14, and at least two unnamed references, questions 161 and I, 68.

224. *QD* 93, 94, and 108–110.

225. *QD* I, 10.

226. *QD* 55.

227. *QD* 32.

228. *QD* 119.

229. An unnamed reference, in *QD* I, 82.

230. *QD* 126.

231. Forty-nine incidences.

232. The Apostle, thirty-nine times, using both the title and his name.

233. Twenty-one times.

234. Sixteen times.

235. *QD* 50.

236. The word "principles" is taken from Karl Froehlich, "Introduction," *Biblical Interpretation in the Early Church* (Philadelphia: Fortress, 1984), 1.

237. For articles on Maximus's use of Scripture, see Polycarp Sherwood, "Exposition and Use of Scripture in Maximus as manifest in the *Quaestiones ad Thalassium*" *Orientalia christiana periodica* 24 (1958), 202–7; Paul Blowers, "The Analogy of Scripture and Cosmos in Maximus the Confessor"; George Berthold, "Levels of Scriptural Meaning in Maximus the Confessor" SP 27, 129–43; Rene Bornert, "Explication de la liturgie et interprétation de l'Écriture chez Maxime le Confesseur" SP 10, 323–27; John Kirchmeyer, "Un commentaire de Maxime le Confesseur sur le Cantique?" 406–13; and Lars Thunberg, "Early Christian Interpretations of the Three Angels in Gen 18," SP 7 (TU 92), 568–69.

238. Blowers, *Exegesis*, 57.

239. *QD* 182, for example, discusses all three. Many have written about this "three-fold spiritual development," as Thunberg calls it. See Thunberg, *Microcosm*, 332–61; Larchet, *La divinisation*, 451–57, 488–93, 495–96); and Sherwood, *The Ascetic Life*, 87–88, 98, to name a few.

240. There is always the possibility that Maximus may have Eph 6 in mind when he includes weaponry and other military terms.

241. Origen used many of these tools; see Henri Crouzel, *Origen*, trans. A. S. Worrall (Edinburgh: T&T Clark, 1989), 65–66. For more on the distinction between allegory and typology in Origen, see Peter W. Martens, "Revisiting the Allegory/Typology Distinction: The Case of Origen" *JECS* 16, 3 (2008), 283–317. Paul's use of allegory (Gal 4:22–26, for example) and typology (1 Cor 10:1–5) is well known, (Froehlich, *Biblical Interpretation*, 8–10), and though certain stories may have been enhanced by the evangelists, there are traces of allegory in Jesus's parables (Matt 13:3–9; 18–23; 24–30; 37–43). Blowers mentions specific forms such as typology, allegory, tropology, etymology, arithmology, and extrapolations from Biblical terms or language under the title of anagogy in his work on the *QT* in *Exegesis*, 196–228. For more on the role of arithmology in early Christian writings, see Joel Kalvesmaki's doctoral dissertation, *Formation of the Early Christian Theology of Arithmetic: Number Symbolism in the late second and early third centuries*, (PhD diss., The Catholic University of America, 2006).

242. The word διδασκαλία (*didaskalia*, "teaching") occurs thirty-five times in the *QD*; διδάσκαλος (*didaskalos*, "teacher") appears ten times; and various forms of διδάσκω (*didasko*, "I teach") appear eleven times.

243. For background on the significance of numbers in Hellenistic thought, see a writing attributed to Iamblicos, *The Theology of Arithmatic: On the Mystical, Mathematical and Cosmological Symbolism of the First Ten Numbers*, trans. Robin Waterfield (Grand Rapids, Mich.: Phanes, 1988). Many thanks to Joel Kalvesmaki for bringing this book to my attention. For background on the significance of numbers in the OT and NT, see "numbers" in Paul Achtemeier, *Harper's Bible Dictionary* (San Francisco: Harper & Row, 1985) 711–12.

244. Peter van Deun states, "Il ne faut pas toujours interpréter de la meme facon tel ou tel nombre" in "La symbolique des nombres dans l'oeuvre de Maxime le Confesseur (580–662)" Byzantinoslavica LIII (1992) fasc. 2, 238.

245. For other biblical examples of threes, see Achtemeier, *Harper's Bible Dictionary*, 712.

246. For the significance of the number five, see Iambicos, *The Theology of Arithmetic*, 55–63, and Plato, *Timaeus*, 32c.

247. Biblical symbols of the number forty include the days and nights of rain (Gen 7:12), Jesus's temptation in the wilderness (Mark 1:12), and Israel's wandering in the wilderness (Num 14:20–23).

248. The number seven is related to the number twenty-eight (there are twenty-eight days from new moon to new moon) by adding the numbers from one to seven. For the properties of the number seven, see Iambicos, *The Theology of Arithmetic*, 87–100. See also, Plato, *Timaeus*, 38d–39c.

249. Hippocrates also spoke of seven ages: child (from birth to the loss of one's baby teeth), boy (until puberty, at age fourteen), adolescent (until the growth of the beard), youth (until full growth of the body), man (until age forty-nine), elder (until age fifty-six), and an old man (beyond age fifty-six). See Iambicos, *The Theology of Arithmetic*, 87–88.

250. The number fifty also represents scientific knowledge (*QD* 49) and divine things (*QD* 155).

251. *QD* I, 78 addresses the third and fourth generations or transgressions.

252. One wonders if Maximus had access to any of the Christian allegorization lists that circulated at the time. *Papyrus Michigan Inv. 3718*, dated to the seventh century, reproduces a passage from Matt 19:24 ("it is easier for a camel to go through the eye of a needle than for a rich man [to enter] the kingdom of heaven") and lists the camel as Judas, the needle's eye as salvation, and the rich man as the devil (Froehlich, *Biblical Interpretation*, 79).

253. Philo, *Legum allegoriarum II*, 24.

254. *Vita Sabae* 33.

255. "Poemen," *Apophegmata Patrum*, 115.

256. *QD* I, 30.

257. *QD* 41.

258. The four colors of the rainbow represent the four basic elements (red represents fire, green represents earth, blue represents water, yellow represents air) and the four humors (blood, phlegm, black bile, yellow bile) that make up the earthly flesh of the Lord; see also, Iamblicos, *The Theology of Arithmatic*, 5.

259. Judg 7:3.

260. Ibid.

261. Judg 7:5–6.

262. Josh 10:22–26.

263. Josh 8:29.

264. Once in *QD* 90 and twice in *QD* 1, 8.

265. Paul Blowers calls Maximus's definition of allegory "curious" (*Exegesis*, 197) and suggests that the comments have "the look of a handbook definition that Maximus has perhaps reproduced" (*Exegesis*, 197). Blowers devotes several pages in his book to Maximus's use of typology, allegory, and tropology (*Exegesis*, 197–203).

266. Anagogy as a method of interpretation is also mentioned in *QD* 29, 38, 162, and I, 35.

267. The interrogations of *QD* 77 and 178 also request an anagogical interpretation.

268. The critical edition of the *LA* is found in *Maximi Confessoris Liber Asceticus*, ed. Steven Gysens, CCSG 40 (Turnhout: Brepols, 2000), 5–123. While other texts by Maximus may include some statement about having been asked to produce the treatise (see the "Introduction" to his *Myst.*, PG 91.657C–660A or "Prologue" to his *EOD*, CCSG 23, 28.35–36), the *LA* does not.

269. He acknowledges that there are various methods, *QD* 30.

270. *QD* II, 18.

271. Lampe, in *A Patristic Greek Lexicon*, states that Ναζιραῖος can be translated as Nazarite or ascetic; see page 896. See also, Basil of Caesarea, *Epistle* 44.1 (PG 32.361C) and Gregory Nazianzus, *Oratione* 42.26 (PG 36.489C).

272. *QD* 68.

273. Ibid.

274. Num 6:3–4.

275. James Mays, *Harper's Bible Commentary* (San Francisco: Harper & Row, 1988), 187.

276. Mays, *Harper's Bible Commentary*, 186. Mays also states that translating these skin diseases as leprosy is incorrect. Leprosy in the OT affected human beings, fabrics, and houses, but the leprosy of the OT is not the same disease known as leprosy today. See, "leprosy" in Achetmeier, *Harper's Bible Dictionary*, 555.

277. Anger, θυμός, is mentioned twenty times in the *QD*.

278. Maximus also uses the phrase "natural contemplation," φυσικὴ θεωρία.

279. There are 214 instances of the word Θεός (*theos*), 177 instances of κύριος (*kyrios*), 196 instances of λόγος (*logos*), 102 instances of πάθος (*pathos*), 82 instances of νόμος (*nomos*), 79 instances of νοῦς (*nous*), and 63 instances of πνεῦμα (*pneuma*).

280. Thirteen times: *QD* 17, 29, 30, 80, 87, 130, 142, 145, 162, 185, 187, 190, and I, 68.

281. This question provides two of the three times the word ἀπόφασις (*apophasis*) is mentioned in the *QD*. The other incidence is in *QD* 73.

282. Thunberg lists several more precise formulations of *praxis*, including practical philosophy, virtue, or ethical philosophy; see *Microcosm*, 335.

283. Though there is one example where knowledge is used as the mode, along with action, by which one gains supreme power, *QD* 80.

284. Thunberg also lists more precise definitions of *theoria*: knowledge, natural contemplation, natural philosophy, and gnostic contemplation. See *Microcosm*, 335.

285. For more on Maximus's sentence structure, see Carl Laga, "Maximus as a Stylist in *Quaestiones ad Thalassium*" in *Maximus Confessor: Actes du Symposium sur Maxime le Confesseur, Fribourg, 2–5 septembre 1980*, Felix Heinzer and Christoph von Schönborn, eds. Paradosis 27. (Fribourg: Éditions Universitaires, 1982), 139–46. The author begins by paraphrasing Photios's evaluation of Maximus's style: "His style is artificial, impenetrable, lacking of restraint, and so dissolute that it disheartens even his most enthusiastic supporters." While Laga points out some of the difficulties, namely, that the text should not be read aloud because of the difficulty in following the sentences,

he also states that Maximus's style is one where the author is purposely trying to shorten his sentences by omitting certain grammatical structures. This is not what Burton-Christie means by the phrase "asceticism of language" (see "Oral Culture," 416), but perhaps the greatest difficulty in translating the Confessor's works comes when trying to "fill in the blanks" or identify the specific subjects and objects of sentences.

286. 1 Cor 15:26.

287. Exod 16:20.

288. *QD* 183, where the one who practices virginity does so as an expression of love for the Lord. See also *QD* 7, where, since Melchisedek did not have a wife, bishops who serve as priests should not be married.

289. *QD* 184.

290. *QD* 40.3, 6, and 13.

291. The word *Theotokos* is translated literally as "God-bearer" or more generally as "Mother of God" (Lampe, 639). See *Theotokos* in *Encyclopedia of the Early Church*, vol. 2 (New York: Oxford University Press, 1992), 833.

292. Maximus uses the word *gnosis* both as basic human knowledge and as knowledge of God. The *gnosis* that refers to God, according to Maximus, plays an essential role in the union of the human being with God (*theosis*) and is given by God. This knowledge is beyond human understanding and provides the person with an experience of God that takes place through the encounter with the energies of God (Larchet, *La divinisation*, 680). For a general explanation of *gnosis*, see Angelo DiBerardino, ed., *Encyclopedia of the Early Church*, vol. 1 (New York: Oxford University Press, 1992), 352, and "knowledge of God" in the same, 355–56; see also, Harry Austryn Wolfson, *The Philosophy of the Church Fathers: Faith, Trinity, Incarnation* (Cambridge, Mass.: Harvard University Press, 1976), 498–500.

293. Christopher Stead, *logos* in the Routledge Encyclopedia of Philosophy, Version 1.0, (London: Routledge, 1998); and Wolfson, *Philosophy of the Church Fathers*, 177–78; 192–286. Larchet, in *La divinisation*, 112–23, speaks of *logos* in terms of divinization : "Il definit par avance sa fin, le but vers lequel il doit tendre et dans lequel il trovera son accomplissement, et cette fin est qu'il soit uni a Dieu et devienne dieu par participation." For more on the *logos* in general, see Sherwood, *The Earlier Ambigua*, chap. 4; Louth, *Maximus*, 57; and Thunberg, *Microcosm*, 415–18. For the relationship between *Logos* and word/Scripture, see Blowers, *Exegesis*, 102–12, 119–24. For the ancient idea of the *logoi* of creation, see Robert Lamberton, *Homer the Theologian* (Berkeley: University of California Press 1986), 39. Maximus developed the theory of the *logoi* to refute Origenism (see *Amb.Io.* 7, PG 91.1068D–1101C and Sherwood, *The Earlier Ambigua*, chap. 4), and he drew from the writings of Dionysius the Areopagite (*Amb. Io.*7, PG 91.1080B and 1085A), where Maximus specifically mentions Dionysius; for more on the *logoi* in Dionysius, see *Divine Names* 5, 5–10, PG 3.820A–825B, though Thunberg mentions other possible predecessors (*Microcosm*, 73n157). For more on the *logoi* in Maximus, see Dalmais, "La theorie des 'logoi,'" 244–49 and "La manifestation du Logos dans l'homme et dans l'Église: Typologie anthropolgique et typologie ecclésiale d'apres Qu. Thal. 60 et la Mystagogie" in *Maximus Confessor: Actes du Symposium sur Maxime le Confesseur Fribourg, 2–5 septembre 1980*, ed. Felix Heinzer and Christoph von Schönborn, Paradosis

NOTES TO PAGE 38

27 (Fribourg: Éditions Universitaires, 1980), 13–25; Alain Riou, *Le monde et l'eglise*, 54–63 and 88–92; Thunberg, *Man and the Cosmos: The Vision of St. Maximus the Confessor* (Crestwood, N.Y.: St. Vladimir's Seminary Press, 1984), 132–40; John Meyendorff, *Byzantine Theology: Historical Trends and Doctrinal Themes*, rev. 2nd ed., 131–34; Joost van Rossum, "The λόγοι of Creation and the Divine 'energies' in Maximus the Confessor and Gregory Palamas," StPatr 27, Elizabeth Livingston, ed. (Louvain: Peeters, 1993), 213–17; and Perl, *Methexis*, 147–59 and 166–79.

294. *Amb.Io.* 41, PG 91.1312B.

295. Thunberg, *Microcosm*, 400–4.

296. *Amb.Io.* 10, PG 91. 1129BC.

297. *Amb.Io.* 41, PG 91.1315B.

298. *QT* 28, CCSG 205.42–45.

299. *Amb.Io.* 10, PG 91.1204D–1205A.

300. Thunberg, *Microcosm*, 73n157.

301. This word has been translated as "ascetic struggle" [see George Berthold, "Chapters on Knowledge," II.94, *Maximus Confessor: Selected Writings*, CWS (Mahwah, N.J.: Paulist Press, 1985), 168, and Louth, *Maximus*, 97] and "training" [see Benedicta Ward, "Traditions of Spiritual Guidance," in *Signs and Wonders: Saints, Miracles and Prayers from the 4th Century to the 14th* (Brookfield, Vt.: Ashgate, 1992), 61]. For more concerning Christ's struggle with the devil, see *CC* II.13 (Ceresa-Gastaldo, 94–96). For Christ, the battle with the devil is extrinsic, while for the monk (or layperson, since *askesis* is for all Christians, see Louth, *Maximus*, 35) the battle is intrinsic, considered to be a war of the passions and virtues (Sherwood, *The Ascetic Life*, 83–84). Maximus, in his discussion with Pyrrhus, describes *askesis* as the separation of the soul from the deceit that takes place as a result of being immersed in the perceptible things, whereby the virtues depart from their natural (understood here as unfallen) character (*DP*, PG 91.309C).

Sherwood refers to the technique of *askesis*, which includes "control of the passions and the right use of natural powers," along with the "attainment and understanding of knowledge" through contemplation (*theoria*); see *The Ascetic Life*, 84. For Maximus, "control" and "understanding" cannot be separated. Therefore, *askesis* is what enables one to outlast spiritual contests (*GC* II.94, PG 90.1169BC), to move beyond the accomplishment of the virtues (*GC* II.69, PG 90.1156BC), is made more brilliant by the practice of the virtues (*GC* II.51, PG 90.1148B), is necessary for fighting the passions (*GC* II.94, PG 90.1169BC), is necessary in order to mortify one's parts of the body (*GC* II.95, PG 90.1169C), is characterized by strength (*GC* II.96, PG 90.1172B), and consists of prayer, natural contemplation, and virtuous activity.

Jean-Claude Larchet sees an overlap between the words *praktike* and *askesis*. Larchet states: "*Praxis*, which Maximus calls practical or ethical philosophy, constitutes the first degree of the spiritual life and identifies itself with the practice of the commandments, or, still, with *askesis*, which does not consist solely in the acts of mortification of the flesh (fasting, sleeplessness, work) but in all work which, in one way, serves to combat the passions and purify the *nous*, the soul and the body, and in another way, the practice of the virtues." See *La divinisation*, 452. This translator would prefer to translate *askesis* as "ascetic discipline."

302. *QT* 65, PG 90.741B, CCSG 22, 259.128–29; *Amb.Io.* 10, PG 91.1204A; *Amb.Io.* 42, PG 91.1325A; *Op.* 23c, PG 91.268A. For references to the translation of the word *nous* as mind in 1 Cor 2:16 and Rom 11:34, see Nestle-Aland, *Greek-English New Testament* (Stuttgart: Deutsche Bibelgesellschaft, 1992). *Nous* is considered to be the highest part of the soul, the reasoning part, distinguished from the sensible part (Sherwood, *The Ascetic Life*, 84). Maximus also calls the *nous* "the inner man" (*CC* 4.50, Ceresa-Gastaldo, 214), which gives consent to sin (Thunberg, *Microcosm*, 112). The highest function of the *nous* is to contemplate the divine realities, in particular, the Holy Trinity. The term appears most often in Maximus's ascetical writings where the work of the passions is addressed, and it is said to distract the *nous* from contemplation. The *nous* is responsible for the relationship between the human being and God (*CC* 1.50, Ceresa-Gastaldo, 66; 1.68, 74), and in relation to God, the *nous* represents the human being as a whole, something not to be contrasted with the remainder of the human being.

It is through contemplation (*theoria*) that the *nous* perceives the divine energies present in creation (the *logoi*) passing through them to God by the Spirit (*CC* II.26, Ceresa-Gastaldo, 102).

303. *CC* II.52, Ceresa-Gastaldo, 118.

304. *QT* 22, from Larchet, *La divinisation*, 502.

305. *LA* 19, PG 90.925D.

306. See ἀπάθεια, LS, 174. For a history of the word *apatheia*, see John Bamberger, "Introduction," *Evagrius Ponticus: The Praktikos & Chapters on Prayer* (Kalamazoo, Mich.: Cistercian Publications, 1981), n233.

307. See θέωσις, Lampe, 649. For a study on the use of the word *theosis* in Maximus, see Stephen James Juli, *The Doctrine of Theosis in the Theology of Saint Maximus the Confessor* (STL thesis , The Catholic University of America, 1990), chap. 3.

308. Ἐτυμολογέω means to "investigate a word and find its origin" (Lampe, 554), and ἐτοιμολογία means "readiness of speech" (Lampe, 554). For more on orthographic variants in the papyri of the Roman and Byzantine periods, see Francis T. Gignac, *A Grammar of the Greek Papyri of the Roman and Byzantine Periods*, vol. 1 (Milan: Instituto editoriale cisalpino–La gorliardica, 1976), 57–60. For the specific variations between *oi* and *u*, see the same, 197–99.

309. John Dewar Denniston, *The Greek Particles*, 2nd ed. (Oxford: Oxford University Press, 1978) 369–74.

310. *QD* 30, 55, 87, 92, I, 8, I, 30.

ST. MAXIMUS THE CONFESSOR'S
Quaestiones et dubia TRANSLATION

1. Exod 4:6.
2. John 1:18.
3. Eph 5:20.
4. Gen 11:1–9; see *QT* 28.29 (CCSG 7, 203).
5. Gen 11:2.

6. See also, *QD* 126, *CC* I.84 (Ceresa-Gastaldo, 82), *CC* II.59 (Ceresa-Gastaldo, 70), *CC* II.68 (Ceresa-Gastaldo, 126), *CC* III.4 (Ceresa-Gastaldo, 144), *CC* III.11 (Ceresa-Gastaldo, 148), *CC* III.59 (Ceresa-Gastaldo, 172). For more on the effects of eating, in general, see Clement of Alexandria, *Paed.* 2.1.2 (PG 8.37–432) and Aristotle, *Nich. Eth.* 3.13.1118a38.

7. Gen 11:4.

8. Gen 11:17.

9. Kgdms 16:23 .

10. Kgdms 17:34–36. On the interpretation of the lion and bear as anger and desire, respectively, see *QT* 53 (CCSG 7, 431). For the lion as anger, see *V. Sab.* 33; *Apoph. Patrum*, "Poemen" 115.96; John Moschus, *Spir. Pratrum* 107 (PG 87.2965C–70B).

11. John 3:5.

12. Matt 3:11; Luke 3:16.

13. See also, *QD* III, 1 for more on the divine marks.

14. Gregory Nazianzus, *Or. XI, In Pent.* 2 (PG 36.444B–C).

15. John 20:22.

16. Φυσικῆς θεωρίας. For more on natural contemplation, see *Amb.Io.* 10 (PG 91.1133A–1127C), and Evagrius, *Keph. gnost.* 1.27 (PO 28, 29).

17. See *QD* 34, 35.

18. Gen 14:20.

19. Gen 14:23.

20. Gen 14:18.

21. Heb 5:6 and 10 (Ps 109:4).

22. Gen 14:18.

23. Amos 7:14. *Physiologus* 48 also provides a spiritual interpretation of the fig tree [Dieter Offermanns, *Der Physiologus nach den Handschriften G und M*, Beitrage zur Klassischen Philologie 22 (Meisenheim: Verlag Anton Hain, 1966), 157)], though it differs from that of Maximus.

24. Mal 4:2.

25. Or copper.

26. Num 21:8–9.

27. See *QD* 122.11.

28. This phrase, "the rust of sin," is also found in Origen, *Ex. Ps.* (PG 17.128C); John Chrysostom, *In sanc. Jul. martyr.* (PG 50.671); Theodoret, *Int. xii proph.* (PG 81.1937A); and Cyril of Alexandria, *Ex. Ps.* (PG 69.948AB).

29. Acts 2:31.

30. Nazianzus, *Or. XLV, In s. Pascha* 22 (PG 36.653B).

31. Ibid., 653C.

32. See also, *QD* 30 and *QD* II, 18.

33. Rom 7:14.

34. Lev 23:3.

35. Lev 23:15–16.

36. Lev 25:4.

37. Lev 25:10.

38. In *CC* IV.54 (Ceresa-Gastaldo, 216) Maximus cautions his reader regarding any thought of attaining perfect detachment.

39. Other questions that address the four levels of transgression are *QD* I, 31; *QD* I, 33; and *QD* I, 78. See also, *CC* III.74 (Ceresa-Gastaldo, 178–80).

40. Σουμανίτιδος.

41. Kgdms 4:32–35.

42. Or rod, see Exod 7:9–8:13.

43. Kgdms 4:29–31.

44. Matt 1:2–26.

45. Luke 3:23–38.

46. The πρόθεσις (*prothesis*), a rite of preparation before the Eucharist, see prothesis, in William Jardine Grisbrooke, *The New Westminster Dictionary of Liturgy and Worship*, J. G. Davies, ed. (Philadelphia: Westminster, 1986), 449–50.

47. Luke 1:26–38.

48. Luke 2:8–14.

49. Eph 1:23.

50. Josh 9:2a–e.

51. Josh 5:2.

52. Cor 3:3.

53. Josh 9:2b.

54. Jer 7:18. The phrase, "cakes for the army of heaven" was commented upon by several writers: Epiphanius, *Pan.* 79.8.1 (GCS 3, 482); Chrysostom, *In Gen.* (PG 54.408); Theodoret, *Int. Jer.* (PG 81.552AB); and Cyril of Alexandria, *Com. Is.* (PG 70.552A).

55. Jer 1:15.

56. Theses sacrifices are described in Leviticus: for the sheep, see Lev 1:10; the cow, Lev 1:10; the goat, Lev 3:12; and the pigeon and dove, Lev 1:14.

57. See Matt 4:2.

58. Aristotle mentions the ox's heart but says it has three cavities; see *De part. an.* III.4, (Bekker), 666b23.

59. Or different parts of the intestinal tract. According to Aristotle, the camel has three parts while the cow or ox has four; see *De part. an.* 674a30–674b17.

60. A phrase found most often in the Macarian *Hom.*; see homilies 3.2, 3.8, and 3.9 (GCS 1, 30.9, 33.30, and 34.7).

61. Τὸ δεξιόν αὐτῆς κέρας. One translation of the phrase is "chief strength" (1 Macc 9:1) from Bagster's translation [*The Septuagint Version of the Old Testament and Apocrypha* (London: Samuel Bagster and Sons, 1879)]. The horn is also a symbol of power and can even be translated as arm of the cross of Christ; see Lampe, 747. This term is found in 1 Macc 9:1 and, as a military term, refers to the right wing of the army; see Cassius Dio, *Hist. Rom.* 75.6.3; Josephus, *Ant. Jud.* 19.91; and Herodotus, *Hist.* 6.111.

62. Matt 17:24–27.

63. Heb 4:15.

64. This passage also refers to the two birth stories; see Gen 1:27 and 2:21–23.

65. For Origen on *apokatastasis*, see *De Prin.* 1.6.2.

66. *Epignosis* is found ten times in the *QD* (*QD* 19, *QD* 35, *QD* 57, *QD* 91, *QD* 99, *QD* 105, *QD* 155, *QD* 168 (ll. 9 and 11) and *QD* I, 5.

67. Bel 1:1–22.

68. See Gen 11:9.

69. The term "kingly *nous*" is found in *QD* 165 and *QT* 64 (CCSG 22,

207) and in *QT* 64.322 and 328 (CCSG 22, 207); also in Philo, *De mut. nom.* 112 (*Philo V*, Loeb, 198); Gregory of Nyssa, *De op. hom.* (PG 44.156D); and Chrysostom, *Hom. in Matt.* (PG 58.651).

70. Bel 1:14.

71. Cor 15:23–24.

72. Cor 15:26.

73. Gen 9:12–17.

74. The four elements correspond to the four colors of the rainbow: fire is red, air is yellow, water is blue, and earth is green.

75. Lev 7:26, 17:12–14.

76. See 2 Cor 5:15; Rom 6:10; Gal 2:19. Anger, according to Nemesius, heats the blood around the heart; see *De nat. hom.* 20.1 (Morani, 81).

77. Exod 29:12; Lev 1:5.

78. Exod 21:28–36.

79. Gen 37:3, 9–10.

80. Origen also speaks of the multicolored coat in term of the virtues; see *Sel. Gen.* (PG 12.128CD).

81. Or sacrosanct; see πρόσθετος, Lampe, 1171.

82. Eph 5:20.

83. Ps 39:7; in some mss. ὦτία is inserted instead of σῶμα; see *Septuaginta: Id est Vetus Testamentum graece iuxta LXX interpreted edidit Alfred Rahlfs*, vol. II, Alfred Rahlfs, ed. (Stuttgart: Deutsche Bibelgesellshaft, 1979), 41; see Heb 10:5.

84. Or blood of the passion of Christ.

85. Exod 13:21–22.

86. Exod 16:20.

87. See Aristotle, *Nich. Eth.* 2.8.1108b and 9.1109a.

88. The phrase is also found in Philo (see *Leg. alleg.* 2.78) and Chrysostom (*In ep. I Cor.* [PG 61.152]).

89. The LXX (Rahlfs) has μή, without any alternatives, in the apparatus on page 122.

90. Exod 21:22–23. For an interpretation comparing the woman to the soul, see Origen, *Homily X on Exodus* 3 (PG 12.369B).

91. Exod 21:22.

92. Num 35:6.

93. Num 35:14.

94. Num 25:14.

95. Num 35:25 and 28.

96. The phrase, τελείαν ἀπάθειαν, is found in *QD* 10, *QD* 154, *QD* 170, *QT* 55.476 (CCSG 7, 509), *CC* IV.54 (Ceresa-Gastaldo, 216), *Myst.* 24 (PG 91.708C), *LA* 44 (CCSG 40, 119), and in Philo, *Leg. alleg.* 3.131–132 (Loeb, 389–90).

97. Cor 5:16.

98. Gen 30:37–38.

99. Gen 31:19.

100. Gen 35:4.

101. The term πτερνιστής (vanquisher) to describe Jacob is found in Philo several places but as one who vaquishes the passions, see *Leg. alleg.* 2.89 (Loeb, 280). See also, Maximus, *QD* 191; and Cyril of Alexandria, *Com. Is.* (PG

70.558D), *Com. xii proph.* 1.247.3 (Pusey), 2.552.22 (Pusey), and *Glaph. Pent.* (PG 69.161A; 168D; 229D).

102. See *QD* 38.27–28.
103. Cor 10:5.
104. See Gen 35:4
105. Col. 2:3.
106. Gen 38.
107. Rom 9:5.
108. Matt 15:24.
109. See Judg 2:17.
110. See Gen 38:18.
111. Kgdms 20:1–13. See also the entire passage from Cyril of Alexandria, *In Reg. III* (PG 69.692BC).
112. Hab 2:15.
113. Judg 11:34–38.
114. Judg 11:1.
115. Judg 11:2.
116. Judg 11:33.
117. Judg 11:30–31.
118. See Rom 9:5.
119. See John 1:11.
120. See Eph 5:20.
121. Eccl 10:18.
122. The voluntary and involuntary temptations are also mentioned in *QD* 195, *QT* 27.125–6 (CCSG 7, 199), *QT* 47.200 (CCSG 7, 325), and *QT* 49.47 (CCSG 7, 353).
123. John 2:1–11.
124. See also, *QT* 51.37 (CCSG 7, 397), *QD* 52.24 (CCSG 7, 415), and *EP* 343 (CCSG 23, 22). This connection is also made in Cyril of Alexandria, *Col. vet. test.* (PG 77.1269C and 1276B).
125. John 2:3.
126. See *QT* 25.31–36 (CCSG 7, 169).
127. John 2:4.
128. Cor 14:22.
129. John 2:5.
130. Understood here as the Mother of God.
131. Rom 10:17.
132. John 2:6.
133. John 2:10.
134. The Baptist.
135. Matt 11:11; see Luke 7:28.
136. Lev 11; Deut 14:3–20.
137. Φλέγμα in the *QD*, but βδέλυγμα in the LXX (perhaps the result of phonological problems). See Lev 11:10.
138. Rom 9:11–13.
139. Sus 1:42.
140. For the difference in Maximus between προαίρεσις, βούλησις and θέλησις, see PG 91.13A.
141. Rom 8:2.

142. Rom 8:6.
143. Isa 1:13–14.
144. See also, 1 Tim 19:2, 1 Pet 3:16, and Maximus, *QT* 62.119 (CCSG 22, 177), *QT* 63.516 (CCSG 22, 179), and *Myst.* 24 (PG 91.717A).
145. Gen 18:2.
146. See Gen 19:1.
147. See also, *QT* 28.12 (CCSG 7, 203) and *EOD* 453 (CCSG 23, 53) and Nazianzus, *Carm. dog.* 413.1.
148. Gen 19:15–22.
149. See Maximus, *Ep.* 1 (PG 91.377A).
150. Gen 19:26.
151. Gen 19:32–36.
152. On the importance of consent, συγκατάθεσιν, see *QD* 10, *QD* 39, *QD* 46, *QD* 77, *QD* 78, *QD* 193, *QD* I, 31, *QD* I, 33, and *CC* I.83 (Ceresa-Gastaldo, 82).
153. See also, *QT* 61.29 (CCSG 22, 85), and Aristotle, *Nich. Eth.* 10.4–5.1174a–1176a.
154. Deut 23:4 and Exod 20:5; see *QD* I, 78.1–3.
155. "Dirty rag," see Liddell and Scott, *A Greek-English Lexicon* (Oxford: Oxford University Press, 1889, rev. ed 1968), 715. See also, Achtemeier's definition of the word on page 849 of *Harper's Bible Dictionary*: "an obscure term of abuse, probably from the Aramaic meaning 'empty one.'"
156. Matt 5:22.
157. Ps 13:1.
158. Deut 32:6.
159. Judg 19:1–30.
160. Judg 20:21; 20:25; 20:35–46.
161. Judg 21:6.
162. Judg 20:47.
163. See 1 Cor 10:4.
164. Tim 4:2.
165. Matt 25:1–12.
166. Gen 2:8.
167. Gen 2:9.
168. Also found in Didymus the Blind, *Frag. Ps.* 465.45.
169. Κακοῦ, from *Vat.gr. 435*; see Declerck, apparatus, line 25, p. 38.
170. John 21:9.
171. Luke 19:1–10.
172. Rom 8:6.
173. Luke 19:5.
174. Luke 19:8.
175. For more on Maximus's understanding of prayer, see *CC* IV.64 (Ceresa-Gastaldo, 220), *CC* II.61 (Ceresa-Gastaldo, 122), *CC* I.11 (Ceresa-Gastaldo, 52), *CC* II.6 (Ceresa-Gastaldo, 92), and *CC* III.47 (Ceresa-Gastaldo, 164). See also for his understanding of formless prayer, *CC* II.91 (Ceresa-Gastaldo, 122).
176. Deut 32:32.
177. Num 6:3–4.
178. "Strong drink" is wine that has been fermented with sugar. See σίκερα, LS, 729.

179. This liquid from the pressed remains has the highest alcoholic content.

180. Philo also defines Sodom as blindness; see *De ebr.* 222.6 (Philo III, Loeb, 432) and *De som.* (Philo V, Loeb, 530).

181. See Num 6:3.

182. Num 6:5.

183. See also, *QD* 67 and 68.

184. See *QD* 67.2.

185. Judg 16:19.

186. See Judg 16:17.

187. This is a phrase Chrysostom uses; see *In asc.* (PG 52.793) and *In ep. Eph.* 2 (PG 62.25).

188. Judg 16:21.

189. Eph 6:14.

190. Eph 6:11.

191. Nazianzus, *Or. XLV in s. Pascha* 18 (PG 36.649A).

192. Eph 6:14.

193. Eph 6:14.

194. Cor 4:10.

195. Cor 4:10.

196. Eph 6:16.

197. Eph 6:15.

198. Eph 6:17.

199. This passage is similar to 1 Cor 13:7, but the biblical passage refers to love, not faith.

200. Eph 6:17.

201. See Nazianzus, *Or. XXXIX, In s. lum.* 15 (PG 36.352D). The *QD* text reads ἡ διαιροῦσα τὸ χεῖρον ἀπὸ τοῦ κρείττονος.

202. See *QT* 10 (CCSG 7, 85).

203. 1 Kgdms 22:18.

204. There are three hundred five priests, according to 1 Kgdms 22:18.

205. Does Maximus confuse the story? Doek tends the sheep of Saul; see 1 Kgdms 21:8.

206. 1 Kgdms 22:19.

207. Also known as the Nicene-Constantinopolitan Creed.

208. Nicene-Constantinopolitan Creed from the Second Ecumenical Council; see *Acta conciliorum* 2.I.II, 80, n14, 1.8.

209. Prov 16:5.

210. Prov 6:1.

211. Prov. 22:27. ·

212. Isa 40:12.

213. Hab 3:3.

214. See also, *QT* 54 (CCSG 7, 461). Philo also interprets the hand as action; see *Leg. alleg.* III.43. 8 (*Philo* 1, Loeb, 328), *Quod deus imm.* 135.4 (*Philo* 3, Loeb, 12). The actions of a virtuous man are supported by education; see *Leg. alleg.* 2.90.3 (*Philo* 1, Loeb, 282). Hand is interpreted as "good works" by Athanasius, *Ex. Ps.* (PG 27.217A) and by Origen, *In Jesu*, Homily 25.2 (GCS 30, 449.25).

215. For knowledge as water, see *QT* 16.70 (CCSG 7, 109) and *QT* 40.139 (CCSG 7, 275).

216. Eph 1:10.

217. 4 Kgdms 20:1–7; Isa 38:1–22.

218. 4 Kgdms 6:4–6.

219. Luke 3:9; Matt 3:10.

220. Irenaeus, *Adv. Haer.* 5.17.4 (SC 153, 232.1–8). See also, Jer 23:29.

221. John 21:11. Evagrius also comments on this passage of Scripture; see *Chapters on Prayer* in *Evagrios Ponticus: The Praktikos & Chapters on Prayer*, trans. John Bamberger (Kalamazoo, Mich.: Cistercian Publications, 1981), 54, especially note 1, for others who have interpreted this passage.

222. Gregory of Nyssa, *Or. I, in Christi resurrect.* (GNO 9, 286.9–12). See also, 1 Pet 3:19, 4:6, and the *Acts of Pilate* v(3)–vi(2) in *The Apocryphal New Testament*, Montague Rhodes James, ed. (Oxford: Clarendon, rev. ed., 1975) 134–136.

223. Or passion.

224. Prov 22:29.

225. Prov 24:16.

226. Gen 3:6.

227. Gen 4:8.

228. Gen 6:3.

229. Gen 6:4.

230. Gen 11:4.

231. Eph 1:12.

232. Eph 1:18–19.

233. Eph 2:10.

234. See also, *QD* 113 and Eusebius of Caesarea, *Com. Ps.* (PG 23.981B).

235. Eph 2:14. Compare with Gregory of Nyssa's *Hom.* VII on the Song of Songs (GNO 6, 201.14).

236. Rom 8:7; the *QD* text says διότι τὸ φρόνημα τῆς σαρκὸς ἔχθρα εἰς θεόν. Maximus includes sections from Rom 8:2.

237. Eph 2:15.

238. Exod 20:15.

239. Matt 5:21–22.

240. Prov 30:4.

241. Eph 1:10.

242. Phil 2:7.

243. Ὀμφαλός, also understood as the god who is seated at the navel of the earth, i.e., the Oracle of Delphi; see Plato, *Rep.* IV.427c.

244. That is, in Origen (*Sel. Ps.* [PG 12.1636D]), Hesychius (*Com. brevis* 123.4.1), Olympiodorus (*Com. Job* [PG 93.194A]), and Cyril of Alexandria (*Com. Is.* [PG 70.704B]).

245. Isa 13:12.

246. Gen 2:12.

247. Judg 16:1. For other interrogations and responses discussing Samson as a type of the ascetic, see *QD* 47, and *QD* 68.

248. Judg 16:19.

249. Ps 51:4.

250. Isa 11:2.

251. Judg 16:26.

252. Judg 16:30.

253. See Rom 8:6.
254. Judg 15:15.
255. For Samson as ascetic, see Origen, *Frag. Lam.* 102.7 (GCS 6, 271.4).
256. See John 1:11.
257. John 19:34.
258. Judg 15:19.
259. John 17:3.
260. See Judg 15:18–19. See also *QD* 95.
261. Judg 16:2.
262. Deut 7:1–2.
263. Judg 3:1–3. *Satraps* were the provincial governors in the time of the Achaemenid Persians; see Achtemeier, 975.
264. Matt 6:17.
265. Rom 7:22.
266. See also, Basil of Caesarea, *Hom.* 1.2 (PG 31.165A).
267. Luke 13:32.
268. See also, *Scholia in Odysseam* 4.188.6 for Herod as "skin-like."
269. Cor 15:50.
270. For blood as anger, see *The Odyssey*, Book 3.455; Galen, *De symp.* 7.192.1 and *De temp.* 1.682.4; and Nemesius of Emesa, *De nat. hom.* 20.1 (Morani, 81).
271. Deut 4:10; Exod 19 and 24.
272. This interpretation of Sinai as temptation is only found in Didymus the Blind; see *Frag. Ps.* 694a.14.
273. Lampe, 907.
274. See Exod 19:10–15.
275. See also, *QT* 48.110–112 (CCSG 7, 337) and *QT* 65.381 (CCSG 22, 273) and 415 (CCSG 22, 277).
276. See Eph 4:7; *Amb.Io.* 10 (PG 91.1153B).
277. Exod 24:1 and 9.
278. Exod 19:24.
279. Exod 19:17.
280. See *QD* 112.11–12.
281. "A word of uncertain derivation and unknown origin and meaning, found in certain psalms in the Old Testament," Achtemeier, 993. The word is also defined as "musical interlude," LSJ, 421.
282. Matt 18:6; Mark 9:42; Luke 17:2.
283. Pet 2:21.
284. Num 15:38.
285. Num 15:32–36.
286. Gen 4:1–16.
287. Rom 8:6.
288. Gen 4:8.
289. Gen 4:15.
290. Gen 4:12.
291. Gen 4:19, 23–24.
292. Matt 18:21.
293. Matt 18:22.

294. These were cultic objects, mentioned as symbols of a private priesthood. See Achtemeier, 1035; see Judg 17:3–5.

295. Judg 8:24–27.

296. A priestly garment; see Achtemeier, 273.

297. Judg 8:27.

298. Judg 6–7.

299. Gen 16:3–4 and 16:15.

300. Gen 16:6 and 21:4.

301. Sarah as "leader" is also found in Philo (*Leg. alleg.* 2.82.1 [*Philo* 1, Loeb, 276], *De cher.* 41.7 [*Philo* 2, Loeb, 32], and *De Abra.* 99.7 [*Philo* 6, Loeb, 52]), in Didymus the Blind (*In Gen.* 114.4), and in Cyril of Alexandria (*Glaph. Pent.* [PG 69.116BC]).

302. Gen 21:2–3.

303. Judg 6:1.

304. Judg 6:2.

305. Judg 6:3–4.

306. Judg 6:4.

307. Judg 6:5.

308. Judg 6:6–8.

309. Judg 6:11.

310. Judg 6:11.

311. Judg 6:12.

312. Judg 6:14.

313. "A dry measure equal to the liquid bath and approximately the equivalent of three-eighths to two-thirds of a bushel." See Achetemeier, 294.

314. Judg 6:17–20.

315. Judg 6:21.

316. Judg 6:37–38.

317. Judg 6:38.

318. Judg 6:39–40.

319. Judg 7:3.

320. Judg 7:5–6. The LXX says 22,000; see Rahlfs, *Septuaginta*, 434.

321. Judg 7:6.

322. Gen 17:15; see *QD* 146.13.

323. Judg 7:6.

324. Judg 7:20.

325. See Heb 4:12.

326. Judg 7:13.

327. Judg 7:13.

328. Matt 28:20.

329. Josh 7:11. Maximus provides an interpretation of these same passages in *Amb.Io.* 10 (PG 91.1120BC).

330. Josh 7:15; Josh 7:20–21.

331. Josh 6:15–16 and 4.

332. Josh 7:21. See also, Matt 25:14–30.

333. They are silver pieces; see Josh 7:21.

334. Gen 12:1.

335. Gen 37–47.

336. See Job 1:13–2:13.
337. Sir 11:58.
338. This phrase, "the unsteadiness of the human faculty of free choice" is also found in Chrysostom's fifty-ninth homily, *De Ioan.* (PG 59.192B).
339. Ps 118:1.
340. Ps 118:1.
341. Ps 3:7.
342. The verb ἐκμοχλεύω, translated here as "disturb," also means "to force open with a crowbar," LSJ, 514.
343. Ps 80:3.
344. Nazianzus, *Or. XX, De dogmat. et constit. episc.* 12 (PG 35.1080B4–5).
345. See also, *QD* 29, *QT* 56.89 (CCSG 22, 9), and *QT* 63.494–5 (CCSG 22, 177). The *logoi* of virtues are also found in *QT* 34.22 (CCSG 7, 235) and *QT* 55.262 (CCSG 7, 495); the *logoi* of knowledge are found in *QT* 3.53 (CCSG 7, 57) and *QT* 53.74 (CCSG 7, 435).
346. "Roman silver coin representing a worker's daily wage," Achtemeier, 237. For a more detailed explanation of the significance of the coin in the biblical passage, see Kenneth Jacob, *Coins and Christianity*, 2nd ed. (London: Seaby, 1985), 27–28.
347. Matt 22:19, Mark 12:15–16, Luke 20:24.
348. Matt 22:21; Mark 12:7; Luke 20:25.
349. Matt 10:23.
350. See also, *QD* 145.
351. Ibid.
352. Matt 12:20.
353. See also, Origen, *Ex. Prov.* (PG 17.237D).
354. Matt 13:26 and 30.
355. Matt 13:19.
356. Ps 80:4.
357. See also, *QD* 155 and *QD* 182.
358. Lev 23:24.
359. The Feast of Yom Kippur; see Lev 23:27.
360. The Feast of Sukkot; see Lev 23:34.
361. Gen 2:17.
362. Gen 3:19.
363. Gen 9:1–7.
364. Gen 17:10.
365. Exod 20:2–10.
366. John 2:2, 4:10.
367. Basil, *Hom. de ieium* I.5 (PG 31.69B).
368. Basil, *Hom. in Ps.* I.3 (PG 29.213CD).
369. Nazianzus, *Or. XL, In s. Baptisma* 27 (PG 36.397C).
370. Isa 32:20.
371. Nazianzus, *Or. XL, In s. Baptisma* 27 (PG 36.397C).
372. Ps 30:3.
373. Nazianzus, *Or. XL, In s. Baptisma* 33 (PG 36.405B); see Matt 15:21.
374. Nazianzus, *Or. XL, In s. Baptisma* 33 (PG 36.405B); see Luke 8:44, Matt 9:20.
375. Nazianzus, *Or. XL, In s. Baptisma* 33 (PG 36.405B); see Luke 8:44, Mark 5:29.

376. Nazianzus, *Or. XL, In s. Baptisma* 33 (PG 36.405B).
377. John 5:7.
378. Nazianzus, *Or. XL, In s. Baptisma* 33 (PG 36.405C).
379. Ibid.
380. Gen 19:24.
381. Ps 11:6.
382. Matt 25:41.
383. Ps 96:3.
384. Nazianzus, *Or. XL, In s. Baptisma* 36 (PG 36.412A).
385. See also, *QD* III, 1.
386. See *QD* III, 1.10–13.
387. See *QD* 19.12–21.
388. Nazianzus, *Or. XVI, In patr. tac.* I (PG 35.936A).
389. Theodoret, *Int. Ps.* 35.10 (PG 80.1124C).
390. Nazianzus, *Or. XVI, In patr. tac.* 4 (PG 35.937CD); Ps 36:6.
391. Ps 57:5.
392. Isa 28:17.
393. Nazianzus, *Or. XVI, In patr. tac.* 4 (PG 35.937D–940A); Matt 20:11–12.
394. Ps 74:9.
395. Isa 51:17.
396. Nazianzus, *Or. XVI, In patr. tac.* 4 (PG 35.940A4–9).
397. See also, Dionysius the Areopagite, *De div. nom.* 4.18–35 (PG 3.716A–736B).
398. Nazianzus, *Or. XXXII, De mod. in disp.* 27 (PG 36.205A13–14).
399. See also, *GC* I.82 (PG 90.1117A), *GC* I.83 (PG 90.1117A), and *OD* 450 (CCSG 23, 53).
400. Nazianzus, *Or. XXIII, De pace* III.8. Opuscule 1 (PG 90.1036C) addresses the topic of the monad and triad; see also, *QT* 28.4–25 (CCSG 7, 203), *QT* 44.7 (CCSG 7, 299), and *Amb.Io.* 10 (PG 91.1184, 1185A, 1195CD–1196B) .
401. Gen 1:26.
402. Ezra 10:3.
403. Basil, *Hom. in Ps. I*, 1 (PG 29.209A–212A).
404. See Eccl 10:4.
405. Basil, *Hom. in Ps. I*, 1 (PG 29.212A).
406. Basil, *Hom. in Ps. I*, 1 (PG 29.212C).
407. 4 Kgdms 3:15; 1 Kgdms 15:16.
408. 1 Kgdms 16:23.
409. Basil, *Hom. in Ps. I*, 2 (PG 29.212D).
410. Nemesius of Emesa, *De nat. hom.* 17.219 (Morani, 75).
411. Rom 11:32.
412. Rom 14:2.
413. Exod 20:21.
414. Exod 24:1–2.
415. Rom 15:8.
416. Ps 48:13.
417. Gen 17:10.
418. Rom 13:11.
419. Song 5:2.

420. Cor 15:29.
421. Acts 10:11–12. See also, *QT* 27.48–64 (CCSG 7, 193) and *Myst.* 2 (PG 91.669C).
422. Ezek 1:16.
423. Acts 10:11.
424. Acts 10:13.
425. Acts 19:9.
426. John 19:33.
427. John 19:32; Matt 27:38; Mark 15:27.
428. Gen 1:26.
429. Rom 8:29.
430. Col 1:18.
431. See Rom 8:6.
432. Acts 9:7.
433. Acts 21:40 and 22:9. Chrysostom has two interesting interpretations of these passages; see *Hom. XIX, de Act.* (specifically, PG 60.153) and *Hom. XLVII, de Act.* (PG 60.329).
434. Acts 9:5 and 22:8.
435. Hos 11:8.
436. Ps 104:25. The biblical passage reads καρδίαν αὐτῶν, "their heart."
437. Maximus, *Amb.Io.* 7 (PG 91.1081A).
438. Ibid. (PG 91.1081B).
439. Ibid. (PG 91.1328B). See also, *QT* 16.82–85 (CCSG 7, 109) and *QT* 27.75–77 (CCSG 7, 195).
440. Exod 5–12.
441. Origen, *Com. Johan.* 20.10.78.4 (SC 290, 196). See also Gregory Nazianzus, *In patr. tac.* (PG 35.940A).
442. See *QD* 9.7–8.
443. Josh 24:17; Exod 3:8.
444. Lev 11:45.
445. Exod 12:21–29.
446. Ps 75:11.
447. Cor 14:19.
448. See *QD* 41, *QT* 64.360 (CCSG 22, 209), and *QT* 65.515–6 (CCSG 22, 283). See also, EP 61–3 (CCSG 23, 6–7).
449. Rom 1:25.
450. Luke 14:18–20.
451. The etymology is found in *Fragmenta varia* Category 7, treatise 39, frag. 361, 3. See also, *Etymologicum Gudianum* (G.298.10) and *Scholia in Homerum* (*Scholia in Odysseam* 18.2.3).
452. Matt 20:1–16.
453. Job 1–42.
454. Rom 9:2.
455. Isa 5:2.
456. Nilus, *Com. Cant.* 61.31 (SC 403, 304).
457. Song 4:8.
458. See Basil, *Hom.* (PG 29.293D); Procopius, *Com. Is.* (PG 87 (2).1888B); and Hesychius, *Com. brevis* 36.35.3 (Jagic).
459. Ezek 6:3; Mic 6:1.

460. Ps 145:9.
461. See *QD* 140
462. Job 24:8.
463. Cor 10:4.
464. Nazianzus, *Or. XIX, Ad Iul. tribut. exaequat.* 8 (PG 35.1052B).
465. Ibid., (PG 35.1052BC).
466. Ps 2:11.
467. Ps 18:10.
468. John 4:18.
469. See *QT* 10.44 (CCSG 7, 85) and *CC* I.81 (Ceresa-Gastaldo, 80).
470. Basil, *Epist.* 45.1.1 (PG 32.1217A).
471. Gen 41:1–7. See *QT* 26.141 (CCSG 7, 181).
472. For other interpretations of "cows," see *QD* 177, *QD* 95, and *QD* 125.
473. Luke 18:2–8.
474. Luke 18:2.
475. See *QD* 134.
476. Luke 18:7.
477. Ezek 2:10.
478. Ezek 3:1–2.
479. Acts 2:1–4.
480. Dionysius the Areopagite, *De cael. hier.* 6.2 (PG 3.200D).
481. Eph 1:23.
482. Eph 1:10.
483. Cor 11:31.
484. Deut 6:4.
485. Acts 2:3.
486. Acts 20:16.
487. Council of Nicea, Canon 20, (Mansi II.684A).
488. Acts 22:25, 27.
489. Acts 22:28.
490. Amos 4:8.
491. See *QD* 90.
492. Amos 8:11.
493. Amos 5:3.
494. The word "all" may also be translated as "full," Lampe, 1345, C. The number ten was considered to be the perfect number because the sum of the numbers one through four equals ten.
495. Or power. Ten to the first power equals ten; ten to the second power equals one hundred; ten to the third power equals one thousand; and ten to the fourth power equals ten thousand.
496. Gregory of Nyssa, *Contra Eun.* 2 (GNO 1, 428.3) and Dionysius the Areopagite, *De div. nom.* 12.4.2 (*Corpus Dionysiacum* 1, 227.8).
497. Gen 17:15; see *QD* 80.107.
498. Amos 5:18–19.
499. See *QD* 3l for an interpretation of lion as anger; see also, Origen, *In Jer.* (PG 13.321D), and Chrysostom, *In ep. I Cor.* (PG 61.238D) and *Frag. Job* (PG 64.565D). For an interpretation of the bear as desire, see *QT* 53.22 (CCSG 7, 431).
500. For the interpretation of the house as soul, see also, Philo, *De cher.* 101.1 (*Philo* 2, Loeb, 68); *Quod deus imm.* 150.8 (*Philo* 3, Loeb, 86); Origen, *Sel.*

Ps. (PG 12.1641D); Athanasius, *Ex. Ps.* (PG 27.153D).

501. See Origen, *Schol. Cant.* (PG 17.265A) and Chrysostom, *In epistulam ad Ephesios* (PG 62.169A).

502. Ps 11:7.

503. See *QD* 80, *QT* 5.27 (CCSG 7, 65), *QT* 65.654 (CCSG 22, 293). See also, Gregory of Nyssa, *In Cant.* 7.4.5 (GNO 6, 240.10); *De inst.* (GNO 8 (1), 51.7); *In ins. Ps.* 2.15 (GNO 5, 161.20); Chrysostom, *In ep. Heb.* (PG 63.211); Didymus the Blind, *Com. Ps. 22–26* 67.27; *Frag. Ps.* 525.1; Cyril of Alexandria, *Com. Is.* (PG 70.453C); and most obviously, Macarius, *Hom.* 50 (GCS 1, 30.9, 33.30, 34.7, 70.18, 75.9, 86.14, 91.2, 93.3, to name a few references).

504. Prov 25:17.

505. Gen 31:39.

506. Deut 21:1–4.

507. Lev 10:1–2; Num 3:4 and 26:61.

508. Rom 12:1.

509. Luke 24:18, 32.

510. Lev 2:1–6.

511. Num 29:12.

512. Num 29:12–32.

513. Matt 18:3.

514. Num 16:35.

515. Num 16:37.

516. Rom 10:2.

517. Deut 23:18.

518. Ps 21:7.

519. See Origen, *Sel. Ps.* (PG 12.1253C) and Chrysostom, *In ep. I Thes.* (PG 62.425). See also, *QD* 184 and *QT* 64.484 (CCSG 22, 217).

520. Gen 3:24. See *QT* 43.1–5 (CCSG 7, 293), *QT* 44.63 (CCSG 7, 301–2), and *CC* II.93 (Ceresa-Gastaldo, 140).

521. This exact interpretation is found in Didymus the Blind, *Frag. Ps.* 825.13. See also, Athanasius, *Ser. ann.* (PG 28.940A); Dionysius, *De cael. hier.* 7.1 (*Corpus Dionysiacum 2*, 27.8); and Theodoret, *Int. Ez.* (PG 81.829C).

522. Cor 3:12–15.

523. See *QD* 139. The stones are interpreted as thoughts in Chrysostom, *De jej.* (PG 60.711) and Macarius, *Hom. 1–22, 24–27* (GCS 1, 205.10); wood is interpreted as attachment to perceptible things or the perceptible things themselves; see Origen, *Sel. Gen.* (PG 12.100A) and Didymus the Blind, *Com. Zac.* 4.30.2 and 4.35.2.

524. Ps 85:16.

525. 2 Kgdms 24:1.

526. Chr 21:1.

527. See *QD* 83.

528. Cor 4:4.

529. See Maximus, *Ep.* 26 (PG 91.617A) and *QD* 83.2.

530. Chr 21:14; see 2 Kgdms 24:15.

531. Amos 8:11.

532. Mark 2:4.

533. Phil 2:7.

534. Dan 3:6. For more on the voluntary and involuntary temptations, see *QD* 34 and *QD* 194.

535. Dan 3:46.

536. The word Λίνα may also mean vestments; see Lev 6:3, 16:4.

537. The blessed children are Shadrach, Mesach, and Abednego; see Dan. 3:51.

538. Dan 3:91–92.

539. Dan 3:50.

540. 4 Kgdms 2:23.

541. See also, *QT* 55.478 (CCSG 7, 509).

542. Luke 14:31–32.

543. The kingly *nous* is also found in *QD* 20 and *QT* 64.322 (CCSG 22, 207), and in Gregory of Nyssa, *De op. hom.* (PG 44.156D) and Chrysostom, *Hom. in Matt.* (PG 58.651).

544. Luke 14:31.

545. Luke 14:32.

546. Gen 3:16–19.

547. Luke 11:14.

548. Luke 14:28–30.

549. See *Catenae in Lucam* (115.31), for exactly the same wording.

550. Luke 19:10.

551. Gen 32:30; see *QD* 25.4 and *QD* 80.9.

552. Matt 15:24.

553. Gen 17:5.

554. Matt 15:26–27; Mark 7:27–28.

555. 2 Kgdms 20:7.

556. 2 Kgdms 20:21.

557. 2 Kgdms 20:21–22.

558. 2 Kgdms 20:8–10.

559. 2 Kgdms 3:27.

560. 2 Kgdms 3:29. See also Maximus's commentary on Psalm 59 in *Maximi Confessoris Opuscula*, 2–22.

561. 2 Kgdms 3:29.

562. See Heb 4:12.

563. 2 Kgdms 15:32–34.

564. 2 Kgdms 15:34.

565. 2 Kgdms 15:32.

566. Eph 1:23.

567. See I Cor 6:15.

568. See Acts 17:28.

569. See Maximus, *Amb.Io.* 7 (PG 91.1080C).

570. Josh 8:29. Adonibezek is the king of Jerusalem (see Josh 10:1–26) and was not hanged on a double tree but was hanged along with four other kings on five trees. The king of Ai was hanged on the double tree.

571. See John 12:31, 14:30, 16:11; Josh 8:29.

572. 3 Kgdms 22:19.

573. See Nemesius of Emesa, *De nat. hom.* 2.8–9 (Morani, 23) and Clement of Alexandria, *Strom.* 6.17.155.3.7 (SC 466, 370).

574. Luke 13:11.

575. Hab 3:17.

576. See Amos 8:11.

577. Matt 5:41.

578. Matt 5:39.

579. Matt 26:29; see Mark 14:25.

580. Rom 14:17.

581. Gen 6:3.

582. Gen 5:32, 6:6, 7:1. These passages give the one hundred years some context. Noah lived over six hundred years.

583. Acts 20:9.

584. See *QD* 89.

585. Matt 20:1–16.

586. Jonah 1:3. See also, *QT* 64.187 (CCSG 22, 199) and *QT* 64.242–5 (CCSG 22, 201).

587. Jonah 1:3.

588. See Jonah 1:4.

589. See Jonah 2:1.

590. Jonah 3:3.

591. Jonah 4:7–8.

592. Ps 21:7.

593. Jonah 4:11.

594. See Nazianzus, *Apol.* (PG 35.441BC) and Basil, *Hom. in illud* (PG 31.205C).

595. 3 Kgdms 17:6.

596. John 1:11.

597. Ps 18:5.

598. Ps 71:7.

599. Amos 5:18.

600. Rom 8:6.

601. Ps 71:8.

602. Joel 2:20.

603. See Hesychius, *In s. Step.* 17.4 (Michel Aubineau, *Laudatio s. Stephani*, 328–350).

604. John 3:8.

605. See *Myst.* 1 (PG 91.665B).

606. Matt 12:31; Mark 3:28–29; Luke 12:10.

607. Matt 9:34, 12:24; Mark 3:22; Luke 11:13.

608. Matt 7:1; Luke 6:37.

609. Mark 9:1.

610. Matt 16:28.

611. See Matt 17:1–2, Mark 9:2–3, and Luke 9:28–29.

612. Matt 17:1–9; Mark 9:2–10; Luke 9:28–36.

613. Matt 17:1–2; Mark 9:2–3; Luke 9:28–29.

614. Luke 9:28.

615. See Origen, *Com. Matt.* 258.11 (GSC 40) and Cyril of Alexandria, *Com. Luc.* (PG 72.588.D).

616. See *QT* 4.9 (CCSG 7, 61).

617. Matt 17:3–4; Mark 9:4–5; Luke 9:30–33.

618. Exod 34:28; 3 Kgdms 19:8.

619. Matt 4:2; Mark 1:13.

620. Exod 16:35.

621. Gen 15:13; Acts 7:6.

622. Matt 5:17.

623. John 1:29.

624. See *QD* 34 and *QT* 27.124–6 (CCSG 7, 197–9).

625. See Plotinus, *Enn.* 2.3.8.13; Eusebius of Caesarea, *Praep. ev.* 15.22.49.1 (SC 352, 338); Pseudo-Galen, *Def. med.* 19.383.10; Aristotle, *Rhet.* 1362b13, 1361a4; Posidonius, *Frag.* 10.12.

626. Cor 14:15.

627. Ps 50:7. See *Amb.Io.* 42 (PG 91.1317A and 1309A).

628. Rom 9:3.

629. Rom 9:3.

630. Eph 5:2, 25.

631. Gal 3:13.

632. Specifically, one sins through one's thoughts; see Evagrius, *Prak.* 48 (SC 171, 608).

633. An *assarion* was a valuable coin equivalent to twelve ounces of bronze. During the time of Augustus it was issued in copper. See James E. Spaulding, *Coin of the Realm: An Introduction to Numismatics* (Chicago: Nelson-Hall, 1984), 55 and 92. See also, Matt 10:29.

634. Rom 7:22; see Eph 3:16.

635. Cor 4:16.

636. 4 Kgdms 2:11.

637. 4 Kgdms 2:14.

638. Ps 49:20.

639. See Diadochus Photike, *Cap. char.* 100 (SC 5ter, 163).

640. Thess 4:17.

641. John 5:24.

642. Matt 16:23; Mark 8:33.

643. John 5:22.

644. John 8:15.

645. John 12:48.

646. Acts 1:1.

647. Prov 25:21–22.

648. Rom 8:6.

649. Ps 101:7. See *Physiologus* 4 (Offermans, 28–31) and Declerck's comparison of the two (José Declerck, "Remarques sur la Tradition du *Physiologus* Grec," Byzantion 51, fasc. 1 (1981), 148–58. See also, Eusebius of Caesarea, *Com. Ps.* (PG 23.1256A).

650. See *QD* 9. For the snake as the originator of evil, see Romanus the Melodist, *Cant.* 43.17.3 (SC 128, 520); and the *Acta Phillipi* 111.3 [Maximilianus Bonnet, ed., *Acta Apostolorum Apocrypha* vol. II, 2 (Zurich: George Olms Verlag, 1990), 43].

651. Rom 6:11.

652. John 19:34; Matt 27:49.

653. Ps 103:17.

654. Ps 103:17. See *Physiologus* 47 (Offermanns, 155).

655. Deut 5:9.

656. Amos 1:9. See *QD* 10 and *QD* I, 78.

657. Matt 5:29–30; Mark 9:43 and 45.

658. See Heliodorus, *Aeth.* 6.8.6.6.

659. Hab 3:11.

660. Mal 4:2.

661. Pet 4:6.

662. Gen 7:6–24.

663. Ps 45:11. See *QD* 189.

664. Matt 24:36; Mark 13:32.

665. See Plato, *Reg.* IX.863c; Proclus, *In Plat. Alc.* 200.18 and *In Plat. Parm.* 989.17.

666. See Nemesius of Emesa, *De nat. hom.* 8.45 (Morani, 64).

667. Other commentators on the monastic habit include Evagrius, *Prak.* (PG 40.1220C–1221C) and Dionysius the Areopagite, *De eccl. hier.* 6.3.3 (*Corpus Dionysiacum* 2, 118), both of whom are sources of Maximus's thought. See also, Eustratius, *V. Euty.* (PG 86 (2) 2296A); Cyril of Scythopolis, *V. Sab.* 54 (Schwartz, 147.7); and *V. Theo.* 5 (Schwartz, 240.8).

668. See Declerck's critical edition, line 4 of the apparatus, page 156. I have chosen to translate τόπον over τρόπον.

669. Job 40:16.

670. Ps 37:8.

671. Gal 6:14.

672. Eph 6:17.

673. Matt 5:16.

674. Phil 3:20.

675. The entire passage is found in Isidore of Pelisium, *Ep.* 1, 122 (PG 78.264C).

676. John 14:27.

677. Liturgy of St. Mark [Frank Edward Brightman, *Liturgies Eastern and Western*, vol. I (Oxford: Oxford University Press, 1896), 119].

678. Rom 8:35.

679. This entire passage is found in Isidore of Pelusium, *Ep.* 1, 221 (PG 78.321BC).

680. Cor 15:29.

681. The entire passage is found in Isidore of Pelusium, *Ep.* 1, 457 (PG 78.433BC).

682. Ps 150:3.

683. Ps 150:3.

684. Ps 150:4.

685. Ps 150:4

686. Ps 150:5. Clement of Alexandria, *Paed.* 2.4 (PG 8.441B). See also, Basil, *Hom. in Ps. I* (PG 29.212B).

687. Cor 15:51.

688. For information on the two variants, see *Novum Testamentum Graece*, Stuttgart: Deutsche Bibelgesellschaft, 1979, apparatus, 469.

689. Cor 5:3.

690. Song 5:2.

691. Gal 5:12.

692. Deut 23:4; Exod 20:5; see *QD* 39.32–34.

693. Ps 86:7.

694. Lev 13:10–13. Macarius devotes almost half of his Homily 44 to the topic of leprosy (GCS I, 255–59), though several others have written on it: see

Chrysostom, *In ep. Tit.* (PG 62.681); Theodoret, *Quaestiones in libros Regmorum et Paralipomenon* (PG 80.605B); and Cyril of Alexandria, *De adoratione et culte in spiritu et veritate* (PG 68.245D).

695. Gen 9:22–25.

696. See Nemesius of Emesa, *De nat. hom.* 43 (PG 40.792B); Maximus, *Amb.Io.* 10 (PG 91.1189AB).

697. Ps 132:1.

698. Ps 132:2. The response to this question is found in Origen, *Sel. Ps.* (PG 12.1652A).

699. Ps 132:3. The response to this question is found in Origen, *Sel. Ps.* (PG 12.1652B).

700. See Chrysostom, *Frag. Prov.* (PG 64.729).

701. Ps 132:3.

702. Dionysius the Areopagite, *De div. nom.* 4.3 and 18 (PG 3.713D10–716A1).

703. Mark 10:25; Matt 19:24.

704. Matt 7:14.

705. Eph 2:14.

706. Gen 1:26.

707. Gen 1:27.

708. Wisdom of Solomon 2:23; see Nemesius of Emesa, *De nat. hom.* 1.9–10 (Morani, 15); Clement of Alexandria, *Strom.* 6.12.97.1.2 (SC 446, 254); and Cyril of Alexandria, *De incar.* (PG 75.1448A).

SELECTED BIBLIOGRAPHY

PRIMARY LITERATURE

Edition of the *Quaestiones et dubia*

Maximi Confessoris Quaestiones et dubia. Greek text edited by José H. Declerck. CCSG 10. Turnhout: Brepols–Leuven, 1982.

Other Works and Lives of St. Maximus the Confessor

Massimo Confessore: Capitoli sulla carita. Verba Seniorum, n.s. 3, A. Edited and translated by Aldo Ceresa-Gastaldo. Rome: Editrice Studium, 1963.

Maximi Confessoris Ambigua ad Ioahannem. Edited by Eduardus Jeauneau. CCSG 18. Turnhout: Brepols–Leuven, 1988.

Maximi Confessoris Liber Asceticus. Greek text edited by Peter van Deun. CCSG 40. Turnhout: Brepols–Leuven, 2000.

Maximi Confessoris Opuscula exegetica duo. Edited by Peter van Deun. CCSG 23. Turnhout: Brepols–Leuven, 1991.

Maximi Confessoris Quaestiones ad Thalassium. I. Quaestiones I–LV, una cum latine interpretatione Ioannis Scotti Eriugenae. Edited by Carl Laga and Carlos Steel. CCSG 7. Turnhout: Brepols–Leuven, 1980.

Maximi Confessoris Quaestiones ad Thalassium. II. Quaestiones LVI–LXV, una cum latine inerpretatione Ioannis Scotti Eriugenae. Edited by Carl Laga and Carlos Steel. CCSG 22. Turnhout: Brepols–Leuven, 1990.

Neil, Bronwen, and Pauline Allen. *The Life of Maximus the Confessor Recension 3*. Early Christian Studies 6. Strathfield, NSW, Australia: Pauls, 2003.

Relatio Motionis. Text edited by François Combefis. PG 90.109C–129D. Edited by J.-P. Migne. Paris, 1850.

Scripta Saeculi VII: Vitam Maximi Confessoris Illustrantia una cum latina interpretation Anastasii Bibliothecarii iuxta posita. Edited by Pauline Allen and Bronwen Neil. CCSG 39. Turnhout: Brepols–Leuven, 1999.

S. P. N. Maximi Confessoris opera omnia. Greek texts edited by François Combefis and Franz Oehler. PG 90 and 91. Edited by J.-P. Migne. Paris, 1850, 1863.

Translations of Works by Maximus the Confessor

Disputation with Pyrrhus of Our Father among the Saints Maximus the Confessor, The. Translated by Joseph P. Farrell. South Canaan, Pa.: St. Tikhon, 1990.

Maxime le Confesseur. Ambigua. Foreword, translation, and notes by Emmanuel Ponsoye. Introduction by Jean-Claude Larchet. Commentaries by Father Dumitru Staniloae. Collecton l'Arbe de Jesse. Paris: L'Ancre, 1994.

Maxime le Confesseur: L'agonie du Christ. Translation by Marie-Helene Congourdeau. Les Peres dans la foi. Paris: Migne, 1996.

Maxime le Confesseur: Lettres. Translation and notes by Emmanuel Ponsoye. Introduction by Jean-Claude Larchet. Paris: Cerf, 1998.

Maxime le Confesseur: Opuscules théologiques et polémiques. Translation and notes by Emmanuel Ponsoye. Introduction by Jean-Claude Larchet. Paris: Cerf, 1988.

Maxime le Confesseur: Questiones à Thalassios. Translation and notes by Emmanuel Ponsoye. Introduction by Jean-Claude Larchet. Collection l'Arbe de Jesse. Paris: L'Ancre, 1992.

Maxime le Confesseur: Questiones et difficultés. Translation and notes by Emmanuel Ponsoye. Introduction by Jean-Claude Larchet. Paris: Cerf, 1999.

Maximus Confessor. *Centuries sur la charite.* Translated by Joseph Pegon. Paris: Cerf, 2006.

Maximus Confessor. *La Mystagogie.* Translated by Marie-Lucie Charpin-Ploix. Paris: Migne, 2005.

Maximus Confessor: Selected Writings. Translated by George C. Berthold. Preface by Irénée-Henri Dalmais. Introduction by Jaroslav Pelikan. CWS. Mahwah, N.J.: Paulist Press, 1985.

Maximus the Confessor. Selected texts translated with a preface and introduction by Andrew Louth. Early Church Fathers. London: Routledge, 1996.

Maximus the Confessor and his Companions: Documents from Exile. Edited and translated by Pauline Allen and Bronwen Neil. Oxford: Oxford University Press, 2002.

Maximus the Confessor. *On the Cosmic Mystery of Jesus Christ: Selected Writings of Maximus the Confessor.* Translated by Paul Blowers and Robert Wilken. Crestwood, N.Y.: Vladimir's Seminary Press, 2003.

Maximus the Confessor: The Ascetic Life and Four Centuries on Charity. Translated with an introduction by Polycarp Sherwood. ACW 21. Westminster, Md.: Newman, 1957.

Editions of Other Patristic Sources

Acta Conciliorum Oecumenicorum. Edited by Eduardus Schwartz. Continued by Johannes Straub. 4 Tomes. Berlin: Societatis Scientiariarum Argentoratensis, 1914–40.

Anastasius Sinaita. *Quaestiones et responsiones centum quinquaginta quatuor.* Greek text edited by Jacob Gretser (1617). PG 89.312–824. Edited by J.-P. Migne. Paris, 1865.

Apophthegmata Patrum. Collectio alphabetica. Greek text edited by J.-B. Cotelier (1647). PG 65.71–440. Edited by J.-P. Migne. Paris, 1864.

Asterii Sophistae commentariorum in Psalmos quae supersunt. Accedunt aliquot homiliae anonymae. Edited by Marcel Richard. CSCO, fasc. suppl. 16. Oslo, 1956.

Barsanuphius and John: Questions and Answers. Greek text edited and English translation by Derwas Chitty. PO 31, fasc. 3. Paris: Firmin-Didot, 1966.

Beauti Joannis Eucratae (John Moschos). *Liber qui inscribitur pratum*. Greek text edited by J.-P. Migne. PG 87. Paris, 1860.

Chronicon Pascale. PG 92. Edited by J.-P. Migne. Paris, 1885.

Complete commentary of Oecumenius on the Apocalypse (The), now printed for the first time from manuscripts at Messina, Rome, Salonika, and Athos. Greek text edited by Herman Charles Hoskier. Ann Arbor: University of Michigan, 1928.

Cyrille de Jérusalem. *Catéchèses Mystagogiques*. Introduction, critical text, and translation by Pierre Maraval. SC 126 bis. Paris: Cerf, 1988.

Der Physiologus nach den Handscriften G und M. Edited by Dieter Offermanns. Beitrage zur Klassischen Philologie 22. Meisenheim: Verlag Anton Hain, 1966.

Diadoque de Photiki: Oeuvres spirituelles. Greek text edited with a French translation by Edouard des Places. Rev. ed., SC 5. Paris: Cerf, 1966.

Expositio in Proverbia Salomonis. Edited by Constantin Tischendorff. *Notitia editionis codicis bibliorum Sinaitici*. Leipzig: Bruckhaus, 1860.

Grégoire de Nysse. *La vie de Moise*. Introduction, critical text, and translation by Jean Daniélou. SC 1 bis. Paris: Cerf, 2000.

Grégoire de Nysse. *Traité de la Virginité*. Introduction, critical text, and translation by Michel Aubineau. SC 119. Paris: Cerf, 1966.

Grégoire de Nysse. *Vie de Sainte Macrine*. Introduction, critical text, and translation by Pierre Maraval. SC 178. Paris: Cerf, 1971.

Gregorii Nysseni Opera. 9 vols. Edited by Werner Jaeger, Hermann Langerbeck, and Heinrich Dôrrie. Leiden: Brill, (1960) 1967.

Hesychii Hierosolymorum presbyteri. *Laudatio s. Procopii Persae*. AnBoll 24. Brussels: Société Bollandistes, 1905.

John Chrysostom. Sur la vaine gloire et l'Education des Enfants. SC 188. Edited and translated by Anne Marie Malingrey. Paris: Cerf, 1972.

John of Ephesus. *Lives of Eastern Saints*. Edited and translated by Ernest Walter Brooks. PO 18. Paris, 1925.

Kyrillos von Skythopolis. Edited by Eduardus Schwartz. TU 49, 2. Leipzig: Heinrichs Verlag, 1939.

Les Sentences des Péres du Désert. Solesmes, France: Bellefontaine, 1985.

Makarios/Symeon: Reden und Briefe: Die Sammlung I des Vaticanus Graecus 694 (B). Greek texts edited by Heinz Berthold. GCS. Berlin: Akademie-Verlag, 1973.

Nemesius of Emesa. *De natura hominis*. Greek text edited by Morani. Leipzig: Bibliotheca Scriptorum Graecorum et Romanorum Teubneriana, 1987.

Origen. *Traité des Principes* I. Henri Crouzel and Manlio Simonetti. SC 252. Paris: Cerf, 1978.

Origenes Werke. 12 vols. Greek and Latin texts edited by Paul Koetschau et al. GCS. Leipzig: Heinrichs Verlag; and Berlin: Akademie-Verlag, (1899) 1955.

Procopius. *Opera Omnia*. Edited by Jacobus Haury. Munich: Sauer Verlag, 2001.

Pseudo-Dionysius Areopagita. *De Coelesti Hierarchia, De Ecclesiastica Hierarchia, De Mystica Theologia, Epistulae*. Translated by Gunter Heil and Adolf Martin Ritter. Vol. 2 of *Corpus Dionysiacum*. PTS 36. Berlin: de Gruyter, 1991.

Pseudo-Dionysius Areopagita. *De Divinis Nominibus.* Translated by Beate Regina Suchla. Vol. 1 of *Corpus Dionysiacum.* PTS 33. Berlin: de Gruyter, 1990.

S. Dionysius Areopagite opera omnia quae extant. Greek texts edited by Balthasar Cordier (1634). Edited by J.-P. Migne. PG 3. Paris, 1889.

Saint Ephrem the Syrian. *Works.* 7 vols. Greek texts edited by Konstantinos G. Frantzola. Thessalonica: To Periboli tis Panagias, 1988–98.

S. P. N. Basilii Cesareae Cappadociae archiepiscopi opera omnia quae extant. PG 31. Edited by J.-P. Migne. Paris, 1885.

S.P.N. Gregorii episcopi Nysseni operae quae reperiri potuenrunt omnia. PG 44–46. Edited by J.-P. Migne. Paris, 1863.

Τοῦ ἐν ἁγίοις πατρὸς ἡμῶν Ἰωάννου τοῦ Χρυσοστόμου τῶν εὑρισκομένων τόμος ά–ή Ἑρρίκου τοῦ Σαβιλίον ἐκ παλαιῶν ἀντιγραφῶν ἐκδουθείς. Greek text edited by H. Saville. Eton, 1612–13.

Theodore Synkellos' *De obsidione Constantinopolitana sub Heraclio imperator* in *Analecta Avarica,* Edited by Ludwik Sternbach. Cracow, 1900.

Theodoret of Cyrus. *Histoire des Moines de Syrie.* 2 vols. SC 234 and 257. Introduction, critical text, and translation by Pierre Canivet and Alice Leroy-Molinghen. Paris: Cerf, 1977, 1979.

Theodosiani Libri. Edited by Theodor Mommsen and Paul Meyer. Berlin: Weidmannos, 1905.

Translations of Patristic Texts

A Select Library of Nicene and Post-Nicene Fathers of the Christian Church. Second Series, reprint. Edited by Philip Schaff and Henry Wace. Grand Rapids, Mich.: Eerdmans, 1979.

Basil of Caesarea: The Letters I. Translated and edited by Roy Deferrari. Cambridge, Mass.: Harvard University Press, 1972.

Cyril of Scythopolis: The Lives of the Monks of Palestine. Translated by Richard M. Price. Annotated by John Binns. CS 114. Kalamazoo, Mich.: Cistercian Publications, 1991.

Evagrios Ponticus: The Praktikos, Chapters on Prayer. Translated and annotated by John Bamberger. Kalamazoo, Mich.: Cistercian Publications, 1981.

Iamblicus. *The Theology of Arithmetic.* Translated by Robin Waterfield. Grand Rapids, Mich.: Phanes, 1988.

Nemesius of Emesa. *On the nature of Man.* In *Cyril of Jerusalem and Nemesius of Emesa.* Edited by William Telfer. Library of Christian Classics 4. Philadelphia: Westminster, 1955.

Pachomian Koinonia. 3 vols. Translated by Armand Veilleux. CS 45–47. Kalamazoo, Mich.: Cistercian Publications, 1981.

Pseudo-Macarius: The fifty spiritual homilies and the Great Letter. Translated by George Malony. Preface by Kallistos Ware. CWS. Mahwah, N.J.: Paulist, Press, 1992.

St. Gregory of Nyssa: Commentary on the Song of Songs. The Archbishop Iakovos Library of Ecclesiastical and Historical Sources 12. Translated by Casimir McCambley. Brookline, Mass.: Hellenic College Press, 1987.

Theodoret: A History of the Monks of Syria. CS 88. Kalamazoo, Mich.: Cistercian Publications, 1985.

Three Byzantine Saints: Contemporary Biographies of St. Daniel the Stylite, St. Theodore of Sykeon, and St. John the Almsgiver. Translated by Elizabeth Dawes and Norman Baynes. Oxford: Basil Blackwell, 1948. Reprinted, Crestwood, N.Y.: St. Vladimir`s Seminary, 1996.

Whitby, Mary, and Michael Whitby. *Chronicon Pascale 284–628 AD.* Translated Texts for Historians 7. Liverpool: Liverpool University Press, 1989.

SECONDARY LITERATURE

Allen, Pauline. "Blue-print for the Edition of *Documenta ad vitam Maximi Confessoris spectantia.*" In *After Chalcedon: Studies in Theology and Church History offered to Professor A. Van Roey for his Seventieth Birthday.* OLA 18 (1985): 11–21.

Bardy, Gustave, "La littérature patristique des 'Quaestiones et Responsiones' sur l'Écriture sainte." *RB* 41 (1932): 210–36, 341–69, 516–37; and *RB* 42 (1933): 14–30, 211–29, 328–52.

Berthold, George. "Cappadocian Roots of Maximus the Confessor, The." In *Maximus Confessor: Actes du Symposium sur Maxime le Confesseur, Fribourg, 2–5 septembre 1980*, 51–59. Edited by Felix Heinzer and Christoph von Schönborn. Paradosis 27. Fribourg: Éditions Universitaires, 1982.

———. "History and Exegesis in Evagrius and Maximus." In *Origeniana Quarta: Die Referate des 4. Internationalen Origeneskongresses.* Innsbruck: 2–6 September 1985, 390–404. Edited by Lothar Lies. Innsbrucker theologische Studien 19. Innsbruck: Tyrolia-Verlag, 1987.

Blowers, Paul M. *Exegesis and Spiritual Pedagogy in the "Quaestiones ad Thalassium" of St. Maximus the Confessor.* An Investigation of the *Quaestiones ad Thalassium.* Christianity and Judaism in Antiquity 7. Notre Dame: University of Notre Dame Press, 1991.

———. "Gentiles of the Soul: Maximus the Confessor on the Substructure and Transformation of the Human Passions." *JECS* 4:1 (Spring, 1996): 57–85.

Brock, Sebastian. "An Early Syriac Life of Maximus the Confessor." AnBoll 91. Brussels: Société Bollandistes 1973: 299–346.

Brown, Peter. *Body and Society, The.* New York: Columbia University Press, 1988.

———. *Society and the Holy in Late Antiquity.* Berkeley: University of California Press, 1982.

Bulloch, Vern L., and James A. Brundage, eds. *Handbook of Medieval Sexuality.* New York: Garland, 1996.

Burton-Christie, Douglas. "Oral Culture, Biblical Interpretation, and Spirituality in Early Christian Monasticism." *The Bible in Greek Christian Antiquity.* Edited and translated by Paul Blowers. Notre Dame: University of Notre Dame Press, 1977, 415–40.

Butler, Michael. *Hypostatic Union and Monothelitism: The Dyothelite Christology of St. Maximus the Confessor.* (PhD diss., Fordham University, 1994).

Cameron, Averil. "Models of the Past in the late Sixth Century: The Life of the Patriarch Eutychius." In *Changing Cultures in Early Byzantium.* Variorum, 1996.

———. *Procopius and the Sixth Century.* London: Routledge, 1996.

Canart, Paul. "La deuxieme lettre à Thomas de S. Maxime le Confesseur." *Byzantion* 34 (1964): 415–45.

Chadwick, Henry. "John Moschos and his friend Sophronius the Sophist." *Journal of Theological Studies* 25 (1) (1974).

Charanis, Peter. "The Monk as an Element of Byzantine Society." *DOP* 25:61–84.

Chitty, Derwas. *The Desert as City: An Introduction to the Study of Egyptian and Palestinian Monasticism under the Christian Empire*. Oxford: Basil Blackwell, 1966.

Dagron, Gilbert. "Les moines et la ville. Le monaschisme à Constantinople jusqu`au concile de Chalcédoine." *Travaux et Mémoires* 4 (1976): 229–76.

Daley, Brian. "Apokatastasis and 'Honorable Silence' in the Eschatology of Maximus the Confessor." In *Maximus Confessor: Actes in Symposium sur Maxime le Confesseur, Fribourg, 2–5 septembre 1980*, 309–39. Edited by Felix Heinzer and Christoph von Schönborn. Paradosis 27. Fribourg: Éditions Universitaires, 1982.

Dalmais, Irénée-Henri. "L'anthropologie spirituelle de saint Maxime le Confesseur." *Recherches et débats* 36 (1961): 202–11.

———. "L'oeuvre spirituelle de saint Maxime le Confesseur. Notes sur son developpement et sa signification." *La Vie Spirituelle*, Supplement 6 (1952).

———. "La doctrine ascétique de saint Maxime le Confesseur d`aprés le *Liber Asceticus*." *Irénikon* 26 (1953): 17–39.

———. "La manifestation du Logos dans l'homme et dans l'Église: Typologie anthropologique et typologie ecclésiale d`aprés Qu. Thal. 60 et la Mystagogie." In *Maximus Confessor: Actes du Symposium sur Maxime le Confesseur, Fribourg, 2–5 septembre 1980*, 13–25. Edited by Felix Heinzer and Christoph von Schönborn. Paradosis 27. Fribourg: Éditions Universitaires, 1980.

———. "La théorie des 'logoi'des créatures chez saint Maxime le Confesseur." *RSPT* 36 (1952): 244–49.

———. "La vie de Saint Maxime le Confesseur reconsidérée?" StPatr XVII, 1 (1982): 26–30.

Daniélou, Jean. *L`etre et le temps chez Gregoire de Nysse*. Leiden: Brill, 1970.

Daniélou, Jean, and Henri Marrou. *The Christian Centuries: The First Six Hundred Years*. 3 vols. Translated by Vincent Cronin, Paramus, N.J.: Paulist Press, 1964.

Davis, Leo Donald. *The First Seven Ecumenical Councils (325–787): Their History and Theology*. Collegeville, Minn.: Liturgical Press, 1983.

Declerck, José H. "La tradition des 'Quaestiones et dubia' de S. Maxime le Confesseur." In *Maximus Confessor: Actes du Symposium sur Maxime le Confesseur, Fribourg, 2–5 september 1980*. Felix Heinzer and Christoph von Schönborn, eds. Paradosis 27. Fribourg: Éditions Universitaires, 1982, 85–96.

———. "Remarques sur la Tradition du *Physiologus* Grec." *Byzantion* 51, fasc. 1 (1981): 148–58.

Delehaye, Hippolyte. "Byzantine Monasticism." In *Byzantium: An Introduction to East Roman Civilization*. Norman Baynes and Henry St. Lawrence Beaufort Moss, eds. Oxford: Clarendon, 1949.

Denniston, John Dewar. *The Greek Particles*. Oxford: Oxford University Press, 1950.

Devreesse, Robert. "La fin inédite d'une lettre de saint Maxime: Un baptême forcé de juifs et de samaritains à Carthage en 632." *RevScRel* 17 (1937): 25–35.

———. "La vie de s. Maxime le Confesseur et ses recensions." AnBoll 46 (1928): 5–49.

———. "Le text grec de l'Hypomnesticon de Théodore Spoudée." AnBoll 53 (1935): 49–80.

DiBerardino, Angelo ed. *Encyclopedia of the Early Church*. 2 vols. New York: Oxford University Press, 1992.

Dörrie, Heinrich. "Erotapokriseis" (A. nichtchristlich). *Reallexikon für Antike und Christentum 6*.

Dörries, Hermann. "Erotapokriseis" (B. christlich). *Reallexikon für Antike und Christentum 6*.

Farrell, Joseph. *Free Choice in St. Maximus the Confessor*. South Canaan, Pa.: St. Tikhon's Seminary, 1989.

Florovsky, Georges. *The Byzantine Fathers of the Sixth to Eighth Century*. The Collected Works of Georges Florovsky 9. Translated by Raymon Miller, Anne-Marie Döllinger-Labriolle, and Helmut Schmiedel. Vaduz, Liechtenstein: Büchervertriebsanstalt, 1987.

Follieri, Enrica. "Dove e quando mori Giovani Mosco?" *Rivista di studi bizantini e neoellenici* N. S. 25 (1988): 30–34.

Frend, W. H. C. *The Rise of Christianity*. Philadelphia: Fortress, 1984.

———. *The Rise of the Monophysite Movement*. Cambridge: Cambridge University Press, 1972.

Garrigues, Juan Miguel. *Maxime le Confesseur: La charité, avenir divin de l'homme*. ThH 38. Paris: Beauchesne, 1976.

Giannelli, Carlo. "Una 'editio maior' delle 'Quaestiones et Dubia' di S. Massimo il Confessore?" Πεπραγμένα τοῦ θ Διεθνοῦς Βυζαντινολογικοῦ Συνεδρίου ΙΙ, Ἑλληνικὰ, Παράρτημα, 9, ΙΙ (1956): 100–11.

Gignac, Francis T. *A Grammar of the Greek Papyri of the Roman and Byzantine Periods*. 2 vols. Milan: Instituto editoriale cisalpino-La gorliardica, 1976.

Gray, Patrick. *The defence of Chalcedon in the East (451–553)*. Leiden: Brill, 1979.

Grumel, Venance. "Notes d'histoire et de chronologie sur la vie de saint Maxime le Confesseur" *Echos d'Orient* 26, 1927.

Guillaumont, Antione. *Aux Origines du Monaschisme Chrétien*. Spiritualité Orientale 30. Bellefontaine, 1979.

Haldon, John F. *Byzantium in the Seventh Century: The Transformation of a Culture*. Rev. ed. Cambridge: Cambridge University Press, 1997.

Hausherr, Irenee. *Penthos: The Doctrine of Compunction in the Christian East*. CS 53. Kalamazoo, Mich.: Cistercian Publications, 1982.

———. *Philautie: De la tendresse pour soi à la charité selon saint Maxime le Confesseur*. OrChrAn 137. Rome: Pontifical Institute of Oriental Studies, 1952.

Hussey, Joan M. *The Orthodox Church in the Byzantine Empire*. Oxford: Clarendon, 1986.

Jili, Steven James. *The Doctrine of Theosis in the theology of Saint Maximus the Confessor*. STL thesis, The Catholic University of America, 1990.

Jones, John D. *Pseudo-Dionysius Areopagite: The Divine Names and Mystical Theology.* Milwaukee, Wisc.: Marquette University Press, 1980.

Kaplan, Michel. "L'hinterland religieux de Constantinople: moines et saints de banlieue d'aprés l'hagiographie."In *Constantinople and its Hinterland.* Cyril Mango and Gilbert Dagron, eds. Hampshire, GB: Variorum, 1995, 191–205.

Karayiannis, Vasilios. *Maxime le Confesseur: Essense et Énergies de Dieu.* Paris: Beauchesne, 1993.

Kesich, Veselin. *The First Day of the New Creation.* Crestwood, N.Y.: St. Vladimir's Seminary, 1982.

Lackner, Wolfgang. "Der Amtstitel Maximos des Bekenners." *Jahrbuch der Oesterreichischen Byzantinistik* 20 (1971): 64–65.

———. "Zu Quellen und Datierung der Maximosvita (BHG3 1234)." AnBoll 85 (1967): 285–316.

Laga, Carl. "Maximus as a Stylist in *Quaestiones ad Thalassium.*" In *Maximus Confessor: Actes du Symposium sur Maxime le Confesseur, Fribourg, 2–5 septembre 1980,* 136–46. Edited by Felix Heinzer and Christoph von Schönborn. Paradosis 27. Fribourg: Éditions Universitaires, 1982.

Larchet, Jean-Claude. *La divinisation de l'homme selon saint Maxime le Confesseur.* Paris: Cerf, 1996.

———. *Theologie de la maladie.* Paris: Cerf, 1991.

———. *Therapeutique des maladies mentales.* Paris: Cerf, 1992.

———. *Therapeutique des maladies spirituelles.* Collection l'Arbe de Jesse. Paris: L'Ancre, 1991.

Leclercq, Jean. *The Love of Learning and the Desire for God: A Study of Monastic Culture.* 3rd ed. Translated by Catherine Misrahi. New York: Fordham University Press, 1982.

Madden, Nicholas. "The Commentary on the Pater Noster: An Example of the Structural Methodology of Maximus the Confessor." In *Maximus Confessor: Actes du Symposium sur Maxime le Confesseur, Fribourg, 2–5 septembre 1980,* 147–55. Edited by Felix Heinzer and Christoph von Schönborn. Paradosis 27. Fribourg: Éditions Universaires, 1982.

Magerie, Bertrand de. *Introduction a l'histoire de l'exegese.* Vol. 1 of *Les Peres grecs et orientaux.* Paris: Cerf, 1980.

Marrou, Henri I. *A History of Education in Antiquity.* Translated by George Lamb. New York: Sheed & Ward, 1956.

Mays, James. *Harper's Bible Commentary.* San Francisco: Harper & Row, 1988.

Meredith, Anthony. *Gregory of Nyssa.* London: Routledge, 1999.

Meyendorff, John. *Imperial Unity and Christian Divisions.* Crestwood, N.Y.: St. Vladimir's Seminary, 1969.

Meyendorff, Paul. *St. Germanus of Constantinople on the Divine Liturgy.* Crestwood, N.Y.: St. Vladimir's Seminary, 1984.

Montmasson, E. "La chronologie de la vie de Saint Maxime le Confesseur." *Echos d'Orient* 13 (1930): 149–54.

———. "La doctrine de l'apatheia d'apres s. Maxime." *Echos d'Orient* 14 (1911): 36–41.

Nellas, Panayiotis. *Deification in Christ: Orthodox Perspectives on the Nature of the Human Person.* Translated by Norman Russell. Crestwood, N.Y.: St. Vladimir's Seminary, 1987.

Nestlé, E., and Kurt Aland. *Greek-English New Testament*. Stuttgart: Deutsche Bibelgesellschaft, 1992.

Nichols, Aidan, OP. *Byzantine Gospel: Maximus the Confessor in Modern Scholarship*. Edinburgh: T&T Clark, 1993.

Nussbaum, Martha. *The Therapy of Desire: Theory and Practice of Hellenistic Ethics*. Princeton: Princeton University Press, 1994.

Olster, David. *The Politics of Usurpation in the Seventh Century: Rhetoric and Revolution in Byzantium*. Amsterdam: Adolf M. Hakkert, 1993.

Ostrogorsky, George. *History of the Byzantine State*. Rev. ed.. Translated by Joan Hussey. New Brunswick, N.J.: Rutgers University Press, 1969.

Pelikan, Jaroslav. "Council or Father or Scripture: The Concept of Authority in the Theology of Maximus Confessor." In *The Heritage of the Early Church: Essays in Honor of Georges Florovsky*. David Neiman and Margaret Schatkin, eds. OrChrAn 195. Rome: Pontifical Institute of Oriental Studies, 1973.

———. *The Spirit of Eastern Christendom (600–1700)*. Vol. 2 of *The Christian Tradition: A History of the Development of Doctrine*. Chicago: University of Chicago Press, 1974.

Perl, Eric. *Methexis: Creation, incarnation, deification in Saint Maximus Confessor*. PhD diss., Yale University, 1991.

Richard, Marcel. "Les veritables 'Questions et reponses' d'Anastase le Sinaite." *Bulletin de l'Insitut de Recherce et d'Histoire des Textes* 15 (1967–78): 39–56. Reprint ed. *Opera Minora* 3. Edited by Eligius Dekkers, Maurice Geerard, Albert van Roey, and Gerard Verbeke. Turnhout: Brepols, 1977.

Riedinger, Rudolf. "Die Lateran Synode von 649 und Maximos der Bekenner." In *Maximus Confessor: Actes du Symposium sur Maxime le Confesseur, Fribourg, 2–5 septembre 1980*. Edited by Felix Heinzer and Christoph von Schönborn. Paradosis 27. Fribourg: Éditions Universitaires, 1982.

Riedinger, Utto. "Die 'Quaestiones et Dubia' (Erotapokriseis) des Maximos Homologetes im Codex *Vaticanus graecus 1703* (s. 10)." *Byzantinischneugriechische Jahrbucher* 19 (1966): 260–76.

Riou, Alain. *Le monde et l'eglise selon Maxime le Confesseur*. ThH 22. Paris: Beauchesne, 1973.

Rorem, Paul. *Biblical and Liturgical Symbols within the Pseudo-Dionysian Synthesis*. Studies and Texts 71. Toronto: Pontifical Institute of Medieval Studies, 1984.

Rubenson, Samuel. "Christian Asceticism and the Emergence of the Monastic Tradition." In *Asceticism*. Vincent Wimbush and Richard Valantasis, eds. Oxford: Oxford University Press, 1995.

Schönborn, Christoph von. "Plaisir et douleur dans l'analyse de saint Maximus d'apres les *Quaestiones ad Thalassium*." In *Maximus Confessor: Actes du Symposium sur Maxime le Confesseur, Fribourg, 2–5 septembre, 1980*, 273–84. Edited by Felix Heinzer and Christoph von Schönborn. Paradosis 27. Fribourg: Éditions Universitaires, 1982.

———. *Sophrone de Jérusalem: Vie monastique et confession dogmatique*. ThH 20. Paris: Beauchesne, 1972.

Schoors, Antoon "Biblical Onomastics in Maximus Confessor's 'Quaestiones ad Thalassium.'" *Philohistor, Miscellanea in honorem Caroli Laga septuagenarii*. Antoon Schoors and Peter van Deun, eds. OLA 69 (1994): 257–72.

Scott, Alan. *Origen and the Life of the Stars*. Oxford: Clarendon Press, 1991.

Sevcenko, Ihor. "The Definition of Philosophy in the *Life of Saint Constantine*." *For Roman Jakobson*. The Hague, 1956, 449–57.

Sherwood, Polycarp. *Annotated Date-List of the Works of Maximus the Confessor, An*. SA, fasc. 30. Rome: Herder, 1952.

———. *Earlier Ambigua of St. Maximus the Confessor and His Refutation of Origenism, The*. Studia Anselmiana, fasc. 36. Rome: Herder, 1955.

———. "Exposition and Use of Scripture in St. Maximus, as Manifest in the *Quaestiones ad Thalassium*." *Orientalia christiana periodica* 24 (1958): 202–7.

Simonetti, Manlio, *Biblical Interpretation in the Early Church: An Historical Introduction to Patristic Exegesis*. English translation by John A. Hughes. Edited by Anders Bergquist and Markus Bockmuehl. Edinburgh: T&T Clark, 1994.

Spidlik, Tomas. *The Spirituality of the Christian East*. Kalamazoo, Mich.: Cistercian Publications, 1986.

Stratos, Andreas N. *Byzantium in the Seventh Century*. English translation by M. Ogilvie-Grant. Amsterdam: Adolf M. Hakkert, I: 602 CE–634 CE, 1968; II: 634 CE–641 CE, 1972; III: 642 CD–668 CE, 1975; IV: 668 CD–685 CE, 1978; V: 686 CE–711 CE, 1980.

Talbot, Alice-Mary. "Bluestocking Nuns: Intellectual Life in the Convents of Late Byzantium." *Okeanos: Essays presented to I. Sevcenko on his Sixtieth Birthday by his Colleagues and Students*. Harvard Ukranian Studies 7. Cyril Mango and Omeljan Pritsak, eds. Cambridge: Ukranian Research Institute, 1983.

Thunberg, Lars. *Microcosm and Mediator: The Theological Anthropology of Maximus the Confessor*. Lund, Sweden: Gleerup, 1965. Reprint, Chicago: Open Court, 1995.

———. "Symbol and Mystery in St. Maximus the Confessor. With Particular Reference to the Doctrine of the Eucharistic Presence." Paradosis 27:285–308.

Trigg, Joseph. *Origen*. London: Routledge, 1998.

van Deun, Peter. "La symbolique des nombres dans l'oeuvre de Maxime le Confesseur (580–662)." *Byzantinoslavica* 53, fasc. 2, 1992.

van Roosum, Joost. "The λόγοι of Creation and the Divine 'energies' in Maximus the Confessor and Gregory Palamas." StPatr 27:213–17.

Viller, Marcel. "Aux sources de la spiritualité de saint Maxime: Les oeuvres d'Évagre le Pontique." *Revue d'ascetique et de mystique* 11 (1930): 156–84, 239–68, 331–36.

Ward, Benedicta. "Traditions of Spiritual Guidance." In *Signs and Wonders: Saints, Miracles and Prayers from the 4th Century to the 14th*. Brookfield, Vt.: Ashgate, 1992, 61–64.

Wesche, Kenneth, trans. *On the Person of Christ: The Christology of Emperor Justinian*. Crestwood, N.Y.: St. Vladimir's Seminary, 1991.

Wilken, Robert. "Maximus the Confessor on the Affections in Historical Perspective." In *Asceticism* 5. Vincent L.Wimbush and Richard Valantasis, eds. Oxford: Oxford University Press, 1995, 412–23.

Wolfson, Harry Austryn. *The Philosophy of the Church Fathers: Faith, Trinity, Incarnation*. Rev. 3rd ed. Cambridge, Mass.: Harvard University Press, 1976.

Wutz, Franz. *Onomastica sacra: Untersuchugen zum Liber Interpretationis Nominum Hebraicorum des Hl. Hieronymus.* 2 parts. TU 41.1–2. Leipzig: Hinrich, 1914–15.
Wybrew, Hugh. *The Orthodox Liturgy: The Development of the Eucharistic Liturgy in the Byzantine Rite.* Crestwood, N.Y.: St. Vladimir's Seminary, 1984.

DICTIONARIES

Achtemeier, Paul. *Harper's Bible Dictionary.* San Francisco: Harper & Row, 1985.
Lampe, Geoffrey William Hugo. *A Patristic Greek Lexicon.* Oxford: Clarendon, (1961) 1968.
Liddell & Scott. *Greek-English Lexicon.* Oxford: Clarendon, 1992.
Kazhdan, Alexander P., editor in chief; Alice-Mary Talbot, executive editor; Anthony Cutler, editor for art history; Timothy E. Gregory editor for archeology and historical geography; Nancy P. Sevcenko, associate editor. *The Oxford Dictionary of Byzantium.* 3 vols. New York: Oxford University Press, 1991.

BIBLICAL AND PATRISTIC
REFERENCES INDEX

General Index

active: 7, 17, 24, 26, 32, 34, 40, 51, 52, 58, 64, 67, 68, 69, 70, 71, 72, 80, 81, 82, 83, 84, 86, 94, 95, 113, 118, 124,127, 131, 134, 136, 137, 139, 152, 155

air: 24, 90, 97, 184, 191

allegoria: 15, 22, 1, 143, 177, 183, 184

anagoge: 15, 17, 18, 20, 22, 31, 46, 58, 59, 64, 68, 83, 124, 130,147, 177, 183, 184, 185

anatole: 23, 68

angels: 112, 115, 129, 144, 154

anger: 24, 26, 33, 44, 52, 54, 55, 58, 66, 70, 79, 81, 100, 104,117, 121, 124, 138, 141, 185, 189, 191, 196, 201

animals: 15,26, 27, 50, 51, 52, 55, 63, 81, 90,108, 111, 126

anthropomorphosis: 22, 26

apatheia: 20, 39, 120, 188

apokatastasis: 10, 13, 190

apophatic: 34, 128

Apophthegmata: 11, 164, 174

Apostle: 28, 44, 45, 49, 69, 82, 88, 91, 136, 137, 144

arête: 17

Aristotle: 21, 23, 108, 189, 190, 191, 193, 205

arithmology: 17, 22, 24, 30, 183

asceticism: 9, 18, 186

askesis: 26, 31, 32, 36, 38, 54, 59, 73, 88, 89, 91, 92, 110, 114, 119, 133, 187

ass: 26, 55, 80 82, 85, 94

Baptism: 26, 28, 31, 87, 94, 102, 103, 134

battle: 27, 33, 45, 67, 125, 133, 136, 137, 187

bear: 26, 44, 117, 124, 125, 189, 201

beings: 24, 28, 29, 38, 47, 52, 59, 60, 62, 63, 71, 73, 76, 78, 83, 99, 110, 112, 113, 120, 128, 131, 134, 136, 144, 145, 148, 154, 155, 156, 185

belly: 27, 28, 63, 149

birds: 63, 145, 146

body: 3, 15, 20, 24, 31, 32, 34, 35, 39, 44, 46, 48, 51, 52, 56, 57, 59, 60, 67, 68, 71, 73, 76, 78, 79, 88, 90, 92, 94, 95, 101, 104, 105, 107, 109, 112, 113, 118, 119, 126, 128, 129, 134, 137, 139, 141, 143, 145, 149, 150, 153, 154, 184, 187

boys: 5, 29, 70, 184

bread: 28, 48, 49, 50, 86, 92, 116, 133, 145

bulls: 29, 50,55, 56

burial: 28, 31, 102, 103, 132, 152

catenae: 19, 20, 181

circumcision: 23, 49, 101, 102

city: 6, 8, 26, 31, 58, 9, 116, 117, 127, 133, 153, 171, 173

Names and Places Index

Aaron: 46, 81, 82, 154, 155
Abel: 83
Abihu: 81, 119
Abner: 127
Abraham: 23, 30, 45, 64, 65, 75, 89, 92, 102, 16, 154, 165
Absalom: 123
Achar: 88
Adam: 62, 77, 78, 92, 141, 142, 145
Adonibezek: 128
Ahab: 60, 129
Ahithophel: 128
Alexandria: 14
Amalek: 85
Amessae: 127
Ammonites: 152
Amos: 46, 116
Anastasius the Apokrisarios: 7
Anastasius, disciple: 6, 7
Apostle (St. Paul): 54, 59, 67, 70, 75, 76, 81, 101, 103, 108, 115, 122, 123, 128, 139, 141, 142, 143, 149, 151, 152, 156
Areopagite. *See* Dionysius
Aristotle: 108

Babylon: 54
Babylonian: 124
Basil: 93, 99
Bel: 54

Benjamin: 66, 67
Bizya, Thrace: 16
Blowers, Paul: 16, 22, 167, 175, 176, 178, 179, 183, 184,186
Bochori: 127

Caesar: 91
Cain: 75, 83
Cana: 23, 61
Canaan: 26, 153, 154
Carthage: 7, 177
Cassian, John: 14
Chalcedon: 8, 169, 172
Christ. *See* Jesus
Chrysopolis (Scutari): 5, 6, 7, 27, 170, 177, 179
Chrysostom: 105
Cleopas: 119
Constans II, emperor: 7
Constantinople: 5, 6, 7, 8, 10, 13, 15, 173
Crete: 7, 171
Cyprus: 7, 171
Cyril of Alexandria: 4, 21, 60, 189, 190, 191, 192, 195, 197, 202, 204, 207
Cyril of Scythopolis: 10, 11, 173, 174, 206
Cyzikos: 6, 11, 12, 171, 173, 174, 175, 177, 178, 179